WOMEN WORLD LEADERS PRESENTS

Restoration

GOD BRINGS BEAUTY FROM ASHES

VISIONARY AUTHORS

KIMBERLY ANN HOBBS

KIMBERLY ANNE KAHN

Acknowledgment

Women World Leaders and the authors of *Restoration* would like to express our sincere gratitude to Connie A. VanHorn.

Connie, your invaluable assistance, guidance, and support have been instrumental in bringing our stories and voices to life on the pages of this book.

In recognition of your time, dedication, and love, we hope this acknowledgment conveys our deep appreciation for your service to our mission of empowering women through sharing God-given testimonies.

Contents

Introduction

Through the eyes of those who had been waiting for God to show up and then experienced His joyful restoration of the shattered pieces of their lives, you will see evidence that God moves in supernatural ways within the surrendered lives of His children. As writers called by God to present this book to you, we pray you will praise our heavenly Father and testify of His greatness along with us as you see His mighty power on display.

God's Word says,

> *The Spirit of the Sovereign Lord is upon me,*
> *for the Lord has anointed me*
> *to bring good news to the poor.*
> *He has sent me to comfort the brokenhearted*
> *and to proclaim that captives will be released*
> *and prisoners will be freed.*
> *He has sent me to tell those who mourn*
> *that the time of the Lord's favor has come,*
> *and with it, the day of God's anger against their enemies.*
> *To all who mourn in Israel,*
> *he will give a crown of beauty for ashes,*
> *a joyous blessing instead of mourning,*
> *festive praise instead of despair.*
> *In their righteousness, they will be like great oaks*
> *that the Lord has planted for his own glory.*
>
> *They will rebuild the ancient ruins,*
> *repairing cities destroyed long ago.*

They will revive them,
  though they have been deserted for many generations.
Foreigners will be your servants.
  They will feed your flocks
and plow your fields
  and tend your vineyards.
You will be called priests of the Lord,
  ministers of our God.

You will feed on the treasures of the nations
  and boast in their riches.
Instead of shame and dishonor,
  you will enjoy a double share of honor.
You will possess a double portion of prosperity in your land,
  and everlasting joy will be yours.

"For I, the Lord, love justice. I hate robbery and wrongdoing.
I will faithfully reward my people for their suffering
  and make an everlasting covenant with them.
Their descendants will be recognized
  and honored among the nations.
Everyone will realize that they are a people
  the Lord has blessed."

I am overwhelmed with joy in the Lord my God!
  For he has dressed me with the clothing of salvation
  and draped me in a robe of righteousness.
I am like a bridegroom dressed for his wedding
  or a bride with her jewels.
The Sovereign Lord will show his justice to the nations of the world.
  Everyone will praise him!
His righteousness will be like a garden in early spring,
  with plants springing up everywhere.
(Isaiah 61:1-11 NLT)

Restoration: God Brings Beauty from Ashes

Sometimes, we can feel like we've lost it all, but God promises to return even more than is stolen from us. We can learn from Job in the Bible. Even though he lost everything—his health, fortune, and even his family—Job kept a humble attitude and trusted that God's ways are far beyond our own ways. In the process, Job honored God, as do the authors of this book. They share their stories of tremendous adversity in an effort to honor God and His ever-steady faithfulness in seeing His children through every situation.

Yes, our loving and devoted God promises us restoration. And although things may not end up looking exactly as they did before our trials, we can trust in His ever-present perfection. When the pain of loss cuts deep and leaves a void, we need to encourage each other to remember God is our sole provider, and He alone can remedy our situation. By standing together, we enable each other to navigate any situation as we keep our focus on Jesus and the restoration He alone can give. No matter your circumstance, if you let Him, you can trust God will renew your heart and life in ways beyond what you can imagine.

May we all claim this promise together: God is able and willing to restore what was lost.

> *Therefore, if anyone is in Christ, he is a new creation. The old has passed away; behold, the new has come* (2 Corinthians 5:17 ESV).

Restoration is often visible on the outside but always begins on the inside; because of this, sometimes our issues take longer to work out than expected. We often require more work, more time, and more effort to reach a state of restoration. God seems to work slowly at times, not because He lacks power, but because He longs to see deep change in us. God can see that which may not be beautiful in us and may not even be visible to others. When we pray for restoration, we must boldly ask God to reveal anything unclean within us and then trust His hand to guide us into becoming all He desires. Through our stories and teachings, we pray you will see God's steady and sure hand waiting to move you on your path to restoration.

> Instead of your shame, there shall be a double portion; instead of dishonor they shall rejoice in their lot; therefore, in their land they shall possess a double portion; they shall have everlasting joy (Isaiah 61:7 ESV).

If you have picked up this book hoping to make something new again or better than its current state, you can trust that our heavenly Father's restoring power is one of the greatest promises from scripture. As we shared with you in Isaiah 61, God will give beauty for ashes, the oil of joy for mourning, the garment of praise for the spirit of heaviness, and He will open the prison doors to set the captives free! He is a faithful God who delivers His promises.

Jesus has already opened the prison doors to anyone in need; we no longer need to stay in the prisons of emotional pain, rejection, disappointment, unforgiveness, worry, depression, anger, addictions, or unhealthy habits. As the writers in this book have dealt with so many of these very issues, we pray that you will be able to make an exchange if you are experiencing pain from your past. You no longer have to be stuck there. You can trade in your pain for God's promise. You can have beauty instead of ashes. We all have a part to play in the process of restoration, though, and it is up to us to search for God's ways and His timing in all of it.

We hope that as you dive into the pages of this book, the truth of God's Word will grip your heart! We pray that you, too, will soon step forward and testify that God alone can restore whatever we've lost, always bringing forth something beautiful... even in the most unlikely places.

Kimberly Ann Hobbs

As the Founder and co-CEO of Women World Leaders, a worldwide ministry empowering women to find their God-given purpose, Kimberly Ann Hobbs oversees all elements of the ministry, including *Voice of Truth* magazine. Kimberly is also the co-CEO of World Publishing and Productions and an international best-selling author, speaker, motivational leader, and life coach.

As part of *Women World Leaders' Podcast,* Kimberly interviews beautiful women from around the world. She also shares daily devotions on the WWL Facebook group and website, womenworldleaders.com.

Kimberly has been a guest speaker on Moody Bible Radio Stations and made appearances on Daystar Television, sharing her passion for bringing women to a closer walk with Jesus through encouragement. She is an artist, with much of her work reaching worldwide, and sits on Kerus Global Education advisory board, helping raise support for South Africa's orphaned children.

Kimberly supports her husband, Ken, in his ministry: United Men of Honor – unitedmenofhonor.com. Together, they serve in missions and ministry and run their own financial coaching business. They have children and grandchildren whom they love very much.

In the Waiting

By Kimberly Ann Hobbs

Our God is the God of Restoration. And our God brings beauty from ashes. But what do we do when restoration and beauty don't arrive when we want them to? Do we wait patiently? Or do we push, trying to "help" God?

When God had me "on hold" for something my heart was in pain over, I had to learn what to do in the waiting. I had to understand that the most important thing I can do as I wait is to actively trust in God's timing while continuing to pray, seeking His guidance, and using the time to deepen my relationship with Him through studying the scriptures, serving others, and seeking His will in my life.

I believe the most excruciating pain a parent can feel is the loss of a child. When physical death strikes, the finality is devastating. However, that is not my story. My daughters are alive, but the fact that I have no relationship with them is an ongoing, raging pain that, in the past, shredded my heart indescribably. I believed in my heart that if I could only get clarity from my daughters as to why they suddenly abandoned our relationship, I would be able to fix it. But fixing the situation was not in my control; I would have to learn this truth with God's help.

The torments in my mind raged as I tried to figure out the "why" of the reality of the present situation. I made every attempt to connect with my daughters, open the door of any painful truths, and apologize where apologies may have been necessary. I did everything I could. All of it was met with unanswered calls, ignored text messages, unresponded to letters, and unacknowledged gifts left on doorsteps. Every step I took was met with a deafening silence of rejection.

Past wounds of my own guilt and shame resurfaced as sadness in my heart, allowing grief to escalate. In the past, I had asked and received forgiveness from my daughters over my mistakes, but nothing in the present seemed to justify this sudden and dramatic change in our relationship. My mind became nothing but a whirlwind of confusion. Their current behaviors were not in my control, and the enemy used our division to drain the life from my soul. Days turned into months, and months into years. Unanswered questions and no responses have now continued for close to eight years. All my greatest joys of being a mother and a grandmother abruptly ended; I was left with nothing but open-ended questions. The wicked spirits haunted and tormented me through countless sleepless nights as the question "Why?" fiercely and relentlessly raged battle in my mind.

As I watched all my friends on Facebook celebrating the joys of motherhood and grandparenting, I cried my eyes out to God, asking Him the same pounding questions, "Why, Lord? What have I done?" I begged Him to help me understand if there was anything I had personally done to cause this division and break in our relationship. I prayed and searched my heart time and time again. I asked family, friends, and anyone who knew my daughters if they had heard anything from them that could help me. No one had answers. I did everything I could do. God remained silent. I even retraced my prayers. I prayed and prayed and prayed for restoration to take place, but nothing came. Still, in faith from the depths of my heart, I believed in restoration and hoped it would come soon.

A shift came when this question arose in my spirit: "Are these feelings of rejection from your children consuming your thoughts and holding you captive, dominating each day with stress and worry?"

Yes, the chains of burden and the torments of thoughts were brutal. The pain of rejection from my children was preoccupying my deepest thoughts and holding me captive from my relationship with Jesus. I couldn't see Him; each day, I could only see my pain from the loss resounding in my head. With faith, I had to gather my courage to emerge from that place of pain and rejection. I knew I no longer wanted to live there because it was debilitating and keeping me from focusing on the Lord. I knew I could only overcome this with God's strength and the power of His Word. Had my desperation of wanting a relationship with my estranged children become an obstacle to my service to God? I realized it had.

I began to lay down my mothering life to God. And in laying down my life, I surrendered the desires of my own flesh—that which I wanted so desperately: a restored relationship with my daughters. I knew I had to release it to God and allow Him to establish a renewed relationship with Him within myself.

> *Trust in the Lord with all your heart and lean not on your own understanding* (Proverbs 3:5 NIV).

I was learning to release my hurts to God so I could love my children more despite the status of our relationship. God allowed me to know He had a plan for their lives, even though I could not see it.

Every person has choices to make throughout their lives, and my children's choices belong to them, not me. I was the one in fear over what I felt was being stolen from me—my relationship with my children and grandchildren. I felt tremendous fear of not being able to be an influence in their lives. Through my shift in perspective, scripture reminded me that all of it, EVERYTHING, belongs to God—even my kids. I needed to back off and begin to trust God and not contaminate HIS ultimate plan for their lives.

We all have a calling in our lives, a purpose God planned for us long ago. The enemy will attack us with whatever tactics he can to distract us, including attaching fear to an area where we are called to serve. And he did just that with me.

When my calling came to begin Women World Leaders, my feelings of unworthiness were heightened as the enemy tried to damage my soul by telling me: "You are not worthy to lead anyone; your own children have rejected you. Who will ever be part of the ministry if you can't even have a relationship with your own daughters?"

The devil spoke this lie to me over and over, tormenting me with my past mistakes, which became giants in my mind. How would I ever know that beyond these enormous giants lay my life's destiny? I had to hear God speak; it was the only way to rise above the lies I believed.

Through my state of hopelessness, I gathered strength to begin restoration by slaying the giants of fear, rejection, and unworthiness with God's undeniable truth. I knew I needed to operate out of the strength God commands versus the fear the enemy dictates. I knew I needed to demonstrate my faith through action and begin a journey with God in the waiting.

God expects us to be strong and have courage—but that courage must not be in ourselves. Even when we want restoration so very badly, we must depend on God alone for it to happen. We must draw our strength from God. "How?" you might ask. Often, we do not realize how strong we really are until being strong and receiving from God is all we have left. God provides for us when we ask Him. We need to let go of whatever holds us back from what the enemy has stolen from us and allow God to take over and heal it.

This was not easy for me back when the pain was raw and real. Oh, how I needed more strength!

We can be in a situation where we want restoration so very badly. But when that longing involves others who may be hindering or hurting us or even keeping us from a tighter relationship with God, we must examine it. We must ask ourselves, *Have I done everything God's Word says to do to make things right in my situation?* In my case, I had. So, the next step was to release both individuals to God. Your situation may be a bit different, but if you ask God what you need to do to foster restoration and then give your situation completely to Him, you can trust He is working.

Because my case involves my children, God had to teach me that my children "belong to Him first." Yes, He gave me the privilege to raise them, and I raised them as best I could with what I knew at the time, but God knows what's best in the now. He is God.

In my situation—longing for restoration with my girls—I had to hand everything over to God. Doing this gave me my first glimpses of beauty from ashes. I watched God pick me up when I was weak and felt Him strengthen me day by day in my weakness.

> *Fear not for I am with you; be not dismayed for I am your God; I will strengthen you, I will uphold you with my righteous right hand* (Isaiah 41:10 ESV).

While we are waiting for restoration in any situation, the only safe place for our vulnerable, hurting hearts is at the feet of Jesus, surrendering our entire situation to Him and telling Him so. And that is exactly what I began to do.

> *Humble yourselves therefore under the mighty hand of God, that he may exalt you in due time* (1 Peter 5:6 KJV).

God will appear in the silence when we are ready! What pleases Him most is our obedience.

In the waiting, I learned that nothing I did on my own worked. Even though my heart still yearned for restoration with my girls, by surrendering the situation and my children's lives to God, I began to see other things

God wanted me to see. I began to see beyond my own wants and needs and recognize that God wanted to birth a ministry in my life. God's timing for my pain of rejection turned into a joy of healing. I believe that in due time, whatever we are seeking to be restored will prove hopeful when we wholeheartedly allow God to be involved.

Two years ago, before this book was even born, I was having a conversation with my co-author of this book. We were relating to each other's prayer hearts about desiring restoration in both our lives with our kids. It was so strong and heavy on our hearts that in that conversation, we felt each other's heartache and pain experienced because of loss. We knew the enemy had been taking something from us and trying to use it to disgrace us over the years. In strength, we encouraged each other with how God was working in our individual stories. We both held on to faith, believing that God would bring beauty from ashes one day and restore what the enemy had stolen. The joy came together with God when we realized a book on restoration could help others. Hence, this book was prayed into being during that two-hour phone conversation.

Fast forward to recently, before publishing. I believed with all my heart that by the time this book was published, I would have my restoration story with my daughters, and it would be a happily ever after story. To be honest, that was one of the reasons I was so eager, hopeful, and excited to enter this journey with all these ladies. But now, despite going to God with my longing, working with the authors, writing the teachings, and spending tremendous time and energy bathed in prayer, I am still "in the waiting."

I even waited until the very last moment possible to begin to write my own chapter, asking God, "Will this be a restoration story about my daughters? Are You going to bring them back to me before the publication of *Restoration,* as I hoped?" Unfortunately, I didn't see any strong indications of that happening. And God whispered in my ear the title, "In the Waiting."

I cried out to Him, "Waiting??? That will be the title of my chapter?"

I still wanted to believe He would restore our relationships. And He did give me glimmers of hope. Over the past few months, due to an accident I recently had, I have heard from both my daughters through text. It brought overwhelming joy to my soul. But our communication ended with the texts. So, I held out again and kept praying for what I'd write about. God said again and again, even louder, "IN THE WAITING." It is all that would resound in the picture of my mind as I prayed to Him over this.

What I have learned and would love to pass on to you if you're waiting on God for restoration or to bring beauty from ashes is this: Know that the God who saved you hears your cries.

> As for me, I look to the Lord for help. I wait confidently for God to save me, and my God will certainly hear me (Micah 7:7 NLT).

As you cry out to God, you can be assured He hears every word of your broken heart and need for restoration. Moreover, God is grieved when we ignore Him. So, use your pain to grow closer to Him. Just as I grieve over my children ignoring me, God grieves over us when we ignore Him in our pain and suffering.

As the chains that so tightly bound me began to break away, I was able to learn and grow with my Lord in the waiting. Women World Leaders was birthed with God during the waiting. Multiple books have been written while I have been on my face before God. God gave me eyes to see that His Word is true. I see it come alive with power each time I need it while waiting.

God tells us to watch with expectancy and be prepared for unexpected answers. As I shared, He gave me hope. He continues to give me hopeful signs that He is working.

At each and every sunrise you will hear my voice as I prepare my sacrifice of prayer to you. Every morning, I lay out the pieces of my life on the altar and wait for your fire to fall upon my heart (Psalm 5:3 TPT).

I pray that scripture can become as liberating to you as it has to me while you are in the waiting. Put your hope in the Word of God. In Him you trust. Trust the words He says to your soul and not what your brain wants you to believe (Proverbs 3:5-6).

When I stopped being passive in my waiting and became active and engaged in my faith, miraculous things began to happen. Although I'm still anticipating the restoration with my daughters and trust that God is working behind the scenes in what I can't see, He has brought me tremendous blessings with more daughters than I can count. How? Through actively starting the ministry of Women World Leaders and partnering with Julie Jenkins to birth a publishing and production company. Now, others have been moved to action by our encouragement in Jesus and because I have chosen to be content with what God has for me in the waiting.

As you wait, I encourage you to maintain your prayer life and communicate with God through prayer, expressing your concerns and desires and asking Him for His patience and understanding. Read the Bible and meditate daily over scriptures that might speak to waiting on God.

> *Wait for the Lord; be strong and take heart and wait for the Lord* (Psalm 27:14 NIV).

> *But those who hope in the Lord will renew their strength. They will soar on wings like eagles; they will run and not grow weary; they will walk and not be faint* (Isaiah 40:31 NIV).

Sharing this story is one of the most difficult things I have ever done as I've battled the fear of people judging me or looking at me differently, but it has been one of the most liberating events I can describe. Connecting with others facing similar situations and sharing our struggles and experiences has truly allowed hope and healing to grow in the waiting. By actively surrendering to God and serving others instead of focusing on our own worries and concerns, we demonstrate faith in action. God will honor your obedience. Examine your motivations and desires and ensure they align with God's will, and He will give you His peace and contentment each passing day you're in the waiting.

When I prayed and God told me to wait and be still, I had to trust Him, even when others advised the opposite. Listen to God's voice. I want restoration more than anyone knows, but God told me to "Be still and wait." And in my obedience to Him, He began to bless me in ways I've never imagined.

God has given me a life worth living and the ability to pour into more women than I could have ever dreamed possible. He has given me His Word as a lamp to my feet and a light to my path. His Word guides me to lead others with strength and honor.

With all my heart, I believe that one day God will bring my waiting season to its appointed end. I pray it is this side of heaven, but I am also prepared if it is not. It is not my will for things to be this way, but I trust God is doing a work in the lives of my daughters. Who am I to stand in His way? When that day of true restoration comes, what a day of rejoicing it will be. Whether it's on earth or in heaven, I will have the joy of complete restoration. It is my promise from God. God does bring beauty from ashes in His time.

Just as God is in control of all that is happening in my life, you can also know that God is in control of your life. He has a plan for you. Trust Him. He will bring restoration and beauty from ashes in His time as He works in your life. He loves you most, and He knows the desires of your heart.

Take delight in the Lord, and he will give you your heart's desires (Psalm 37:4 NLT).

Restoration with Adult Children

By Kimberly Ann Hobbs

The Bible gives us hope for a restored relationship with wayward adult children. Many relationships have been broken and bridges burned between parents and children. Despite how bleak a situation may look, God assures us there is hope. He even gives us examples of that hope in His Word.

The parable of the prodigal son, chronicled in Luke 15:11-32, is one such lesson. In Jesus' illustration, the father welcomes his repentant son back into his life with open arms. This story reminds us that the door is always open for the return of a wayward child. It also suggests that, as parents, we have a responsibility when things go awry—we are to stand with our arms open to our children through continuous prayer and a willingness to communicate, offering our never-ending, Christ-like love. God can move even in seemingly hopeless situations. Never abandon the expectancy of God's restoration when it comes to a parent-child relationship. Trust that God is working as long as you both are breathing.

As parents, we can grow by examining our own past mistakes and practices. Ask God to reveal any area where He is calling you to improve. Then, pray for an opportunity to approach your child and ask for forgiveness for your own shortcomings or errors, even as you seek to forgive your child for theirs. Forgiveness is always a great place to begin. If you feel your child doesn't trust you, it can help to reveal your heart and ask for forgiveness in front of a professional Christian counselor or therapist. A trained third party can provide active support and guidance as you seek to communicate and express accountability.

When reaching out to your child to show love to them, it is wise to sidestep any comments that would encourage their distant behavior to continue. At the same time, recognize it is not the parent's role to continually bail their children out of their situations or shield them from the consequences of their wrong actions. Instead, surrender their behavior to God. Ask Him to protect and guide your child and give you the wisdom of how you can shower them with love without enabling any injurious behavior.

If you feel it is not possible to communicate with your child, take this issue and all that surrounds it to God. Remember, nothing is impossible for Him. Then, persistently engage with them in an honest, open conversation in any way you can—even through social media, texting, or by way of another person you trust. That may be enough to open the door a crack. Express your concerns, but above all, always show love. If there is a response, be sure to listen and be respectful. Always reflect God's character, showing unwavering love and acceptance.

> *Respond gently when you are confronted, and you'll defuse the rage of another. Responding with sharp, cutting words will only make it worse. Don't you know that being angry can ruin the testimony of even the wisest of men?* (Proverbs 15:1 TPT).

Continuously pray and intercede for your child's well-being. God knows your heart and how badly the loss of them in your life hurts. I frankly speak from experience when I share about this. Ask God to draw your children back to you. Do not give up on this prayer! Look into the following scripture and heed the words.

Confess and acknowledge how you have offended one another and then pray for one another to be instantly healed, for tremendous power is released through the passionate, heartfelt prayer of a godly believer! (James 5:16 TPT).

The above scripture is of the utmost importance to memorize. I've personally taken this Word from God to my heart, and He allows me to press on even though I still can remember the mistakes I've made in my past that may have played a role in my distance from my children. God calls us to examine our actions that may have caused or widened the rift we now see. God wants us to cooperate with Him in our growth; He wants our hearts to be right with Him.

> Don't be pulled in different directions or worried about a thing. Be saturated in prayer throughout each day, offering your faith-filled requests before God with overflowing gratitude. Tell him every detail of your life, then God's wonderful peace that transcends human understanding, will make the answers known to you through Jesus Christ. Keep your thoughts continually fixed on all that is authentic and real, honorable and admirable, beautiful and respectful, pure and holy, merciful and kind. And fasten your thoughts on every glorious work of God, praising him always (Philippians 4:6-8 TPT).

May all of us who desire restoration with our adult children understand that restoration might take time. Don't try to be a perfectionist before your children, making them feel like you've never made any mistakes. Let your adult child watch you and see that you struggle or have struggled in your past, just as they might struggle. Let them see you are growing in your faith, hope, and love as God's Word instructs—then wait for this to catch their attention. Allow God to orchestrate progress in your relationship.

Don't ever give up—even if you become weary or frustrated that the restoration is not coming in your desired time. Fully surrender to God's timing. In the prodigal son story, the Bible says, *"But while he was a long way off, his father saw him and was filled with compassion for him"* (Luke 15:20 NIV). Keep your heart full of love, and press on. Patience and perseverance are the efforts that you must exude to reconnect with your loved ones one day.

Restoration: God Brings Beauty from Ashes

*And don't allow yourselves to be weary in planting good seeds,
for the season of reaping the wonderful harvest you've planted is
coming! Take advantage of every opportunity to be a blessing to
others, especially to our brothers and sisters in the family of faith!*
(Galatians 6:9-10 TPT).

Make a resolution today with the Lord; pray that God will keep you faithful in blessing others while you wait. Pray also that your children stay safe in God's care and that God will guide them closer to Himself. Pray that He will continue to make Himself known in their life. Pray that He will melt their stubborn heart and return them to you in full restoration.

Pray this prayer now and trust God as you add your own words and names of your child. Then, believe He will completely restore your broken or damaged relationships.

*Jesus looked at them and said, "With man this is impossible, but with
God all things are possible."* (Matthew 19:26 NIV).

Kimberly Anne Kahn

Kimberly Anne Kahn is a best-selling author and the founder of WildFire International Ministries in Orlando, Florida. Passionate about transformation, she has dedicated her life to revealing the redemptive power of God's love—a love that rescued her from despair and ignited her mission to heal hearts and empower women worldwide. Through her compelling writings and inspirational messages, Kimberly has become a beacon of hope, encouraging the weary and broken to embrace their own journeys of renewal and faith.

Her testimony is a tapestry woven from trials, divine intervention, and perseverance. Each book reflects God's transformative grace, inspiring others to rise above adversity and step into a life filled with purpose, passion, and spiritual abundance. More than overcoming obstacles, her work demonstrates how challenges become opportunities for growth and testimony.

Currently, Kimberly is furthering her biblical studies at Charis Bible College, deepening her knowledge of Scripture to share God's love with greater authenticity. Newly married and living in the charming town of Mount Dora, Florida, she finds joy in her two young grandsons, who remind her daily of life's beauty. Embodying resilience and grace, Kimberly continues to share the power of God's love, igniting healing and renewal.

The Refiner's Fire

By Kimberly Anne Kahn

What comes to mind when you hear the word fire?

For some, it's the roaring destruction of a house engulfed in flames or a forest fire consuming thousands of acres. Others may picture the gentle flicker of a campfire on a cool summer night, the kind that invites quiet reflection beneath a canopy of stars. Whether destructive or comforting, one thing remains true—fire is hot, powerful, and demands respect.

Fire is more than just a force of destruction. It can also provide warmth and security, drawing people together and allowing them to share stories about its beauty. Something is mesmerizing about the way flames dance, a rhythm that soothes and warns of their untamed nature. In many ways, fire mirrors life—it can consume, refine, or illuminate, depending on how we encounter it.

For me, fire is both a haunting memory and an unforgettable experience.

The summer before I started first grade, I experienced a house fire that left an indelible mark on my soul. To this day, a single song takes me back to that night.

I remember the evening before the fire vividly. My mom had just come home with two 45 single records—one for me and one for my younger brother. He repeatedly played his record, filling our home with "Bye, Bye, Miss American Pie" lyrics. Even now, I can smell the smoke when I hear that song.

That night, my mom tucked us into bed as usual. Nothing seemed out of the ordinary. But in the middle of the night, I woke to chaos. My cousin frantically shook me to wake me up. The room was dark, but the glow of red flames pierced through the thickening smoke. The heat was suffocating. Before I could understand what was happening, he scooped me up and carried me across the hall into the bathroom. In a swift motion, he shoved open a tiny window and pushed me through it. I tumbled outside, landing in a world that felt both familiar and terrifying. The night air was thick with smoke, and the house I had always known as home was now a monster—glowing, crackling, devouring everything in its path. My heart pounded as I searched for my family.

Then, I saw him. My little brother was climbing through the same window I had just escaped from. Relief washed over me, but fear still gripped my heart—where was my mother?

Panic spread as my cousin darted through the carport, shouting, "Where is Brenda?"

My mother's car was still in the driveway. No one had seen her. The fire raged, and the weight of the unknown crushed me. Was she still inside? Had she escaped another way?

My cousin desperately attempted to re-enter the house, but the fire's grip was too strong. Time felt frozen. The uncertainty, the helplessness—it was unbearable. And then, suddenly, she appeared. My mother ran toward us, breathless, her face streaked with tears. She found us at the neighbor's house, threw her arms around us, and wept.

It wasn't until later that I learned the truth: My mother had been out with friends that night, leaving her car behind. When the fire started, people assumed she was trapped inside—that misunderstanding fueled the frantic search for her. But the truth inflicted me with an emotional wound. That night, the fire stole more than just our home. It, along with my mom's absence, stole my sense of security, planting seeds of fear that I was abandoned and unprotected.

It wasn't the first time I felt abandoned, and it wouldn't be the last. The flames may have destroyed our home that night, but the feeling of being left behind—of not being protected—was something I carried long after the embers cooled.

My parents were in the middle of a divorce at the time. My mother left my father. She had been having an affair, and in search of something she thought was better, she walked away from our family, taking us with her. I was too young to understand the complexities of adult relationships, but I did understand loss. One day, my dad was there, and the next, he wasn't. The divorce shattered me.

I'd lay awake at night, wondering what I had done wrong. Was I not good enough? Was I the reason she left my daddy? The pain of losing my father felt unbearable, but I held onto the belief that, no matter what, Eddie Ewell was still my daddy. Until the day my mother told me he wasn't.

I don't remember the exact moment she sat me down and said the words, but I do remember how they felt—like the ground had been ripped out from under me.

"Eddie isn't your real father."

I stared at her, my mind reeling. *What?*

"Your biological father is Curtis Gaskin." The man she was married to before Eddie.

No! No, that isn't true. It can't be true. I shook my head, tears burning my eyes. You're lying! I have a father. I know who I am—his little girl. You can't just take that away from me.

But the truth didn't care about what I wanted to believe.

Night after night, I cried myself to sleep, longing for the man I had always called Daddy. The pain of the divorce had already left a wound in my heart, and now, that wound was ripped wide open. If Eddie wasn't my birth father, then who was I? For the first time in my life, I felt utterly lost.

> *Though my father and mother forsake me, the Lord will receive me* (Psalm 27:10 NIV).

I went through many episodes of trauma throughout my lifetime—too many to even write about. But I did not realize for the longest time that my trauma didn't start when I was five years old and sexually abused by a neighbor. It began when I was in the womb.

When I was 18, my mother told me the truth about why she left my biological father. Curtis Gaskin, the man whose name I had once refused to accept, had been physically violent. Not just toward her, but toward me—before I even took my first breath.

When my mother told him she was pregnant, he didn't respond with joy. He didn't place a protective hand on her stomach or dream about the future. Instead, he beat her. Again and again. His goal wasn't just to hurt her—it was to end the life growing inside her. That baby was me. But what the enemy intended for harm, God was already turning for good (Genesis 50:20).

I was supposed to be born on February 14, 1965—a Valentine's Day baby. But God's plan was different. My birth was delayed, and when I finally entered the world four days later, I came fighting for my life.

The umbilical cord was wrapped tightly around my neck, suffocating me. The lack of oxygen caused complications, and the doctors told my mother that I would be mentally delayed and have learning disabilities. But the enemy had underestimated the One who had formed me.

> *For you created my inmost being; you knit me together in my mother's womb. I praise you because I am fearfully and wonderfully made* (Psalm 139:13-14 NIV).

From the very beginning, I was fighting to survive.

Research has confirmed what God has always known—a fetus in the womb can experience trauma. While the dangers of substance abuse during pregnancy are widely recognized, fewer understand the devastating effects of physical abuse. Blunt force trauma can lead to brain injuries, developmental delays, and lasting emotional wounds. High maternal stress levels increase cortisol production, affecting the baby's neurological development. Many enter the world already carrying unseen scars from the trauma they endured before birth. But despite the trauma, I was not an accident. God saw me before I was born; all my days were already written in His book.

> *Your eyes saw my unformed body; all the days ordained for me were written in your book before one of them came to be* (Psalm 139:16 NIV).

For me, survival wasn't something I had to learn—it was all I had ever known. From the day I took my first breath, my body and mind were already operating in survival mode. I was always on edge, scanning for danger. I learned to disconnect from my feelings to avoid pain.

When I was 13 years old, I was skateboarding with my brother when, in a quick flash, I felt my body go empty. I couldn't express joy, pain, love, sadness, or any emotion. I felt dead inside. I thought to myself, *What is wrong with me?* I tried to make myself feel happy—I couldn't. I tried to be angry—I couldn't. Looking back, I believe this was the beginning of me disconnecting from my emotions. It became my survival mechanism, and I carried it into adulthood.

As I got older, I began to heal from my past, but the effects of survival mode lingered. I struggled to focus and experienced fatigue, stomach issues, and muscle tension. I was a reactor, responding out of fear rather than love. My thoughts were lies I believed about myself and others, and I always expected harm or betrayal from people. Though I couldn't always put what I felt into words, the underlying emotions were always the same: rejection, fear, and feeling unloved and unwanted.

The mental delays the doctors predicted weren't just physical; they were emotional. As a baby in the womb, I didn't know the words to describe these emotions, but I felt them. And I felt them deeply; fear was the drive of my life.

> *For the Spirit God gave us does not make us timid, but gives us power, love, and self-discipline* (2 Timothy 1:7 NIV).

The effects of trauma ran deep, but they did not define me. The fire I walked through tried to consume me, but God had a plan more significant than my pain. I didn't just enter the world—I fought my way into it.

> *When you pass through the waters, I will be with you, and when you pass through the rivers, they will not sweep over you. When you walk through the fire, you will not be burned; the flames will not set you ablaze* (Isaiah 43:2 NIV).

Though trauma marked the beginning of my story, it would not have the final say. God had a plan.

I was on my honeymoon with my amazing husband—the man I had longed and prayed for. I had asked God to bring me a godly man who would do ministry with me and stand beside me as we fulfilled His calling. When God answered that prayer, I was overjoyed, full of hope, and excited for what our future would hold. But shortly after we returned from our honeymoon, the enemy came in like a flood.

We didn't see it at first. We were blindsided, unaware of how the enemy used our past wounds against us. He crept in through the cracks, through old traumas, insecurities, and pain we had buried long before we met each other. Triggers we never expected began surfacing, and suddenly, our marriage—only weeks old—was under attack. The fighting became unbearable. Just five weeks into our marriage, my husband left. The pain was unbearable. The devastation shook me to my core. We were on the brink of divorce, and I felt like my prayers had been shattered. I don't know how many times the word divorce came up. Every time we fought, one of us would say it. We had no idea how to deal with the pain, the triggers, the past wounds that were rising to the surface. Anger, resentment, bitterness—they were all eating away at us.

But then, amid my despair, I heard His voice. That still, small, sweet voice of God whispered, "Don't give up." Again and again, those words echoed in my spirit. God would light a flame inside me, giving me strength when I had none. I held onto His voice as I pressed forward, refusing to let go of the promise that He had given me. Day after day, week after week, we tried to fix our marriage ourselves. But no matter how hard we tried, we failed. The battle was too big. We were too weak. Our faith had crumbled, and instead of looking to God, we were drowning in our pain and devastation.

For a long time, I kept our struggles to myself. I didn't want people to see my weakness. I didn't want to be seen as a failure. I had always been the strong one who pushed through and survived. But this? This was different. I was crumbling under the weight of everything, and the loneliness was suffocating.

Before we got married, I heard the Lord say: "I will take care of you."

At the time, I thought it was a promise of a happy marriage, a life filled with joy and purpose with my husband. But I didn't realize what God truly meant.

God's promise to take care of me wasn't only for when things were good. He was talking about the moment I would be on my knees, alone, brokenhearted, crying out to Him for help. He told me, "I will take care of you—when you feel abandoned. I will comfort you—when the pain is too much to bear. I will restore you—even in the deepest wounds that have yet to heal." I thought He was going to restore my marriage. But first, He had to restore me. A few months later, the Holy Spirit said to me: "You are about to go through the fire."

At first, I thought He meant that our marriage was going through a season of refining. I assumed He was preparing us for healing, restoration, and the emergence of something beautiful from the ashes. But I was wrong.

God was taking me through the fire first. This was a process of refining meant just for me.

Like the three Hebrews in the book of Daniel who were bound—hands tied, feet shackled, and completely helpless—when they were thrown into the fiery furnace. They had no control, no escape. The fire was meant to consume them, to be their end.

But God had another plan.

When I finally surrendered my marriage, my traumas, my brokenness—when I laid down the bitterness, resentment, and anger that had taken root in my soul—I was thrown into the fire.

For so long, I thought I had to hold it all together. I thought I had to fight for my marriage, to push through my past, to somehow fix myself. But when I let go, when I finally gave it all to God, I realized that surrender doesn't mean defeat.

Surrender means refinement.

Just like those three men in the furnace, I was not alone. Jesus was there. Not watching from the outside, not distant, not waiting for me to figure it out—He was in the fire with me.

At first, I resisted. The flames burned, bringing up every hidden wound, every buried trauma, every shattered piece of my heart that I had spent a lifetime suppressing. I wanted to run. I wanted to numb the pain. I wanted to retreat back to what was familiar, even if it was broken.

But Jesus was breaking the chains. One by one, every chain that had held me captive—fear, rejection, shame, anger, unworthiness—began to fall. I thought the fire would destroy me. But instead, it set me free.

I am not out of this process yet. The flames are still refining me, still bringing the hidden places to the surface, still stripping away what does not belong. But I am no longer afraid. Because I know that this fire isn't here to consume me; it's here to make me new. God is restoring me. He is taking the burned ashes of my past and turning them into something beautiful.

> He will sit as a refiner and purifier of silver; He will purify the Levites and refine them like gold and silver. Then the Lord will have men who will bring offerings in righteousness (Malachi 3:3 NIV).

The fire may feel unbearable at times.

The process may feel endless.

But I know what waits on the other side: beauty from ashes, strength from sorrow, joy from mourning.

And for the first time in my life, I am not walking through the fire alone.

Jesus is with me. He is refining me. He is restoring me. Before He could restore my marriage, He had to restore me. God is removing the pain, brokenness, and walls I built to protect myself. He is peeling back the layers of wounds I didn't even know were still there. Because fire doesn't consume us—it refines us.

For so long, I thought the fire was a punishment. But now, I see the truth.

The fire wasn't meant to destroy me but to purify me. God is redeeming what was once broken. And when we come through the fire, we won't even smell like smoke. We will be restored. Our relationships will be restored! Because God is bringing restoration. Beauty from ashes!

If you are reading this and find yourself in the middle of the fire, don't give up!

I know what it feels like to be weary, to want to walk away, and to believe that healing is impossible. I see the exhaustion of fighting battles that feel too heavy to carry. I know the pain of wondering if restoration is even possible.

But I also know this: God is faithful. No matter what you have walked through—abuse, trauma, rejection, betrayal, heartbreak, or the deep pain of a broken marriage—God sees you. He has not forgotten you. And He is not done with your story.

The enemy will whisper lies that tell you it's over and that your marriage is too far gone. That your heart is too broken. That you will never heal.

But those are lies. God is a God of redemption. He is the God who restores.

I will restore to you the years that the swarming locust has eaten (Joel 2:25 ESV).

You may feel like your life is in ruins—as if everything has been burned down to nothing but ashes. But let me tell you something about ashes: they are the very thing God uses to create something new, more beautiful, and stronger than before.

> *To all who mourn... he will give a crown of beauty for ashes, a joyous blessing instead of mourning, festive praise instead of despair* (Isaiah 61:3 NLT).

Healing takes time. Restoration takes surrender. And redemption takes trust.

Let God take you through the fire—not to destroy you, but to refine you.

Let Him peel back the layers of pain, not to hurt you, but to heal you.

Let Him restore what is broken—not just your circumstance, but you.

You are not alone. You are deeply loved. And your story is not over.

Hold on, sister. Because on the other side of this fire, you will rise stronger than ever before. And when you do, you will look back and see that even in the fire—He was with you all along.

Restoration Found in God's Word

By Kimberly Ann Hobbs

What better place is there to find instruction and guidance for the soul's restoration than in the Word of God?

> *Restore us, O God; make your face shine upon us, that we may be saved* (Psalm 80:3 NIV).

We all may encounter times when we are searching for divine restoration for our health, relationships, or spiritual brokenness. We would be blessed to remember that even in the most desolate circumstances, our God can bring about complete restoration, ushering in a fresh, clean start.

Far too often, we may feel we face too many obstacles to overcome our brokenness, even becoming intimidated by the mere thought of pursuing restoration. At times, we give up seeking help and throw in the towel long before heading in the proper direction—seeking God in His Word, which would ultimately lead us to a place of healing. We might also become too intimidated to pray—afraid God won't hear our prayers because they are not good or holy enough. If this applies to you, take heart. God wants you to come to Him, and He hears every prayer you offer. God understands your cry for help no matter the words you use or how you say them—because He knows your heart!

By drawing closer to God through prayer and reading His Word, you will find yourself restored in spirit and in truth, which is the best place you could ever be.

When I suffered in brokenness from a life riddled with sin and shame, there seemed no way out of my crippled life and the ugly consequences of my actions. I made the same mistakes over and over, becoming stuck in a cycle of believing I could never heal or find my true identity again. I had nowhere to turn; no one had the answers I wanted to hear or words that could help my situation. So, I was left to make changes based on my own belief system, which was comprised of lies to myself. How could I ever change and get better? My belief system was all screwed up! But when I prayed and read and acted on scriptures, my life was transformed by God. God spoke back to my prayers through His Word.

> *For the word of God is living and active. Sharper than any double-edged sword, it penetrates even to dividing soul and spirit, joints, and marrow; it judges the thoughts and attitudes of the heart* (Hebrews 4:12 NIV).

Bear your soul to the One who loves you most. No matter what your need might be, He will hear your heart. Then go to the Word of God. He will listen to the bellows of your brokenness and guide you through the POWER of His Word.

When we ask God to speak and then follow through by seeking Him in the Bible, He answers. God's Word is our manual and guide to complete restoration.

> *"You will seek me and find me when you seek me with all your heart"* (Jeremiah 29:13 NIV).

If we search for God's answers in His Word while fully committing to align with His truths for restoration, we can trust He will always speak to us. His Word says in Isaiah, *"See, I am doing a new thing! Now it springs up; do you not perceive it? I am making a way in the desert and streams in the wasteland"* (Isaiah 43:19 NIV).

The Bible tells us that God can restore our brokenness and change it into something beautiful and better. Jesus tells us in Matthew 11:28-30 (NIV), *"Come to me, all you who are weary and burdened, and I will give you rest. Take my yoke upon you and learn from me, for I am gentle and humble in heart, and you will find rest for your souls. For my yoke is easy and my burden is light."*

God's Word is a game-changer! God is in the business of transformation; there is no better way to restore our souls than to use His Word to find every answer we need!!!

. . . .

Connie A. VanHorn

Connie A. VanHorn has a heart for encouraging others to find their God-given purpose. She serves on the Women World Leaders' Leadership Team as an ambassador and administrative assistant, is a best-selling author, and writes for *Voice of Truth* magazine. Hoping her story will help someone else, Connie passionately shares how her amazing and loving God spared her, an ordinary woman, and gave her new life.

Connie resides in Winston-Salem, North Carolina, where she has participated in discipleship classes, taught Sunday school, and attended Bible classes at Vintage Bible College.

Being a mother is Connie's greatest accomplishment and her first, best ministry. She dreams of changing the world by sharing Jesus and raising world-changers with a kingdom perspective. She enjoys being active, making bracelets, journaling, writing, and spending time with her family.

Connie dedicates this chapter to her mother, having come to understand her mother's reasons for holding her secrets close to her heart. Life can be tough, especially for women who carry struggles and hide their own childhood traumas. "Thank you for always teaching me about kindness and unconditional love, even though you were hurting and struggling too. I love you always, Mom!"

Secrets in the Bluegrass

By Connie A. VanHorn

They say the Kentucky bluegrass holds secrets that might never be uncovered unless someone goes digging for them.

Very hidden in the heart of the bluegrass lies secrets waiting to be revealed, whispers of my life story that have remained hidden for decades. Until recently.

In a small town in Kentucky, a story of forbidden love took place. It seemed like a chance meeting when two people from very different backgrounds came together, but their connection changed many lives and future generations, including mine.

A divide in the town separated the farm folks from the others in town. Still, a country farm man found himself drawn to a beautiful "non-farm" woman who was trapped in an unhealthy marriage.

Lily, the woman from the poor side of the tracks, held onto their love like a precious gem, burying it deep within her heart. The farm man offered small clues of his affection, like the glass bottle of chocolate milk left on her porch every week, a luxury she could never afford.

Their yearning remained hidden until, over half a century later, the secrets they kept locked away finally came to light, revealing a story of love and commitment that lasted through the years.

These two strangers eventually created a child together, a boy, after which they immediately parted ways, never to mention their secret again. The boy grew up hearing the same whispers that haunted my own childhood.

The farm man and Lily lived in the same town, both married to another. It's unclear whether they kept in touch—although the rental house she lived in was under his family name, and farm-fresh chocolate milk was regularly left on the porch. This hidden truth would accompany them to their graves.

Their son grew up and, at 17 years old, met a girl near the post office.

The boy didn't know much about the girl, except that she was friendly. They engaged in light conversation, and he impulsively invited her over. They spent the day together before she vanished without a trace.

It later emerged that the girl was several years older than him and in an unhealthy marriage; she returned to her life in Florida the day after they met. She had momentarily escaped into the bluegrass, leaving behind her troubled marriage and childhood traumas, struggling with adulthood all at once. She would hide her Kentucky secrets in the deepest parts of the bluegrass.

On that fateful day, these two young individuals also conceived a child -

Hey, that's me!

I am the product of their hidden past, but my journey goes far beyond the bluegrass. Years later, I dived into the secrets of the bluegrass, piecing together the truth about my life and so much more!

In the beginning...

It was the first day of school. New school. New state. Fifth grade. We moved around a lot. I remember walking into the room and seeing bold words on the chalkboard—"Who am I?"

As we took our seats, the teacher introduced herself. She started by saying, "Who am I?"

She went on to explain that we would each take a turn standing up and sharing who we are. She wanted to focus on that concept along with the curriculum as she prepared us for middle school.

I froze. My body went limp as I felt a heat wave consume me.

Who am I? I had no idea what to say. *I don't know who I am, and I surely don't want them to know anything about my life. I don't even like my life. I'm embarrassed. Ashamed.*

This was also the year I experienced firsthand the definition of "bullying."

The teacher called on me to stand up.

"Who are you, Connie?"

I could hear it now. The names that were constantly uttered behind me. "Vanhorn-eee ~ toot toot."

They would mock my words and laugh at my clothing. That summer before school, we started shopping at a store called "Loaves and Fishes." It was a hand-me-down store for mothers in need. I actually loved going there with my mom—it felt like Christmas. But wearing the actual clothes to school was a different story. I was afraid someone would notice an old shirt or dress they had donated.

"Well, Connie... Who are you?"

I sat silent. At that exact moment, a boy from across the room made a noise; the teacher turned her attention to him and skipped right over me. I call that a miracle.

Yet, the boy's actions seemed to start a firestorm. I don't recall his exact ugly noise, but I do remember his name perfectly. It was the first day of a year full of torture and bullying.

And it was only the beginning of my identity crisis. Looking back, I now understand that I searched for my identity in all the wrong places.

I often heard whispers and rumors that my dad was not my real dad, and that my "real" biological father, "JC," lived in Kentucky. This was especially hard to hear at a young age. I loved my dad, but I believed that finding this "other" guy would finally reveal who I truly was and allow me to piece together a puzzle that felt scattered in me.

I carried the name JC in my heart for most of my life, convinced that if I could just locate him, I would find my missing piece. Even though I had a father who loved me and played an important role in my life, I felt an unshakeable need to determine if the secrets and rumors about JC were true.

As the years passed, my longing to find my true identity only deepened, leaving me feeling lost and alone. I couldn't talk to anyone about this part of me. I didn't want to hurt my parents by bringing it up to them. I considered it was best just to look happy! So, I pushed my feelings further and further within me.

I became a runner—whenever life got hard, I would run away, searching for anything and everything to fill the voids, only to come up empty. It wasn't until I decided to take an ancestry DNA test 30+ years later that I felt I might finally find the truth I had been seeking for so long. I was eager to know if JC was indeed my father.

When the day came to receive the results, I could hardly contain my excitement; my hands trembled as I started to read. I was desperate to see JC's name—not because I sought a new father, but because I simply wanted the truth. To my shock, the name JC was nowhere to be found. Instead, I found unfamiliar names that left me more confused than ever. I filtered through these results over the following months; the hurt continued as I dealt with the unsettling realization that the dad who raised me was not my biological father. If he wasn't, and if JC wasn't either, then who was?

At one point, I had the opportunity to connect with JC's wife, and we began to build a friendship. There was a mutual hope between us that JC would be my biological father. She was incredibly kind, welcoming, and an overall loving person. Having recently lost her own daughter, she was open to the idea of me being part of her family, which made me feel even more accepted.

For the first time, I thought I might have a tangible connection—brown hair and brown eyes that mirrored JC's. We all felt a resemblance, and it brought a sense of hope. But even with our growing bond and connection, it still wasn't JC. And with that realization, I found myself in a deeper identity crisis, feeling so lost about who I truly was.

In all my searching for my biological father, I hoped to find something to fill an emptiness within me. I never considered looking up to my heavenly Father for my true identity. I was seeking my identity in the wrong things of this world, when in reality, my true identity was in one source: God.

We are children of God, and our roots, ancestors, and DNA are connected through Jesus. It is in Him that God desires us to discover who we really are. It is in Him that we find the missing piece. Our true identity lies in our relationship with Him and His love for us.

But I was still searching.

> I have been crucified with Christ and I no longer live, but Christ lives in me. The life I now live in the body, I live by faith in the Son of God, who loved me and gave himself for me (Galatians 2:20 NIV).

My search for my biological father lasted for nine months, consuming my thoughts day and night. As I went deeper, I found out that both sides of my biological father's family had large numbers of children—each grandparent had nine kids! With so many people to filter through, the search felt overwhelming and took forever. I also assumed my biological father was around my mother's age, never considering he could have been just a teenager in high school when I was born, which caused me to jump right over his actual name on several occasions. "It can't be this guy. He's too young." That's what I kept saying.

But then, just when I felt the search might never end, I received a message from a kind gentleman. He had heard about my search from his much older brother and believed, deep down, that I was his child. His message felt like hope but was also very scary.

He had been completely unaware of my existence, but he did remember meeting my mom and knew her name. It felt like a connection that God had perfectly woven between us to be revealed one day. When I shared the truth with my other dad, who raised me, he was very supportive. It turned out that I was blessed with two dads who genuinely cared for me and supported me through everything that brought me to this moment.

In my very long search, I uncovered more secrets than I ever thought I would. It turned out that my biological father had a past very similar to my own. He, too, had been told the rumors and whispers about his own father not being his biological dad. It was only after I revealed the truth about my DNA that he uncovered the truths of his own.

Together, we were able to piece together a complicated puzzle that connected our lives in unexpected ways. We uncovered the secrets that had been hidden by those we loved and cared for over the years. This journey not only brought clarity to our own identities but also to the family history that shaped us both.

After finding this piece of my puzzle, I believed I would finally understand who I am and where I truly belong. But that wasn't my reality. Although I felt a sense of relief at having answers to my questions, I still struggled with the same uncomfortable question...

Who am I?

I still struggled with my identity and my place in this world. My journey was far from over, and my search for my true identity and security continued.

For most of my life, I concealed my true self from everyone around me. I unknowingly buried my identity deeper and deeper in that bluegrass, alongside all the other secrets surrounding my existence. As a result, it was difficult for me to view myself in a positive light.

Then, in August 2014, I surrendered my heart to Jesus and began to see myself through His perspective and recognize the woman He intended me to become. However, I was still missing a valuable piece—I had to understand and believe that I belong to God first and can only find my identity in Him. Only when I truly came to know and believe who God is could I actually begin to understand who I am.

That is the key to each of us when we ask, *Who am I?*

We are all made in God's image, fearfully and wonderfully created by His loving hands. We are not defined by the standards of this world (or social media!) but by the love and grace of our heavenly Father.

When we see ourselves as daughters of the King, our perspective shifts. You are cherished and adored by the Creator of the universe. You are chosen, loved, and accepted just as you are. Cracks and all!!

Finding my true identity in Jesus has brought me to a place of hope, where my real purpose started to unfold and His truth about me was revealed, answering the question, Who am I? I started to emerge as more than just a secret from the bluegrass. I no longer had to strive to be someone I wasn't, hiding my identity, but I could believe the truth that I am enough just as I am!

Child of God, your identity is secure in Christ, and nothing can shake the foundation of who you are in Him.

> For I am convinced that neither death nor life, neither angels nor demons, neither the present nor the future, nor any powers, neither height nor depth, nor anything else in all creation, will be able to separate us from the love of God that is in Christ Jesus our Lord (Romans 8:38-39 NIV).

Several years ago, I heard a pastor spend her entire message on who her God is. At that moment, God gripped my heart, and I started to understand where my true identity resides. In Him! It doesn't matter what anyone else says about me. The enemy will try to convince me that I'm worthless and not liked—he wants me to stay in an identity crisis. The same is true for you.

When we don't claim our identity in Christ, the enemy has an open door to our minds and our lives and will work to keep us away from God and our eternal home with Him. Knowing the *TRUTH* of our true identity is a weapon keeping us rooted and on track to the life God meant us to have.

Please read this next part out loud right now and repeat it daily until you know it by heart and BELIEVE IT!

I am my Father's daughter.
I was made in the image of a perfect King.
I am cherished and loved by a good God, even when I don't feel worthy.
I refuse to believe any lies the enemy or the world throws at me.
I belong to a loving Father.
THIS is the TRUTH, and I choose to believe it!

Know who God is and know who you are. You are His beautiful child, created in His image to shine His light in a dark world.

It's so beautiful for me to finally have the right answers to the questions I searched for all those years. I solved my puzzle! This journey has brought me reassurance about my past, which is a wonderful feeling. I discovered that I look exactly like my biological father's mother, someone I never had the chance to meet. I also have another brother whose entire family welcomed me with open arms. He and his wife instantly and proudly became Mamaw and Papaw! It's brought many blessings to my life.

I learned that I inherited my brown eyes from my other grandma, who had the most stunning, big brown eyes. I was the only child in my family with that trait, and now I know this part of my identity is unique and true.

I cherish the traits I received from both sides of my biological family. And I especially hold dear those from my dad who raised me. Even though he and I are not linked by blood, we are connected in many other ways. He's been a constant in my life, and my children have been blessed to call him "Papa." I love all my siblings more than anything in this world and am proud to be like both my dads!

I now realize I didn't need to spend all those years searching for my true identity, though I am grateful that my search brought new people and something very special in my life and my children's lives!

The truth is, my identity was rooted in me long before I was ever born. It's in the One who created me. I am not defined by my past or my DNA but by the love and purpose given to me by my Creator. The voids are starting to close, and I am filled with confidence, knowing that I'm valued and loved just as I am.

God restores our broken pieces and uses them to create masterpieces!

> I praise you because I am fearfully and wonderfully made; your works are wonderful, I know that full well (Psalm 139:14 NIV).

Besides my family, God has blessed me with an incredible group of beautiful warriors. These women, all part of Women World Leaders, welcomed me into their sisterhood and believed in me even when I struggled to see my own worth. They looked beyond my brokenness and helped me find my true purpose. Little by little, it's been nothing but light streaming through the cracks of my wings! See all people through God's eyes!!

Finding my identity in God is a beautiful thing that has changed how I see myself and my place in the world. God healed so many of my broken pieces. He restored relationships that were strained over time, piecing together the torn and broken threads of connection and love. God has truly made beauty from ashes, turning my pain and struggles into something amazing and piecing together a masterpiece as only He can.

I am starting to see through my own cracks and now know that I am His beautiful daughter, perfectly designed for His plans. This truth has filled me with hope and understanding that I am cherished, valued, and made to shine His love and light in a dark world. So are YOU!

You have a loving Father in heaven who loves you more than anything or anyone in this world. He will turn the broken pieces of your life into His beautiful masterpieces. All you have to do is surrender your pieces to Him!

For we are God's handiwork, created in Christ Jesus to do good works, which God prepared in advance for us to do (Ephesians 2:10 NIV).

Da'Quanya Hanson

Da'Quanya Hanson is a disciple of Jesus Christ with a heart for God, His people, and His creation. She was born in Riviera Beach, Florida, and raised with her younger brother, De'Vario, in a Christian home by a single mother, Deidra. Both her brother and her mother went home to be with the Lord, after which the Lord healed Da'Quanya's grief and pain and gave her a vision to nurture "What's Your Seed Ministries," a ministry dedicated to serving inner-city kids.

Da'Quanya has also teamed up with Women World Leaders, which has impacted her love for writing and telling her story with and to other women. Her mission is sharing the Gospel of Jesus Christ through creative outlets, expressing the love of Jesus with meals, clothing, and words of encouragement to the homeless, whom she calls "future homeowners."

She enjoys drives near the beach in her camper van, evangelizing, painting, and sharing hope, joy, and laughs with the broken and forgotten. Being sensitive to Holy Spirit every day is an adventure for Da'Quanya, who is always ready to let her light shine.

But God Meant It for Good

By Da'Quanya Hanson

Can you imagine having your life shattered right before your eyes? Many of us can likely relate to this feeling. We have all faced our share of trials and tribulations at different points in our lives. We have made choices that have led us to unforeseen circumstances and outcomes. My journey began with a pivotal moment that not only changed my life but also affected future generations. The repercussions of my actions ultimately brought me back to God, who renewed my hope and reassured me that He was working everything out for my good.

One day during my senior year of high school, my best friend was driving us to school when she mentioned that she planned to skip class and spend the day at her boyfriend's house. As I listened, a thought crossed my mind: maybe this could be my chance to skip school, too. I asked her if she could drop me off at my boyfriend's place and pick me up later. She looked surprised and asked, "Are you sure?" I nodded, affirming my decision.

In that moment, she turned the car in the opposite direction, and I felt a wave of excitement wash over me, momentarily pushing aside any worries about the consequences of skipping school. This wasn't something I typically did; I valued my education, worked hard for good grades, and never wanted to face the outcome of getting into trouble. But I thought this could be a much-needed escape, a break from the stress I was dealing with at home.

My mother was seriously ill, and her condition had left her unable to care for me and my brother. Weekly dialysis treatments drained her energy, and watching her suffer day after day filled me with fear and frustration about losing her. I buried those feelings deep down, pretending everything was fine. If only I had known how that day would shape my future.

A few weeks after that day I skipped school, I sat down for breakfast one morning and bit into my favorite egg, bacon, and cheese sandwich. I suddenly felt a wave of nausea wash over me. I immediately rushed to the bathroom, barely making it in time to vomit. My cousin, who was eating breakfast with me, heard the commotion and asked if I was okay. I couldn't respond; I was too overwhelmed.

When I finally emerged from the bathroom, my cousin stood there holding a pregnancy test kit and said, "Girl, you might be pregnant. You should take this."

I stared at her in disbelief, quickly snatching the pregnancy test and heading back into the bathroom. To my shock, the results came back positive. My heart raced as I rushed out to show my cousin.

"I'm pregnant," I said, my voice trembling with fear.

She looked at me with disappointment and urged me to consider an abortion, saying I was too young to have a baby. Her words hit me hard, filling me with a sense of dread. The idea of becoming a teen mom terrified me, and the thought of telling my mother about my pregnancy was equally daunting. I felt lost and overwhelmed, as if my entire life had been turned upside down, and I had no idea how to regain control.

My future plans had always included waiting until marriage to have children. I remember a saying I heard from a pastor: "Don't have the marriage before the wedding." At that moment, I realized I was far from either. The dreams

I had of waiting were shattered. My mom had often spoken to me about the importance of saving myself for marriage, sharing her own experiences from her youth and expressing her desire for me to make better choices than she had. I cherished those conversations and tried my best to heed her advice.

The thought of telling my mom that her teenage daughter was pregnant filled me with shame and guilt. I felt completely unprepared to face her or my boyfriend that day, so I decided to wait until the following day to share the news.

The next day, I called my best friend to share the news and express my uncertainty about what to do. She was incredibly supportive and assured me that she would stand by any decision I made, which gave me a bit of relief and the courage I needed to talk to my mother.

That afternoon, I finally told my mom everything. To my surprise, she responded with a calmness that eased my fear. She acknowledged that it would be challenging for me to care for a baby without her support, especially since she knew her time was limited. The love she showed me, without any judgment, only deepened my feelings of guilt. I felt like I had let her down by making a reckless choice while she was battling a serious illness.

I mentioned my cousin's suggestion about having an abortion, and my mom looked at me with concern, simply saying, "It's all going to be alright." Even without saying much else, her presence and love reassured me that things would work out. I could see that she was exhausted and didn't want to carry the weight of my news. I wrapped my arms around her in a hug, holding on to her words and believing that, somehow, everything would be okay.

I soon called my boyfriend to share the big news, and he was extremely excited. He immediately began expressing how he would be there to help me take care of our child and reassured me not to worry about anything. Hearing his confidence and joy and knowing he wanted to keep the baby brought me a sense of peace.

I wanted to share in his excitement, but I struggled to feel that way myself. I didn't want to dampen his enthusiasm, so I chose not to mention my thoughts about having an abortion. I was so confused about my feelings that I couldn't decide whether to keep the baby or not, caught in a conflict between two very different paths.

Hearing my mom's loving concerns, my boyfriend's excitement, my best friend's support, and my cousin's words echoing in my mind, I began to worry about what others might think of me—my family, friends, and classmates. One moment, I felt a glimmer of happiness, and the next, I was filled with disappointment in myself. I longed to pray and seek guidance from God, but shame held me back from asking for His help. I just wanted answers, as the weight of my situation was taking a toll on my mental well-being.

School was back in session, and I was bracing myself to face my classmates. With senior activities and dues approaching, it was a time for seniors to savor their final days together. As everything began to unfold, I knew I needed to make a decision quickly. Inside, I felt a swirl of shame, sadness, confusion, and embarrassment, even as I wore a smile on my face, pretending everything was okay and that I had it all figured out.

My plan was to wear loose-fitting clothes to hide my growing belly. Being petite, it was hard to overlook any weight gain, and my body was going through significant changes. I was struggling with nausea after eating dairy, so I decided to skip school lunches altogether. My breasts felt sore and tender, my face was starting to round out, and I was experiencing strange cravings.

Day by day, it became clearer that a new life was developing inside me, and I was doing everything I could to keep it a secret.

A voice in my head kept urging me, "Have an abortion; you can pretend it never happened, and your life will return to normal." Taking that thought seriously, I started calling abortion clinics to gather the information I needed about the process.

With each call, I felt as though I was preparing to sell a part of myself. The more details they provided, the more numb I became to the entire idea. One common theme among all the clinics was their strong push to get me to come in for an appointment. It felt like an invisible force was propelling me toward that decision.

They asked me questions and emphasized that if I chose to go through with the abortion, I needed to decide soon, as I was further along than most clients, and the cost of the procedure would increase as the baby grew.

I had no idea where I would find the money to pay for the procedure. My boyfriend was excited about becoming a dad, and I felt torn about how to tell him my plans. Ultimately, I had no choice but to share what I was considering regarding our baby and that I needed his financial support. As I finished sharing, he was furious and couldn't believe I would even consider such a thing. His reaction was not what I had hoped for; this led to a heated argument between us. He stood firm in his refusal to help, insisting that it was a decision we both had to make.

Frustrated by his response, I ended the call abruptly. I just wanted to get the procedure done as soon as possible before it became too late. With the pressure of needing to abort my baby before a certain period, my cousin knew I was in need, so she decided to let me borrow the money for the procedure. I called again to the clinic with the lowest fees and scheduled an appointment for the next day.

The next morning, I woke up with a heavy sense of anxiety, knowing I was about to make a choice I might regret. My boyfriend wasn't there to support me, and my mom was in her final days. I felt sad, confused, and utterly alone, unsure of what to expect. As my cousin drove me to the clinic, I remained silent the entire journey, fighting back tears. Deep down, I knew what I was doing felt wrong, but I also felt trapped with no other option.

When we arrived, she parked in front of the clinic and let me out of the car. As I approached the entrance, fear gripped me. The sight of a clinic filled with vulnerable-looking individuals was daunting. Some women were young, while others were older, but they all shared the same fearful expressions I felt. After what seemed like an eternity, my name was finally called, and I was led into the back room. A wave of nausea washed over me as I realized what was about to happen. I lay down, closed my eyes, and surrendered to the moment.

The procedure was over. As I made my way to my cousin's car, I felt both weak and relieved, yet I was physically and emotionally drained. I didn't want to discuss what had just happened. Deep down, I understood that my baby was gone, my uterus was empty, and there was no way to reverse the decision I had made.

Once we arrived at the house, I began to process everything that had occurred in that room. I went into my mom's room to share what I had just done. All she could do in that moment was hold me tightly, and I felt her embrace as a source of comfort. Inside, I wanted to scream and cry.

I sensed that she wanted to say something, to help me in some way. Just having her there with me was enough at that moment. I made a decision to try to forget what I had done and move on with my life as if it had never happened. At least, that's what I thought I would do.

A few days after the procedure, I called my boyfriend to share what I had done and how it all went. Unsurprisingly, he wasn't happy; our conversation quickly spiraled into a confrontation, and ultimately, we broke up. At the time, I struggled to understand why he was so angry with me, but now I see things more clearly. He knew it was our baby growing inside me, and by making that choice, I had taken away his chance to become a father. Although I made the final decision, I realized that my choice affected not only me and the baby but also my boyfriend.

A few months before my high school graduation, my mom went home to be with the Lord, and I was left with the responsibility of taking care of my brother. It was a challenging season, but we eventually moved on with our lives. I started working for a driving company that allowed me the freedom to listen to Christian songs and encouraging messages on the radio each day while making deliveries.

One particular day, I was listening to a woman share her story about having an abortion. I turned the radio up loud enough to hear what she had to say. Hearing her speak about her experience was heartbreaking.

Memories soon came flooding into my mind of being on the procedure bed that day. Years had gone by since that devastating day, and I had eventually put that moment in the past and never talked about it again.

After the woman finished sharing her story, she began to express the forgiveness she received from Jesus Christ after making that decision and how He didn't come to condemn the world but to save us from our sins. I could feel the tears falling from my eyes and my heart rate rising. All the emotions I had buried came up again. I realized that what I had done was truly wrong and wished I could take back what had happened. I suddenly began to confess and repent of my sins to God for aborting my baby. I asked Him for forgiveness and to heal me from the trauma I had experienced that day. A sense of peace washed over me, and I felt His restoration of love covering me like a blanket, causing me to experience His peace. Still trying to focus on driving, I knew in that moment that I was forgiven and had received the restoration from God that I had longed for.

The woman on the radio began to share my favorite verse in Psalms: *You made all the delicate, inner parts of my body and knit me together in my mother's womb. Thank you for making me so wonderfully complex! Your workmanship is marvelous—how well I know it. You watched me as I was being formed in utter seclusion, as I was woven together in the dark of the womb. You saw me before I was born. Every day of my life was recorded in your book. Every moment was laid out before a single day had passed* (Psalm 139:13-16 NLT).

My radical moment with Jesus in the van that day transformed me. At the end of the testimony, they shared how to volunteer at a clinic that offers women who want to abort their babies other options and resources. One amazing tool they provided was free ultrasounds to allow the woman or parents to experience the baby in the womb. I wanted to be a part of that, so I decided to volunteer.

During my interview process, as I began to share my abortion experience, I realized I needed healing from my traumatic experience. The interviewer shared that the clinic had an abortion Bible study I could join to help me heal and move forward on my journey.

That opportunity led me to be able to share my abortion experience on social media, advocating for babies in the womb. My transparency has helped many women reconsider before making a lifetime decision. I have had women share how hearing my story has encouraged them to speak up about their own abortion experiences and others about how they were empowered to not follow through with the procedure. The women often said that the more they educated themselves on the matter, the more they realized that abortion does not only affect the baby's life and the mother's life but many others' lives as well.

The day during my senior year in high school, I became a statistic in America. I became one out of thousands of women who have abortions every year. In 2006, research showed a total of 846,181 abortions were reported by the CDC in the United States. Over the years, the reports have grown. I experienced what our culture accepts as a common occurrence in our nation today.

This subject is devastating to so many, yet our nation is divided between pro-life and pro-choice. I would encourage women who have gone down the path of abortion but wish they had not to get the healing that they need from that life-changing experience. Having personally experienced an abortion, I realize now the importance of the sanctity of life, and as I speak out, I know that what the enemy meant for evil in my life, God has used for good; if I can save just one child and one woman from experiencing the regret I did, sharing my story has been worth it.

A child is a precious gift and a reward from God. Children can bring joy and excitement. Although children can be challenging during moments of messiness, colic, and sleepless nights, we can trust God to use even those difficult moments of parenting for His plans and purposes for our lives.

> *Behold, children are a heritage from the Lord, the fruit of the womb is a regard* (Psalm 127:3 NKJV).

If you are experiencing a pregnancy and seeking wisdom, it isn't a mistake that you just read my story. I pray you will trust God to care for you and your child. His plans of restoration always work out for good.

Restoring Hope

By Kimberly Ann Hobbs

How do we go on when we feel we have lost everything? What do we do when everything has failed and all hope seems gone? People who ask these questions often feel a desperate longing for God to come through for them. The amazing truth is that God sees and hears everything, and He is the only One able to bring hope to our hopelessness. By fully surrendering to God, we open the pathway to restoring hope in our lives.

> *So now wrap your heart tightly around the hope that lives within us, knowing that God always keeps his promises!* (Hebrews 10:23 TPT).

When we accept Jesus as our Savior and Lord, the Holy Spirit comes to live within us, offering assurance that we will spend eternity with God —that is the "hope" the scripture above refers to. No matter what situation we face in life or how discouraged we may get, we can restore our hope by wrapping our hearts tightly around the knowledge that our Lord always keeps His promises.

When your hope is wavering and you need it restored, the best way to do this is to go back to God's Word, the Bible. God wants to meet you there and emphasize His promises to you. We can get so caught up in longing and so badly desire to have our own way that we forget to go to the One who holds all the promises.

Our hope can be restored when we believe by faith that God and His Word are 100% true. It is a deep and powerful belief that God always finishes what He starts in us. Without God, our lives have no hope at all, but the moment we bring Jesus into our heart, we can have hope for any situation we encounter. You may ask why. The answer is that God is our breath of life. Nothing is ever over until He says it is. He is the One who brings hope through the power of the Holy Spirit, which brings life to our body. Something changes deep within us when we set our hope in Jesus Christ. I love the scripture in Isaiah that tells us:

> But those who hope in the Lord will renew their strength. They will soar on wings like eagles; they will run and not grow weary; they will walk and not be faint (Isaiah 40:31 NIV).

When doubt begins to creep in, we often wonder if we've even been hoping for the right thing. Proverbs 13:12 says, *Hope deferred makes the heart sick* (NIV). Take heart! Don't give up. God is able! He is the God of hope.

Trust the Lord and place your restored hope in our heavenly Father, whose ways and plans are far better than yours, and you will experience freedom. You can completely trust and wholeheartedly believe that God knows you fully and loves you completely. Confidently insert the word hope into your life, knowing that your life and future are in God's hands.

Go directly to God in prayer and learn to trust Him with every breath you take and every decision you make, knowing He will always be with you. Read His Word, our truth, and rest in the secure hope of His promises!

> May the God of hope fill you with all joy and peace as you trust in him, so that you may overflow with hope by the power of the Holy Spirit (Romans 15:13 NIV).

Dee Miller

Dee Miller is a speaker, author, and a podcast host of "Picking Up the Pieces." Dee is passionate about walking with others on their journey to discovering their identity in Christ. We all bear God's image and are created in His likeness. Dee supports individuals as well as parents and churches as they navigate the narratives that surround the teachings that tell us to follow our feelings over the Word of God.

Dee is the Founder of MJM Ministry (mjmministry.com). When she left her home state to begin her transition to male, she cut off all communication with her family. MJM is dedicated to her parents, Mary and John Miller, who rushed back into her life at the precise moment the door was reopened. Their unconditional love is what every person should experience.

Dee authored a chapter in Women World Leader's book *Unshakable: God Will Sustain You* that followed her journey to embracing being female.

Stay connected with Dee at Dee@mjmministry.com.

Mother and Daughter Restored

By Dee Miller

Have you worked so hard to please someone in your family, but to no end? I pray my story will encourage you to keep fighting the good fight, trusting our God of restoration.

When I was a child, I could not make my mother happy. I learned it was best to stay out of her sight and not be heard. It was obvious she loved her boys. I longed to be treated like they were treated. As I grew older, I realized I would never please her, so I stopped trying. I attempted to convince myself I did not care; it was less painful. I could not understand why she did not love me; I was her daughter. Trying to understand life's disappointments through the eyes of a child is immensely difficult. I am grateful my mother lived a long life because, during that long life, God worked on my hard heart to restore the relationship between my mother and me to what He intended it to be.

One Sunday evening, I walked into my parents' house to make an announcement. I had made a life-altering decision I knew they would disagree with. I did not care what they thought. I was not there for a consultation, only to drop my bombshell. I had no intention of softening the blow. My exact words were, "I am moving and going ahead with medical intervention to change my gender. The woman you assumed was my roommate is my fiancé."

My mom got up from her chair and left the room. I followed by getting up from my chair and vacating their house. Six years went by without communication. She tried to reach out. I refused. She loved my brothers differently than she had loved me all my life. I did not expect to be supported now. I was happy to be four hundred miles away, building a new life.

In time, I realized I needed to stop pursuing becoming a man. (You can read that story in my chapter in *Unshakable: God Will Sustain You.*) It was a difficult transition returning to being female. It was arduous enough that I had a complete mental breakdown that required a hospital stay. After I was admitted, without my knowledge, a friend reached out to my mom. My family had no idea I had ended my pursuit to become male. Nor did they know I accepted Jesus into my life.

Mom contacted the hospital to see if I would be open to speaking with her. No matter how grown-up or independent I thought I was, hearing that my mom was reaching out to talk to me was somewhat confusing. I had built up walls to keep her out to prevent her from hurting me any longer. *Should I take her call or not?* The choice was mine. At that moment, I was just a shell of a human being. The hospital staff's goal was to help me get better and capable of going home. The idea of releasing me into my mother's care was ideal for them.

At the staff's urging, a call with my mother was scheduled. To my shock, Mom wanted to come stay with me. I did not have a spare bedroom for her to sleep. My bed was a waterbed, and I had cats! My mother was terrified of cats. Surprisingly, none of these things mattered to her. It had been six years since we spent time together; nevertheless, I needed her. *Should I let her come? Do I have any other practical options?* I needed companionship as I began recovering from the breakdown. I was overwhelmed by the need to make any decisions. What better way was there than to allow Mom to come and mother me for a few weeks? So she did.

I still laugh at how well-behaved my cats were. Every night, I would look at them and announce bedtime, to which they would obediently follow me to the bedroom. If you have ever owned a cat, you know this is not normal behavior.

After my mother returned home, I continued to heal and grow my faith in Christ; that's when I heard the Lord tell me it was time to forgive my mother. He wanted me to take one of my weeks of vacation to spend at my parents' home. *Really, Lord? The entire week?* I tried to convince the Lord that a three- or four-day weekend would be enough time. Eventually, I was obedient and scheduled the entire week.

My trip became an annual one, and while I was home each year, my mom made a list of movies we could attend together. One of the theaters in town showed older films and served a meal at your table. We did two of Mother's favorite things at once: eat out and watch a movie. Soon, my annual visit was a highlight of her year.

At one point, my mom injured her back as my dad was preparing to hike the Grand Canyon. I suggested I come to be her caregiver, which would allow my dad to go as planned. They were both shocked I would give up a second week of vacation to do this for them. We planned our schedules to coincide—as my dad drove out, I was driving into their driveway.

I will never forget that first morning I was to care for her. Mom had a physical therapy appointment and came out of her bedroom holding her shoes. I could see the sheepish look on her face as she spoke, "You are going to have to help me put my shoes on." We were not 24 hours into my care for her, and she was now dependent on me. As I fell to the floor to slip her shoes on, I began crying. I was humbled, feeling like I was washing her feet as Jesus taught His disciples. I spent the rest of the week taking her to all her appointments. I also completed all her Christmas gift shopping for every person on her list. It felt like I shopped for a hundred people! By the time my week was up, I felt the shift in our relationship. It was changing.

When we celebrated Christmas that year, I knew I was her favorite. I will remember that Christmas forever.

As my life continued growing with the Lord, even though I moved physically further away from my parents, we talked more often. I prayed, asking God to show me what my mom's life was like as a child so I could have a better understanding of why she was the way she was. God was gracious and gave me glimpses into her life. He gave me empathy for unhealed places in her heart. I believe we both had the same goal for what our mother/daughter relationship should look like. Now, distance and time were our enemy.

When I was diagnosed with uterine cancer requiring a hysterectomy immediately, my parents made the eleven-hour drive twice in one month to be with me. Mom was allowed in the pre-op holding area with me. The only certainty was I had cancer. I did not know what stage it was, nor what treatment would be necessary after surgery. The doctor was expecting complications during surgery—there were no guarantees I would leave the operating room.

In the moments before surgery, I was expecting someone from my church to come and pray with me, but he did not make it. It was only Mom and me amongst the bustling surgical staff. My mom was calm but did not have a calming presence. I was doing my best to be strong for her! When it was my turn to go into the operating room, my mother leaned in and kissed me on my cheek. It was the first time in my life I recall my mother kissing me. I prayed to God, "You cannot let me die in that operating room now!"

I spent three days in the hospital after surgery with my mom at my bedside. She helped me shower and dress and did everything she could to help me. My parents stayed in town for ten days after the operation. Dad would come before sunrise every day to ensure I could get out of bed. Later, he would go back to get my mom. She ensured I had plenty of meals in the freezer, my laundry was done, and everything else she could do to assist me was taken care of. She even learned to like taking a nap with a cat on her lap. After she

Restoration: God Brings Beauty from Ashes

was gone, I said to my friends, "Who was that woman? She looked like my mother, but my mother has never acted like that before."

Over the next year, God told me that my life was going to change drastically. I had completed one mission trip to Kenya and was planning a second trip to Kenya and Uganda. I stressed about crossing the Uganda border, which caused me to have nightmares about going to prison. My mom was not happy about my desire to return to Africa. Imagine her misery if I had told her about my nightmares.

As I was reading my Bible in preparation for my trip, I started having flashbacks of images from my childhood that I hadn't remembered before. The surroundings in these images matched my childhood closet. I referred to them as "blips on the screen." These flashbacks were disturbing and occurred a few times a month.

I traveled to Uganda and returned safely, only to learn that the company I worked for was being sold, and my position would soon be eliminated. The frequency of my "blips on the screen" increased as I tried to find a new job, causing my stress to increase drastically. Subsequently, I relocated in pursuit of new opportunities.

During this time, a friend called to support me in prayer. As we spoke, she described seeing the exact same images that had been troubling me. I was shocked. That moment marked the first time I accepted that the "blips" were indeed flashbacks to events from my childhood, which God was revealing to me.

Flashback is the term used to describe a mental image of a past actual event or a traumatic situation that comes to mind, usually involuntarily. It can last for seconds or hours. Often, it can feel like you are reliving the event. Sometimes, I felt like I was living in the past while trying to function in the present, knowing my mind was trying to get me to react to something that was not happening in the here and now.

What is God trying to show me?

The scene was my childhood closet. I knew I had spent time there.

Wait, why?

The next blip was God showing me what preceded my ending up in the closet. It was a near-death beating by my mother.

What had caused her to be so angry with me?

I could almost hear God say, "Well, I am happy you asked."

It was an attack from my brothers.

Was the attack called for? No!

Was mom's beating? No!

I had put in all this work to have a relationship with my mom, and now this!? *Seriously, God!?*

Interestingly, on the numerous times that God showed this image to me, I was mad that I was still alive.

Why didn't You let me die as a result of the attacks, God? I accused God of loving my mom more than me, saying, *You didn't want her to have to live with killing her child.*

I had so many reasons to be angry at God. *Why am I not in heaven with You? Why did you leave me with that family? All my days were ordained before one came to be, and this! This is the family you chose for me?*

Psalm 139:16 tells us, *Your eyes saw my unformed body; all the days ordained for me were written in your book before one of them came to be* (NIV).

I knew it was God's will that everything He showed me should not affect my current relationship with my mom. It was so difficult not to ask her why she hated me so much when I was a child. To sit at the table with my enemy, peacefully as if nothing had ever happened. Jesus gave me many examples throughout the Gospels of how to handle these situations. My desire to have a loving relationship with my mother had to be stronger than any other feeling.

Slowly, God healed me from this new trauma caused by my flashbacks. Every morning, I took communion and prayed that I would heal—body, soul, and spirit in the fullness that Jesus paid the price for. Eventually, the memories lessened. Though I could still hear the words my mom spoke over me, I now took the opportunity to speak words of truth from the Bible over anything she said to me. She spoke as a frustrated parent. I spoke confidently of who God says I am—His beloved daughter.

I now know that Jesus was in the closet awaiting my broken, bloody body. He spoke love to me while He held me close. The most memorable thing Jesus said to me was, "Mom had a bad day."

I have learned that a bad day is nothing to build a life on. People will always fail us. Jesus never will. I could have chosen to stay angry at my mom. I had a list of things to be angry at God for. In the end, that anger only hurt me. It was taking my peace away. Peace is described as being free from conflict. Being angry would not allow me to be in a relationship with my mother as I had always hoped. I had to understand that my fight was not with her but with the enemy of my soul. Jesus came to earth so I could be free and become who He created me to be. Still, I know the evil enemy, Satan, lurks around every corner, scheming to destroy me. First Peter 5:8 instructs us to, *Be alert and of sober mind. Your enemy the devil prowls around like a roaring lion looking for someone to devour* (NIV).

> For our struggle is not against flesh and blood, but against the rulers, against the authorities, against the powers of this dark world and against the spiritual forces of evil in the heavenly realms (Ephesians 6:12 NIV).

As my mind healed from those images, God blessed me with complete forgiveness for Mom. Our relationship grew stronger. My new job allowed me to visit for a week at Christmas. As she aged, we could only share one movie per visit. She always had one saved on her DVR for us to watch together after Dad went to bed. We never really had heart-to-heart talks. She did not want to talk about things from the past. I wanted to revisit my past to apologize for the anguish I knew I had brought them when I announced my decision to change my gender. An apology was not important to her. For her, what was in the past was over. I felt I had to honor her wishes.

When my dad died, I could not let him have an impersonal funeral, so I wrote and delivered his eulogy. Mom told me I only had five minutes. *No pressure there, Mom.* Before I left to return home, she hugged me tight, kissed me, and told me I did better than she could give me credit.

My relationship with my mom blossomed after my father's funeral. We chatted often about whatever came to Mom's mind. It was a precious time for me. I made the six-hour trip to see her as often as I could.

Then, news came that she had suffered a heart attack. It became apparent that she wouldn't recover; I needed to get there as quickly as possible. The decision was made to take her home under hospice care.

Mom's mind stayed sharp until the end. She was fully capable of making every decision for herself. She lasted an amazing ten days. It took seven for her to lose the strength to speak. I had waited my entire life for her to ask me for my forgiveness, but I finally realized I did not need to hear her ask. I pulled up a chair next to my mother's bed and grabbed her hand. I had never held her hand before—my mother wasn't a person who liked touch. At long last, I spoke forgiveness to her. I spoke of the day she beat me so severely I shouldn't have survived. I didn't want her life to end with her not understanding she had been forgiven for that dreadful act.

"Mama, we had a tough start. God has work for me to do now. And when He is done with me here, I will join you in heaven. I forgive you for everything.

I love you."

She held my hand tightly for the next three hours. If I shifted in the chair, she clenched my hand tighter. During that time, I rested my head on her lap, crying. That was what I had always wanted: to rest my head in my mom's lap.

When her caregiver came to adjust her in the bed, my mom opened her eyes and looked at me as she mouthed, "I love you."

I believe we both wished for more time to keep restoring a relationship that had been stolen away years before. Two days later, my mom took her last breath on earth and transitioned into heaven. She was looking into my eyes, not those of one of her dearly loved sons. It took twenty-some years of restoration work for this moment to occur—for me to be the daughter God created me to be. The ability to be at mother's deathbed signified that all the beauty of our relationship had been restored.

Our God is the God of Restoration. That's what having a relationship with Him is all about. Jesus died on the cross to restore our relationship with God. With that kind of track record, we can trust Him with all our relationships. Give your struggling relationships to God and submit to Him in obedience. He WILL see you through.

Linda McGrane

 Linda McGrane, inspired by her father's medical career, started with a dream to alleviate suffering and bring healing to others. After earning a B.S. from Northwestern University and an M.S. from the University of Missouri and pursuing advanced studies at the University of Wisconsin, she worked in speech-language pathology and special education administration.

Her path initially led her to roles in hospitals and schools, eventually becoming director of special education and then starting her own business.

Personal struggles, including a tough divorce, deepened Linda's faith and shifted her focus. Embracing biblical principles and healing insights from various fields, she has a passion for restoring marriages for God's kingdom.

Linda now partners with her husband, Bill, to counsel couples in crisis and high-level leaders through a proven system with unparalleled results they call S.E.E. This system is custom-designed for couples; Bill and Linda guide and show you how to remove the brick walls dragging marriages down and relearn communication and conflict resolution, and then reintroduce passion, love, and intimacy.

Linda would love to hear from you. Learn more about her and receive a free gift of marriage tips through the following avenues:

Website: mcgrane.com
Email: hello@mcgrane.com

The Blessedness of Answered Prayer

By Linda McGrane

"Kidney failure."

Those words from my doctor left me in shock. In one phone call, everything abruptly changed.

I felt confused and numb. I was healthy. I rarely even took an aspirin.

Shortly before the surprising diagnosis, the Lord gave my husband Bill and me a considerable assignment. We knew He never gives an assignment without the resources to complete it.

> *"You did not choose Me, but I chose you and appointed you that you should go and bear fruit"* (John 15:16 NKJV).

My doctors told me my kidney function had dipped precariously low, and they didn't know why.

I went to the Lord for guidance. Despite my fervent prayers for a creative miracle that would testify of God's healing to the medical community, God spoke to me only once. He told me He would heal me, but it would be a "process." As in Isaiah 50:7 (NKJV), I set my face like a flint on His words.

I feared the idea of a transplant because my body does not like medication. I had almost died from anesthesia complications after a routine operation about 30 years earlier. Plus, I had read research that showed emotions were stored in each cell of our body. My best friend's brother, who was a special forces veteran, had received a heart transplant, after which he had many issues with emotions that he had never experienced before the surgery. He got to the point where he wanted to commit suicide.

My idea of "process" and God's idea of "process" differed. I wrestled with the discrepancy. I often cried out to God. He healed people I prayed for right before my eyes. I returned from healing conferences where I witnessed Jesus' miraculous healing, and yet I did not get healed.

God's silence seemed deafening while the devil's constant whispers of doubt and fear tried to overshadow my faith in God's promise. God had already spoken to me. He was not going to repeat it. He wanted total trust, praise, and worship. Not whining. I had to learn that God's promise of a process did not mean a quick solution to my problem.

A year later, the news came: I was rejected from one hospital's kidney list. In my pride and rebellion, I took this as a sign I would not have to have a transplant. Each test felt like a chance to prove my healing to the doctors. Naively, I thought each completed procedure led to the final hurdle. Then, yet another issue would arise, leading me to realize the journey wouldn't be easy. As hope flickered, I yearned for a miracle every day.

The Bible tells us to rejoice in trials: *Count it all joy, my brethren, when you meet various trials* (James 1:2 RSV). I recommitted to worshiping the Lord, whether healed or not. The Lord challenged my commitment. There were times when prayer and worship seemed impossible. God's silence unnerved me. I was used to hearing from Him on a regular basis. Now, pain and sickness overwhelmed me. In those moments, I learned the importance of clinging to faith even when nothing seems to come out as hoped.

> Let us hold unswervingly to the hope we profess for He who promised
> is faithful (Hebrews 10:23 NIV).

Be still and know that I am God—the beginning of Psalm 46:10 (NIV)—kept coming up. Only in quiet surrender does God truly work in our hearts.

Even though I know that each trial I face, though difficult, ultimately leads to blessings beyond measure, I craved a shortcut. I felt desperate to escape further suffering. Pain wasn't my strong suit. I needed to remember the countless times God had delivered me from my obstacles.

I know that God doesn't respond to mere needs but to acts of unwavering faith. True power comes from surrendering our hearts entirely to His will. I thought I had done this, but the Holy Spirit revealed areas I needed to address for deeper surrender.

I felt overwhelming disappointment when I heard the diagnosis that I had heart failure, too. Then followed by even worse information: I had a rare blood disease that has no cure and a survival rate of less than 1%. Despair engulfed me. I feared I wouldn't have enough faith for healing. For a while, I foolishly tried to manufacture faith on my own, as I forgot to rely on God.

Fear veritably surfaces at the cusp of a breakthrough. It's a desperate attempt from the enemy to steal your promised victory. Stand firm for God. Don't relinquish your prayers. Don't waver in your convictions. Don't settle for anything less. Choose unwavering belief. Heaven accomplishes what we cannot. The path may seem illogical, a hidden trail known only to Him. True faith requires silencing the doubts: *Will He heal me? How can this possibly happen?*

Amid my darkness, God's light shone through. Miraculously, tests revealed my heart failure had vanished, and my blood cancer test was deemed completely inaccurate. That experience taught me to surrender to God even more.

When my kidney continued to get worse, I ended up in the emergency room, unable to speak or see clearly. As I was faced with a terrifying situation, my faith became my anchor. I had to decide whether or not to be treated with a risky medication. The stroke doctor was at least an hour away, detained in an emergency, unable to make a diagnosis. All I could do was pray in my mind: *Jesus, Jesus.*

Then, an unexpected blessing happened. Our Pastor, Cleddie Keith, arrived out of nowhere and prayed for me from outside my room. Moments later, the stroke doctor arrived and, to everyone's surprise, declared the medication unnecessary. My sight and speech began to return, and within hours, I was dismissed. I experienced firsthand the power in the mighty name of Jesus!

Satan challenged my resolve to trust God's process, timing, and purpose. My kidney condition worsened rapidly, unexpectedly requiring dialysis. But complications piled on top of each other. First, the surgery to implant the dialysis catheter caused significant issues. Then, the anesthesia shut down my colon, which led to multiple hospital admissions before dialysis could begin. I felt utterly wretched. Days and nights blurred together. Every breath felt labored. My energy vanished as toxicity levels soared and organs began to fail. I couldn't fathom enduring another minute of that agonizing state.

Tethered to a dialysis machine for eleven hours a day, I began to spiral into despair, desperate for a miracle. Dialysis was grueling. Those long days became my ultimate test of faith. God doesn't always take away the challenges we face. Instead, He walks alongside us—like in

Daniel chapter 3. When three men were thrown into the fiery furnace, God did not keep them from enduring the furnace; instead, He went through the fire with them.

Then, I received a call that there was a deceased donor kidney; I had to be at the hospital within two hours. But there was a hiccup in the plan—what should have been an insignificant detail. I had two days left to finish a ten-day course of antibiotics treating an infection; medical errors had forced me to restart the medication three times. Not having completed the course of antibiotics disqualified me from receiving the transplant even though the infection I was taking the antibiotics for no longer existed. At the time, however, I was scared and not emotionally ready for the procedure. Looking back, God protected me. He had another plan.

I stormed heaven, declaring why I did not want a transplant. Then, in a moment of quiet reflection with the Lord, He finally spoke. "You are dust." I understood that, like any human organ, my kidney was also dust. In an instant, He overcame all my objections. I knew He was preparing me for a kidney transplant. It was crucial for me to feel emotionally ready for a transplant for fear my body might reject the kidney.

Finally, we received fantastic news: a new match. My husband's friend—John, from Michigan—was a potential donor. When we met, I could feel John's love for Christ. It seemed like divine intervention, a direct answer from the Lord. John committed to be the donor. The next night, when I received John's call expecting to make surgery arrangements, things shifted. Although John was still committed, personal obstacles had come up. I was extremely disappointed, but I released John. Then, the Lord told me that he had fulfilled his purpose—he had been there to prepare me to emotionally accept God's ultimate plan, not share his kidney.

Just as the two disciples on the road to Emmaus walked in despair, not recognizing Jesus beside them (Luke 24:13-32), despair clouded my vision. God had promised healing, yet here I was—faced with the news I was about two weeks from death.

However, God intervened with a radical twist of fate. His restoration plan unfolded in a way I never could have imagined. Michael, a man from Tennessee who planned to retire in a lakeside cabin, found an unexpected turn in his life. Michael had left his long-held job of more than 20 years and relocated to Cincinnati, where he and his wife bought a home in my neighborhood.

Miraculously, a neighborhood magazine featuring my story sat on his kitchen counter courtesy of his realtor. Michael felt an undeniable pull to the article. That very same night, while dining with his wife in a Cincinnati restaurant, a powerful message resonated within him, which he believed to be a divine instruction. He was to donate his kidney to me.

With unwavering conviction, Michael declared himself a perfect match. The doctors, skeptical of divine intervention, were unconvinced. Testing began, a hurdle Michael faced with resolute faith.

Then, on a joyous Easter Sunday, Michael stood at my doorstep, a beacon of hope. The tests confirmed he was a miraculous match. My energy was dwindling rapidly; surgery was scheduled immediately. It felt like a divine gift, a last-minute answer to a desperate prayer.

Two days before surgery, everything seemed to be on track. I was elated and filled with hopeful anticipation. But then my vision blurred, and I lost my speech yet again. Hope vanished like smoke. Panic surged. My weakened state fueled my fear that I would no longer be a candidate for a kidney transplant.

Two days later, both Michael and I were in the hospital, prepped and ready. But just before wheeling us into surgery, the surgical team assembled in my room, their faces grim.

Their verdict: the surgery was too risky to proceed. My recent episode of vision and speech malfunction left them concerned about my ability to survive the operation.

Bill and I were more disheartened when we learned the new requirement for a battery of tests with countless specialists before the doctors would even consider rescheduling the surgery. I doubted we would be able to navigate that new hurdle in time.

Despite the setback, unexpectedly, doors began to open. Appointments materialized, and tests were completed with remarkable efficiency. It felt like divine orchestration. Miraculously, the surgeries were rescheduled for one week later, May 8th, 2018.

My daughter, a doctor herself, had suggested a particular surgeon due to his exceptional skills.

While requesting a specific surgeon wasn't an option, her recommendation lingered in my mind.

With the new surgery date came a new surgical team. Eight, a number symbolizing new beginnings, felt particularly significant. New doctors and nurses would be involved, and to our utter astonishment, the very surgeon my daughter had suggested was assigned to my case.

That was an answer to our prayers. We had fervently asked the Lord to handpick everyone who would care for Michael and me. In this unexpected turn of events, we saw a glimpse of His handiwork.

When I emerged from surgery, Mary, my recovery nurse, greeted me. The fact that she had the same name as my dear mother, who had passed years before, comforted me. In the ICU, another comforting presence was a nurse named John, the same name as my deceased brother. The coincidence extended even further when my nurse on the regular floor introduced himself as Johnny, the nickname I used for my brother. These echoes from the past felt like gentle reminders of Christ's unwavering love, which surrounded me, even in the hospital's sterile environment.

The medical marvels continued. Michael's kidney functioned flawlessly within me. The doctors were astounded and called it a perfect match. His magnificent organ, significantly larger than average, had brought my toxicity levels down from critical to healthy so fast they had never witnessed such a rapid improvement. The anesthesiologists were equally impressed. Unlike the complications I experienced during dialysis tube insertion, the transplant surgery caused no organ shutdown. A swift recovery seemed imminent, a testament to God's intervention and Michael's selfless gift. Then, I experienced a chilling setback. My health abruptly deteriorated. Doctors suspected rejection and readied themselves for another surgery, a prospect that cast a long shadow over my hard-won progress. The mere thought of another surgery filled me with dread. Exhausted and terrified, I fervently prayed against it.

Our pastor's teachings echoed in my mind. He often said I should always seek the Father's perfect will, not mine. But at that moment, all I craved was an escape from the scalpel, a desperate plea that conflicted with the surrender I strived for. I knew better, but I couldn't do better.

I received a lesson etched in pain. While I prayed for relief, I received a harsh reminder that the path to God's perfect will was not always what I envisioned. My answered prayer for no surgery resulted in a three-day delay. Crucially, that delay prevented doctors from discovering that the anti-rejection medication itself was the cause of wreaking havoc on my body and the precious kidney.

For three months after, I returned to the excruciating hell of feeling wretched, not being able to eat, and having so little energy I was in a wheelchair. Everything might have been spared had they discovered the cause and intervened sooner. Instead, I wanted to be the Potter and God the clay.

I learned to thank God when I experienced setbacks, knowing He would set me up for a more significant victory.

> Give thanks in all circumstances; For this is God's will for you in Christ Jesus (1 Thessalonians 5:18 NIV).

I had witnessed that with my friend Fe, from the Philippines. She had been invited to speak at a healing conference in Cincinnati. Months prior to the event, the Lord had given her specific instructions for what to speak about—the story of the woman with the issue of blood (Luke 8:43-48). Fe was not to lay hands on anyone; those seeking healing needed to reach out on their own, to touch the hem of Jesus' garment.

There was immense resistance to Fe attending the conference. Some organizers did not want her there, yet she found herself on the speaker's list just a few days before. Fe called me and urged me to attend. With each passing day, my condition worsened, which made the prospect of travel impossible. But on the day of the talk, an unwavering conviction gripped me—I had to be there.

I attempted to get ready, but debilitating weakness and relentless nausea threatened to derail my plans. I feared becoming ill in church. Bill practically carried me to the car. The journey was a blur of stops for anti-nausea medication.

When we reached the church with the help of kind strangers, Bill helped me to the front of the room. As Fe's message about faith and healing resonated through the room, a feeling of powerful hope surged within me. When the altar call was made, Bill guided me forward.

I didn't feel anything at all during the altar call. Disappointment rose within me as I saw everyone around me getting healed. My hopes sank as I wondered if I would ever be cured. I did not notice that I could walk back to the pews without help. Bill noticed it first. He said, "Look at how you're walking." *I could walk, which starkly contrasted with how I entered the church with Bill's and other's assistance.*

It wasn't a dramatic shift but a gradual change that awakened me to my miracle. *I was healed!* I noticed I felt a lot better. For instance, at lunch, I could eat one whole sandwich instead of one bite. When we came home, I could walk for 20 minutes without stopping.

The journey to healing was arduous, littered with moments of doubt and despair. Yet, looking back on it, I am filled with immense gratitude. The Lord orchestrated every twist and turn, leading me to the perfect kidney donor.

Because of my story, 90 people offered to be kidney donors. People's lives were saved because, when tested, doctors found illnesses before they became issues. Others found faith in Christ.

God's plan is always greater than our own. He showed me that if we entrust ourselves to Him, He cannot fail. He was always working, even in the quiet moments when He seemed distant and I feared He had left me. What we see as the answer or what we desire may not be the answer at all, but in His perfect wisdom, He guides us toward a future brighter than we can imagine.

> *"As the heavens are higher than the earth, so are my ways higher than your ways and my thoughts than your thoughts"* (Isaiah 55:9 NIV).

Fe had prophesied over me 20 years before, saying, "Beauty for Ashes." Perhaps she meant that I would write my story in a chapter for this book, *Restoration: God Brings Beauty from Ashes.*

I believe God's light can illuminate your path forward, too. May my story serve as a beacon of hope to remind others that faith is a journey, not a destination. With unwavering trust, we can climb even the most challenging mountains.

Claiming Restoration by Faith

By Kimberly Anne Kahn

Faith is the substance of things hoped for, the evidence of things not seen (Hebrews 11:1 NKJV).

Faith comes in different forms. There's natural human faith—relying on our senses—and then there's supernatural faith, as described in Hebrews 11:1. This faith transcends what we see or feel; it's a deep trust in God's promises, power, and love.

I appreciate how Kenneth Hagin, a Christian minister and founder of Rhema Bible College, describes faith as "grasping the unrealities of hope and bringing them into the realm of reality." This supernatural faith doesn't originate from human reasoning or ability—it grows out of the Word of God.

So then faith comes by hearing, and hearing by the word of God (Romans 10:17 NKJV).

I learned an important lesson about faith after I relied on myself for years, doing things independently but thinking I was walking in faith. The more I trusted in my own abilities, the more frustrated I became, never finding true peace. Everything changed when I immersed myself in the Word of God. One life-altering truth became clear: *I can do nothing without Him, but He can do everything. No matter the situation, I need Jesus!*

Restoration: God Brings Beauty from Ashes

The more time I spent with the Lord, the more sensitive I became to God's voice and grew in faith. One day, He showed me a vision.

In the vision, I saw myself standing with both hands out in front of me with my palms up. I looked to my right hand, and I saw Jesus standing there. The peace, joy, and love I experienced in His presence was freeing. Then I looked at the other hand and saw corporate business. I could feel the weight of the hustle and bustle of working in the corporate world and doing things in my own strength. I quickly looked back at my right hand and recognized that Jesus was overpowering the weight of the world with His peace.

Then I heard Jesus' voice: "You can have the corporate world and work long hours without peace, or you can have what I have for you—what I've called you to do."

Without a second thought, I said, "I choose what you have for me, Lord."

Suddenly, the joy of the Lord was upon me; I knew He was about to do something great!

Three months later, the company I worked for shut down. The board president, in tears, told me I was being let go. But instead of fear, I felt a profound peace—I knew God was at work. She looked at me, confused, and asked, "Aren't you upset?"

I responded, "No. I trust in God. He will take care of me."

Though the reality was that I had just lost my job and had no income—no way to pay rent or provide for myself—I made a choice to stand on the promise God gave me: "I will never leave you; I will always provide for your every need."

We find God's promises in the Bible.

For He Himself has said, "I will never leave you nor forsake you" (Hebrews 13:5 NKJV).

Because I chose to believe God's truth, I had faith—*the substance of things I hoped for.* Even when I couldn't see it, God was already working things for my good behind the scenes; He was moving.

We may say that God's Word is good, but we will never know until we have acted on it and reaped its results. Faith is giving substance to things hoped for. I went to work; I acted on God's Word. I had hope that all my needs would be taken care of, and as I acted on God's Word, my faith offered the substance I hoped for. Hope says, "I'll have it sometime." Faith says, "I claim it now."

If you find yourself in a position where nothing is working out, you may be trying to do things in your own strength. Step back and ask yourself where your faith is coming from. Are you banking on your ability to do things independently or trusting that God will do exceedingly abundantly more than you could ask or imagine?

It only takes a little faith....

Jesus said that even faith the size of a mustard seed can move mountains. It's amazing to think that such a tiny seed can grow into something big and beautiful. Just like that mustard seed, a small amount of faith can blossom into bold, daring faith that sustains us as we rely on and trust God.

Every single step you take in faith, no matter how small, is a step toward something greater. As you grow in Christ, your faith will grow and strengthen, allowing you to face life's challenges with confidence and hope.

Always hold onto the promises of God, for He is faithful and true. Even in moments of doubt or struggle, never give up. Trust that God is working in your life, and believe He has incredible plans for you. Your faith can move mountains, and with each passing day, you can become a bright light and encouragement to others. Keep believing, keep persevering, and watch how God transforms your life in ways you never imagined!

. . . .

Kelly Williams Hale

 Kelly Williams Hale is a speaker, author, and life coach. She is passionate about Jesus and encourages others to deepen their personal relationship with Him.

Her teaching and online courses help Christian women walk in their unique calling to bring God glory. Partnering with the Holy Spirit, Kelly teaches women how be courageous and confident in Christ. Her speaking topics include spiritual growth, emotional resilience, and leadership.

She is happily married (third time's a charm!), a mom of three—each born a decade apart— delivering her youngest at 44 years old.

Kelly is living proof that our mess truly becomes our message and past mistakes don't define future success.

You're invited to join the Facebook group, Sisters Who Shine, or visit thebebravelife.com for more information.

Failure, Forgiveness, and Faith

By Kelly Williams Hale

They triumphed over him by the blood of the Lamb and by the word of their testimony (Revelation 12:11 NIV).

I think I drove my mom a bit crazy when I was a little girl.

To this day, she'll remind me about the battles we had over my "girly" bobby socks. When I started school, she wanted me to wear the ones with lacy ruffles, but I hated them. I tugged, pulled, and whined until the socks were replaced. That tension over fashion continued well into high school. If she saw something hideous, her first thought was, *Kelly would probably like that.*

Even then, I had this need to express myself—my way.
Oh yes, you shaped me first inside, then out;
  you formed me in my mother's womb.
I thank you, High God—you're breathtaking!
  Body and soul, I am marvelously made!
  I worship in adoration—what a creation!
You know me inside and out,
  you know every bone in my body;

You know exactly how I was made, bit by bit,
  how I was sculpted from nothing into something.
Like an open book, you watched me grow from conception to birth;
  all the stages of my life were spread out before you,
The days of my life all prepared
  before I'd even lived one day.
(Psalm 139:14-16 MSG)

. . . .

I've always been a creative at heart. My earliest memories are filled with crayons, music, and the endless worlds I built when I played pretend. Once, I even staged a "wedding" with the son of my parents' friends. We were maybe seven years old.

Drawing, though—that was my happy place. I would spend hours sketching anything I saw. Endless renditions of The Pink Panther, Snoopy, and Tweety. It felt like magic to recreate these characters on paper, pencil flowing with an ease and joy that felt like... well, a gift.

Now there are varieties of gifts, but the same Spirit; and there are varieties of service, but the same Lord; and there are varieties of activities, but it is the same God who empowers them all in everyone (1 Corinthians 12:4–6 ESV).

By high school, I realized portraits were my specialty. My art teacher planted that seed. We spent weeks studying each part of the human face—eyes, noses, ears, mouths. I became an observer of details: symmetry, asymmetry, and the subtleties that make us unique. I saw beauty in it all.

When the assignment came to draw a self-portrait, I was ready. I set up a mirror outside, leaning it against a tree. With my sketchpad and ebony pencil in hand, I went to work. Hours passed as I studied my reflection, capturing every shadow and line. I finished, and for the first time, I looked at my face and thought, *It's beautiful.*

Then, I shared it in class.

A random comment—something offhand, probably not even meant to hurt—changed everything. I can't remember who said it or the exact words, but I heard: "crooked," "off-center," and "weird."

My face.

That day, another seed was planted: insecurity. It took root and began to choke the joy I'd felt in expressing myself.

> *What's the price of a pet canary? Some loose change, right? And God cares what happens to it even more than you do. He pays even greater attention to you, down to the last detail—even numbering the hairs on your head! So don't be intimidated by all this bully talk. You're worth more than a million canaries* (Matthew 10:29-31 MSG).

As a kid, I often wished I were an only child. Babysitting my three little brothers was no walk in the park. Once, after a particularly long day watching them during Spring Break, my mom came home, and I told her, "They hate me!"

I was the bossy big sister at home. But at school, I was a wallflower—desperate to fit in yet hyper-aware of anyone who didn't. I easily made friends with the kids who sat alone and seemed left out.

I became the peacemaker, the adapter, the one who could blend in and make others feel comfortable. Friends confided in me, and I took on their burdens with an open heart. I didn't realize it then, but God had given me another gift: the gift of encouragement.

> *God has given each of you a gift from his great variety of spiritual gifts.*
> *Use them well to serve one another. Do you have the gift of speaking?*
> *Then speak as though God himself were speaking through you. Do*
> *you have the gift of helping others? Do it with all the strength and*
> *energy that God supplies. Then everything you do will bring glory to*
> *God through Jesus Christ* (1 Peter 4:10-11 NLT).

It came naturally to me, woven into my DNA. But back then, I felt flawed, insignificant, and unworthy.

Still, I had dreams.

. . . .

At 19, I found out I was pregnant.

My high school sweetheart, Charlie, and I got married in a whirlwind shotgun wedding. My dreams of art school were put on hold. I became a wife and mommy, and though the transition was hard, I didn't lose hope. My dreams simply grew bigger—they now included my baby girl.

I thought God might be disappointed in me, but He wasn't. He was there, quietly working behind the scenes. He had plans for my life that I had yet to understand.

> *Here's what YAHWEH says to you: "I know all about the marvelous*
> *destiny I have in store for you, a future planned out in detail. My*
> *intention is not to harm you but to surround you with peace and*
> *prosperity and to give you a beautiful future, glistening with hope"*
> (Jeremiah 29:11 TPT).

. . . .

By 22, I was divorced. A single mom.

Life at that crossroads was messy and uncertain. But I still had dreams. I went back to art school, determined to create a better future for my daughter and me. I worked hard, balancing classes with motherhood, fueled by sheer determination and a deep sense of hope.

But insecurity clung to me. Trauma responses guided many of my decisions during that season. I wasn't living. I was surviving.

> A thief has only one thing in mind—he wants to steal, slaughter, and destroy. But I have come to give you everything in abundance, more than you expect (John 10:10 TPT).

In my late 20s, I met my second husband.

He was charming, fun, and seemed to have it all together. But hindsight is 20/20, and now I see the red flags I chose to ignore.

I'd always believed I could "love people better." I thought my love could fill their emptiness, just as I hoped they could fill mine. But that's a God-sized job. Only He can fill the cracks in our hearts.

Looking back, I don't regret those choices. Each misstep and moment of disappointment—it all became part of my evolution. God never left me, even in my mess. He was there through the tears and the joy, the heartbreak and the hope.

> He has made everything beautiful and appropriate in its time. He has also planted eternity [a sense of divine purpose] in the human heart [a mysterious longing which nothing under the sun can satisfy, except God]—yet man cannot find out (comprehend, grasp) what God has done (His overall plan) from the beginning to the end (Ecclesiastes 3:11 AMP).

HOPE AND HEALING

By my early 30s, I was a single mom again—twice divorced and feeling unqualified for the dreams I still carried. How could God use someone like me? But He met me in that brokenness. He showed me who I was in His eyes: loved, forgiven, brave, and worthy. I truly began to understand that life didn't happen to me; it happened for me.

God was writing a story I couldn't yet understand. Every mistake was preparing me for what was next. I was entering a season of restoration and began to believe that God can truly bring beauty from ashes.

> *For we are God's masterpiece. He has created us anew in Christ Jesus, so we can do the good things he planned for us long ago* (Ephesians 2:10 NLT).

> *To all who mourn in Israel, he will give a crown of beauty for ashes, a joyous blessing instead of mourning, festive praise instead of despair. In their righteousness, they will be like great oaks that the Lord has planted for his own glory* (Isaiah 61:3 NLT).

THE POWER OF PURPOSE

In 2004, I attended a business event that changed my life. The keynote speaker shared his story with such vulnerability and purpose that a spark ignited in me—another seed was planted.

At the time, I was a single mom, freshly divorced (for the second time), and struggling financially. Honestly, I said yes to the business opportunity because I desperately needed the extra income. Little did I know I would leave that training with something far more valuable than financial hope.

The guest speaker that day, Bill, shared his incredible story: Late one night, he was shot at an ATM. What followed was his journey of transformation—from extreme anger to compassionate forgiveness. His message wasn't just about what he endured but about how he overcame adversity.

The passion with which he spoke, the clarity of his purpose, and his ability to move beyond tragedy struck a chord deep within me. That moment was a catalyst for me. I walked out of that room understanding what God had been preparing me for. This was my purpose. To impact people. To help them see that even in the face of heartbreak, tragedy, or seemingly insurmountable challenges, they could move forward. They could forgive. They could create change—first in their own lives and then in the lives of others.

Today, 14 years later, I'm still inspired by that moment. My mission hasn't wavered: To encourage women with hope. Hope that they, too, can change their situation—whether it's financial, spiritual, or even health-related. It's about transformation. It's about believing where you are now doesn't have to be where you stay. There is hope. Change is possible.

> Stop dwelling on the past. Don't even remember these former things.
> I am doing something brand new, something unheard of. Even now
> it sprouts and grows and matures. Don't you perceive it? I will make
> a way in the wilderness and open up flowing streams in the desert
> (Isaiah 43:18-19 TPT).

GOD'S TIMING IS PERFECT

The year I turned 40, I met my husband, Buddy. But first, I met his mom at a home party for my side business. The hostess was the wife of their preacher, and the guests were the women of the congregation. I shared not only the business but also my faith. At the time, God was moving mightily in my life—I was finally paying attention to Him—and I couldn't help but share what He was doing.

Little did I know Buddy's mom was paying attention, too. She told Buddy about me, but not before the preacher's wife informed him I was a "praise-the-Lord kind of girl." (And yes, I do love to praise Him, but maybe not with quite the dramatic flair Ms. Marilyn described!)

When Buddy and I finally met—after two months of emails and one phone call the night before our lunch date—neither of us could have guessed what God had planned. But He knew. Even then, He was weaving together a story far better than anything I could have dreamed.

> *For God is working in you, giving you the desire and the power to do what pleases him* (Philippians 2:13 NLT).

LOOK WHAT GOD DID

One year to the day after Buddy and I met for lunch, he proposed. And in September of 2008, we stood together in Puerto Morelos, Mexico, saying, "I do." Our original plan for a beachside ceremony changed at the last minute when Hurricane Ike decided to make its way toward Texas. Instead, we got married in the courtyard of the house we rented, joined by my old neighbors and friends (who lived in Puerto Morelos), my daughter, Christie (then 21 years old), and my son, Dallas (11 years old). *And* an authentic mariachi band!

When I think back, I marvel at how God orchestrated it all. I was 41 years old, twice divorced, and raising two children from those previous marriages. And there was Buddy, 33, never married, no children of his own, and my perfect partner. Oh, and as for an oldest child marrying an only child? Let's just say God has a sense of humor!

ANSWERED PRAYER

In the early days of our marriage, Buddy would wonder out loud, *"What would a kid of ours look like?"* I wondered, too, but after a few years and no babies yet, I assumed it was too late. After all, I met Buddy when I was 40 and already raising two children. I resigned myself to the fact that our little family was complete.

But God had another chapter of our story yet to write.

Just before our two-year anniversary, we discovered we were expecting. And on March 23, 2011, at 9:16 PM, Austin Thomas Hale made his entrance into the world. I was 44, Buddy was 35, Christie was 24, and Dallas was 13. *Now* our family was complete!

God has a way of surprising us. His plans are always good, and His timing is always perfect—even if it doesn't match ours. Austin is now 13, and every day with him has been a blessing and a beautiful reminder of God's faithfulness.

> *Never doubt God's mighty power to work in you and accomplish all this. He will achieve infinitely more than your greatest request, your most unbelievable dream, and exceed your wildest imagination!* (Ephesians 3:20 TPT).

LESSONS IN GRACE

Marriage has taught me so much—about trust, forgiveness, faith, and, above all, grace. His grace. And the grace He gives Buddy and me to extend to one another daily. It's not always easy, but it's always worth it. Buddy is my biggest fan, the best dad, and the most incredible supporter of every dream God has placed in my heart.

Life isn't easy, and marriage isn't perfect. It takes faith, forgiveness, trust, and a whole lot of love. But through it all, I've seen God's hand at work. I've seen Him turn brokenness into beauty, chaos into calm, and disappointment into delight.

> *My grace is sufficient for you, for my power is made perfect in weakness* (2 Corinthians 12:9 NIV).

Maybe you're in a season where you're questioning His plan. Maybe life hasn't turned out the way you thought it would. I encourage you to praise Him anyway. Praise Him in the waiting. Praise Him in the unexpected. Because even when we can't see it, He's working all things for good.

> *And we know that for those who love God all things work together for good, for those who are called according to his purpose* (Romans 8:28 ESV).

God gave me unique gifts: Creativity. Encouragement. A knack for seeing the beauty and potential in others. And He showed me that these gifts aren't just for me. They are for His glory, to serve and uplift others.

Today, I look back on my life as a tapestry. Every thread—joy and sorrow, strength and weakness, triumph and failure—had a purpose. God used it all.

I've learned that evolution is a process and restoration is a gift. It's not about getting it perfect; it's about growing, learning, and leaning into the One who makes all things new.

Sweet sister, if God can create something beautiful from the ashes of my life, He can do the same for you. He has a plan for your life, and He will use *your* gifts for His glory.

He who was seated on the throne said, "I am making everything new!"
Then he said, "Write this down, for these words are trustworthy
and true" (Revelation 21:5 NIV).

But seek first the kingdom of God and his righteousness, and all these
things will be added to you (Matthew 6:33 ESV).

Maybe you're wondering: *But how can God use me?*

Satan would have us believe that we are too messed up, damaged, and unworthy for God to use us. But God says we are loved, chosen, and forgiven. The evangelist Billy Graham once said: "The unbelieving world should see our testimony lived out daily because it just may point them to the Savior."

You have a message that needs to be shared. We all do. I know my story is not unique; many women have overcome trials and obstacles, hidden sin, and made very public mistakes. The enemy would love for us to keep our stories hidden in shame. But when we share our burdens and past sins with each other, God can use our story to strengthen and encourage others.

Allow me to share a simple ABC approach that can help you move forward and walk in the purpose God has planned for you:

A) ACCEPT. Accept that you make mistakes. God is not surprised by our sin. When we accept that we fall short, we clear the way to move forward.

B) BELIEVE. Believe who God says you are, *fearfully and wonderfully made* (Psalm 139: 14 ESV). Despite how we may feel, God says we are His masterpiece, and He created each of us with a purpose (Ephesians

2:10 NLT). Remember: God doesn't call the equipped; He equips who He calls (Hebrews 13:21 NLT).

C) CONFESS. The Bible says when we confess our sin, *he is faithful and just to forgive us* (1 John 1:9 NLT). Talk to God about your mistakes. Acknowledge them. If possible, talk to a trusted friend. Something powerful occurs in the Spirit realm when we confess out loud. We open the door to freedom. I like to say we can't heal what we don't reveal.

For so many years, I felt "less than," and now I realize my worth in God's eyes.

I pray my story helps you see your value in His eyes, too. Jesus loves you so much and is calling all of us *for just such a time as this* (Esther 4:14 NLT).

Stacy Jo Coffee-Thorne

Stacy Jo Coffee-Thorne is a visionary entrepreneur and community leader who is passionate about empowering others through financial stewardship and Christian values. Based in Stuart, Florida, she is the founder and president of Freedom Support Solutions, a daily money management and accounting firm. In 2021, Stacy Jo launched the Association of Christian Business Women (ACBW) to equip and inspire women entrepreneurs and leaders in their faith and professional journeys.

An advocate for community involvement, Stacy Jo serves on multiple local boards and is active in her church. She enjoys spending time with her husband, Allen, their four adult children, and their church family. A worship leader and performer, she occasionally performs locally with her daughter as part of the duo "Not Sisters."

Certified as a Life Coach, John Maxwell Team member, and Dave Ramsey Master Coach, Stacy Jo is guided by her faith, living by Philippians 4:13: *I can do all things through Christ who strengthens me* (NKJV). Her dedication to service continues to inspire and impact her community and beyond.

From Repentance to Restoration

By Stacy Jo Coffee-Thorne

How did I end up here once again? What is wrong with me that I continually make the same mistakes time and time again?

Those were my questions to God as I sat in disbelief, certain that my world was crashing down around me. I had left everything in Ohio—my family, friends, church, and all I had ever known—to move to Florida and start a new life that I thought would be glorious! And now, this? How could this be happening? After two failed marriages, I could not imagine how I would handle going through this one more time.

My life in Ohio had left me with a lot of pain and shattered dreams that I somehow thought would all disappear once I uprooted and moved my children somewhere new—somewhere we could find a new life. Little did I know that my "new life," despite the initial difficulties and the challenges along the way, would far exceed my hopes and expectations,

Isaiah 61:3 says, *To all who mourn in Israel, he will give a crown of beauty for ashes, a joyous blessing instead of mourning, festive praise instead of despair. In their righteousness, they will be like great oaks that the LORD has planted for his own glory* (NLT).

Nearly three years after all signs pointed to the failure of my third marriage, I was in mourning. I was still grieving all the mistakes I had made throughout my entire life, the devastating loss of my mom just a month after I left her in Ohio to move to Florida, and the ruins of my two initial marriages, leaving me feeling unwanted, ashamed, afraid, and angry. And now, I was mourning my current marriage, which seemed to be lost in the battle of addiction and codependency. I can remember the pain as if it were yesterday. That torment felt as though someone had just reached in and ripped out my heart, leaving nothing but an empty chasm. I cried out to the Lord in desperation and begged Him to rescue us. "God, I am trying to be a good wife. I am doing my best to be a great mom to my kids. I go to church every Sunday and try to do what every 'good Christian' is supposed to do. What more do You want from me? I am desperate, and I can't do this anymore!"

Change was not immediate, but God gave me the strength to hold on, and in hindsight, it didn't take long for the answers to start coming. My husband's sobriety came through the suggestion of a dear friend who guided him into Christ-centered recovery; within the next year and a half, I came out of denial and faced the fact that I could *probably* (I'm laughing at this word now) use some recovery myself. I entered a step study, and as I began to pry up the nails and lift the rug under which I had swept all of my pain and shattered dreams, I started to recognize that God had never intended for me to be a victim—He had created me on purpose and for a purpose. He created me to fight *from* victory via the work that Jesus had already done on the cross, and more so, via the empty tomb! My victory is found in Him!

> But thank God! He gives us victory over sin and death through our Lord Jesus Christ (1 Corinthians 15:57 NLT).

I truly was thanking God. Moving through denial, operating from a grateful heart, and leaving the dreadful victim mentality behind me were my first steps toward true freedom and victory with Jesus!

Before going any further, let's flashback and check out the foundation I had laid. I grew up in church and accepted Jesus as my Savior at an early age. Looking back, however, I realize I had a very superficial knowledge of who God, Jesus, and the Holy Spirit really were. I knew *about* God's Word because of my wonderful mom and grandma. Grandma challenged me with Bible trivia on car rides and insisted on me attending Vacation Bible School each summer and Sunday School each week. I loved placing a gold star on the Bible memory chart every Sunday in class. However, despite knowing I was created to follow Jesus, I only had cognitive head knowledge of who He truly was (is).

Although I knew and often sang the song "Jesus Loves Me" in Sunday School, I lacked HEART knowledge. In all those years, I never grasped the depth or the width of His love for me or that He's had a plan for my life since before I was formed in my mother's womb. I knew about Him, but I didn't know Him...yet.

> *"I knew you before I formed you in your mother's womb. Before you were born I set you apart and appointed you as my prophet to the nations"* (Jeremiah 1:5 NLT).

I had lived my life with all the pain from my past—pain I was never meant to carry. As mentioned earlier, I had swept all my heartache and shattered dreams under the rug, slung it over my shoulder, and then moved to Florida. Carrying all this baggage impeded the plans God had for my life. I had to surrender EVERYTHING to Him to move forward and fulfill the purpose He had for me. God was very clear with me that if my hands were full of things He did not give me, I wouldn't be able to carry the good things He had for me. I had never pondered this before, but He was right! If my hands are full, I cannot pick up something else without setting something down. It just makes sense.

Let me be clear. God did not give me any of the pain from my past. That was the result of poor choices I had made or someone else had made, affecting me and requiring my forgiveness. You see, God gives us free will, and our choices will reap the harvest we sow. We don't always ask for the weeds, but when they come, we have to pull them up by the root and dispose of them properly so they don't grow back. Most often, based on my experience, proper "weed disposal" comes through forgiveness.

As I began to press into the idea that I was not meant to carry the pain that had burdened me for so long, I started letting go of things like sin, shame, and that God-forsaken victim mentality that kept me bound to my soul's satanic adversary. The enemy had my ear for many years because I let him have it. He had me fooled into believing he was right, telling me I was unworthy of love and would never be good enough for anyone. He called me a failure, afflicted me with imposter syndrome, and whispered in my ear that I was created to be used and abused and deserved the inflicted hurt because of what I had done. However, the diabolical reign of this despicable father of lies would soon come to an end! I had had enough! Through a process of restoration, I fully repented of my sin and released my pain of the past. I forgave myself. I was redeemed! From there, I started offering forgiveness to those who had hurt me, lifting the burdensome weight from me, and oh, what a relieving feeling that was!

Matthew's gospel declares a common but highly applicable call for us to relinquish our burdens to Him who came to relieve us. Our Savior Christ declares, *"Come to me, all you who are weary and burdened, and I will give you rest. Take my yoke upon you and learn from me, for I am gentle and humble in heart, and you will find rest for your souls"* (Matthew 11:28-29 NIV). Of course, I appreciate His precious offer of rest for my soul. However, so much more so, I value how *"learning from Him"* enriches the rest of my blessed days.

As I was praying about this chapter and struggling with what to write, God gave me beautiful instructions regarding the steps to restoration. It took me a little while to wrap my heart and head around it, but He said, "Repentance leads to redemption, redemption leads to relationship, and relationship leads to full restoration."

As I thought about this, I applied it to my experience. When I repented of my past, giving it all over to Jesus, I received the full redemption I had been seeking. I had repented when I accepted Jesus as my Savior, but at twelve years old, I had not yet experienced the turmoil that the enemy had for me. At sixteen, I repented again, but within two years, I made poor choices that put me on a slippery downward spiral that eventually led to alcohol, drugs, promiscuity, and even suicidal attempts. The enemy's lies kept me entangled in that lifestyle until I was twenty years old. Then, just as I was married for the first time and pregnant with my first child, satan brought new lies and sins to use against me.

But God had now heard my cry! He knew I sought full restoration but that I needed help getting there. He made a way for my repentance and redemption, but having never grasped the depth of my Savior's love for me, I limited myself. Even as I knew I had been forgiven and redeemed and had gained eternal salvation, I also understood there was so much to *learn from Him* concerning His *abundant life* for me on this side of heaven. I was listening.

I had always felt there was more. There had to be more, but what? A genuine relationship with God our Father—THAT WAS IT! That was what I had been longing for all my life. That was the key to filling the void inside me— an authentic relationship with my Jesus, my Savior, MY REDEEMER! It was not about talking to Him one time, asking for my free gift of salvation, and then going on with my life. It was about a relationship. God wanted a relationship with me even more than I wanted one with Him. When you are in a true relationship with someone, you want to spend time with them. You long to be with them—to walk with them, talk with them, and know more about them. I wanted more of God. I NEEDED more of Him immediately!

> *This is the message from the one who is the Amen… "Look! I stand at the door and knock. If you hear my voice and open the door, I will come in, and we will share a meal together as friends"* (Revelation 3:14, 20 NLT).

This revelation was the missing piece that not only restored my relationship with God through His son Jesus, but also restored my relationships with others. Just as He restored me and brought me NEW LIFE, He also restored my relationships with my husband and children! Why had I waited so long to seek Him?

As the Lord began to heal my relationship with my husband, I recognized the necessity for us to take the same steps that had been required to restore my relationship with my Savior. My husband and I had to repent for the hurtful things we had done to one another and extend forgiveness to each other. Through that redemption, our relationship was restored. Just as God restored my relationship with Him, as we leaned into Him and followed His commands, God faithfully restored our marriage. All glory to God! Our marriage is now stronger than ever, and we even lead a ministry together in Christ!

The enemy tried to destroy what God had brought together, but God's promises are true, and His Word never returns void. The Lord's Word says that when we return to God, He will repay what the enemy has stolen. We take our God-given authority over satan seriously and daily cast him and his minuscule minions to judgment at the feet of Jesus! We claim what is rightfully ours in Jesus's name. From our marriage and family to our businesses and finances and all points in between, we take authority over it all in Jesus's name; we consecrate it all to the Father, in Jesus's name, and we cleanse it all as we have been cleansed, by the blood of Jesus! It's payback time, satan!

Restoration: God Brings Beauty from Ashes

> *"Even now," declares the Lord, "return to me with all your heart...I will repay you for the years the locusts have eaten—the great locust and the young locust, the other locusts and the locust swarm—my great army that I sent among you. You will have plenty to eat, until you are full, and you will praise the name of the LORD your God, who has worked wonders for you; never again will my people be shamed"* (Joel 2:12, 25-26 NIV).

I wish I could say I woke up one morning to an instantly transformed relationship with my husband. However, as with anything worth having, the restoration of our marriage has been a process. However, the changes I've seen in the last eleven years—and even more so during the most recent five years—have been astounding. The Holy Spirit continues drawing out lies hiding underneath our denial and exchanging them for God's truth. I joyfully declare that I am no longer a slave to the lies of the enemy! I am worthy! I am worthy of love and belonging! God has plans for me and has equipped me to carry them out! He is using what the enemy meant for evil for His good! I believe that I am forgiven, but more so, I know who holds the key to the truth, and I go directly to Him when the enemy comes with his wicked chatter.

The new life I've been granted on this side of heaven through the restorative power of the Holy Spirit is certainly a life worth living. I see God's hand at work daily in my personal life through my relationship with Jesus, my husband, my children, and others with whom I come into contact. I personally stand in faith, believing that God supplies all my needs and abundantly more! As a business owner, I emphatically declare that Jesus Christ, the King of kings and Lord of lords, *is* the CEO of my businesses, and I will seek first the kingdom of God.

Now, my life is full of the fruits of the Spirit—love, joy, peace, patience, kindness, goodness, faithfulness, gentleness, and self-control—for which

I am grateful daily, especially in the midst of trials. I live with faith and the expectancy of what God will do, and I strive daily to be a Proverbs 31 woman. Solomon—noted as the wisest man of all time (except, of course, for Jesus)—scribed the Lord's perception of a godly wife.

> *A wife of noble character who can find?*
> *She is worth far more than rubies.*
> *Her husband has full confidence in her*
> *and lacks nothing of value.*
> *She brings him good, not harm,*
> *all the days of her life.*
> *She selects wool and flax*
> *and works with eager hands.*
> *She is like the merchant ships,*
> *bringing her food from afar.*
> *She gets up while it is still night;*
> *she provides food for her family*
> *and portions for her female servants.*
> *She considers a field and buys it;*
> *out of her earnings she plants a vineyard.*
> *She sets about her work vigorously;*
> *her arms are strong for her tasks.*
> *She sees that her trading is profitable,*
> *and her lamp does not go out at night.*
> *In her hand she holds the distaff*
> *and grasps the spindle with her fingers.*
> *She opens her arms to the poor*
> *and extends her hands to the needy.*
> *When it snows, she has no fear for her household;*
> *for all of them are clothed in scarlet.*
> *She makes coverings for her bed;*
> *she is clothed in fine linen and purple.*
> *Her husband is respected at the city gate,*
> *where he takes his seat among the elders of the land.*

She makes linen garments and sells them,
   and supplies the merchants with sashes.
She is clothed with strength and dignity;
   she can laugh at the days to come.
She speaks with wisdom,
   and faithful instruction is on her tongue.
She watches over the affairs of her household
   and does not eat the bread of idleness.
Her children arise and call her blessed;
   her husband also, and he praises her:
"Many women do noble things,
   but you surpass them all."
Charm is deceptive, and beauty is fleeting;
   but a woman who fears the LORD is to be praised.
Honor her for all that her hands have done,
   and let her works bring her praise at the city gate.
(Proverbs 31:10-31 NIV)

The new life I've found on this side of heaven is a VICTORIOUS LIFE IN CHRIST! I claim what He has done in me and through me and what He will continue to do next as I surrender to His good, perfect, and pleasing will. His purpose for me will be fulfilled.

Thank you, Lord, for full restoration in You!!

Restoration Through Forgiveness

By Kimberly Anne Kahn

How can you tell if you have truly forgiven someone who has hurt you? This question has been on my mind lately as I've been navigating my own restoration journey while writing this book. Unbeknownst to me, one thing preventing complete restoration in my own story was unforgiveness I harbored in my heart.

Several months after my husband left our marriage, I consistently asked God to send us the counselors we needed, as nothing else we tried seemed to work. God answered my prayers, and things began to change weeks after we started to work with the counselors. The Lord began to heal our wounds.

However, I felt like I was on an emotional roller coaster.

Because I honestly thought I had forgiven my husband, it surprised me to realize I hadn't fully forgiven everything. I had said the words, "Lord, I forgive him," and didn't think much more about it afterward. But as I continued my counseling sessions and focused on my healing, the Lord brought forth random dreams about situations from my childhood, past relationships, and my marriage.

I started to realize I still had unresolved feelings in my heart, causing resentment and anger toward others I thought I had forgiven. There were situations I had not fully let go of; the file for those unresolved issues was still open.

What is an open file? When I learned of "open files," I envisioned the movie *Bruce Almighty*, starring Jim Carrey as Bruce and Morgan Freeman playing

Restoration: God Brings Beauty from Ashes

the role of God. There is a scene where Bruce talks with God in a vacant building. God tells Bruce that everything he has said and done is in the file cabinet across the room. As snarky as he was, Bruce looked at the file cabinet and said, "Oh, one drawer just for me." When he walks over to pull the drawer out, the drawer rapidly flies open and keeps going and going until it stops clear across the room.

To me, these files represent unresolved issues—unfinished business that still demands our attention. An "open file" may indicate unforgiveness we need to address. Once we offer forgiveness and fully release any ill feelings to God, He destroys the file forever. Forgiveness isn't just about releasing a person—it's about making peace with the hurt, closing the file on the pain, and allowing proper healing. It's about choosing peace over resentment and grace over bitterness as we surrender the weight of past wounds to God.

As I navigate my own healing, I'm learning that forgiveness is not just a one-time decision but an ongoing journey. Some wounds take time to heal, and that's okay.

> Then Peter came up and said to him, "Lord, how often will my brother sin against me, and I forgive him? As many as seven times?" Jesus said to him, "I do not say to you seven times, but seventy-seven times" (Mathew 18:21-22 ESV).

How do we recognize that there may still be some unforgiveness in our hearts? One of my favorite prayers is, *Search me, O God, and know my heart: try me, and know my thoughts: And see if there be any wicked way in me, and lead me in the way everlasting* (Psalm 139:23-24 KJV).

Are you holding on to unforgiveness and unresolved matters in your life? Sometimes, we don't even recognize the weight we carry until God shines a light on it. Allow God's light to search your heart and pull up any unforgiveness you may still have. Trust in Him and know that He will reveal it to you.

I recognized I hadn't forgiven my husband for leaving our marriage. The hurt continued to resurface each time I was triggered, making me angry. I knew the file was still open, and I needed to heal this area of my life and continue to forgive until the matter didn't arise any longer.

Dear Father,

Thank You for the gift of forgiveness and the grace You so freely extend to us. Lord, I ask that You search my heart and reveal any areas where I still hold on to unforgiveness. Help me to surrender every hurt, every wound, and every unresolved matter into Your hands. Give me the strength to truly forgive, not just with my words but with my heart, so I can experience pure restoration as You intended.

Father, I trust You to heal my relationships and the broken places within me. Teach me to love as You love and to release the weight of past pain so that I may walk in the freedom and peace You have promised. Thank You for Your patience as I navigate this journey and for Your unfailing love that carries me through. May my heart remain open to Your guidance, and may I continue to grow in Your grace.

In Jesus' name, Amen.

. . . .

Barbara Wooden

 Barbara Wooden is a Florida girl with a Florida family history going back at least eight traceable generations. She grew up in Miami and graduated from the University of Miami. After graduation she lived and traveled around the world doing Marketing and Advertising for fast food companies like Burger King Corporation, McDonald's, Wendy's, and Church's and Popeyes Chicken.

Barbara is currently back living in South Florida working in the Investment and Insurance industry.

Barbara never married; she focuses most of her spare time doing mission work with her church. Her hobbies include traveling, reading, tennis, and loving the Lord. Wooden is also an avid sports fan having spent time during college working in the sports department of both the Miami Hurricane and Miami Herald Newspapers,

Barbara gives thanks for what each new day brings and has enjoyed working on this *Restoration* project.

From Brokenness to Beloved

By Barbara Wooden

My life has been a series of trials and moments of grace, starting with the unexpected pregnancy of my mother and proceeding to the traumatic experiences of my childhood. I faced rejection, isolation, and a constant battle with feelings of inadequacy. My story has continued through dark times, where my faith, echoing through scripture by my mother, along with perseverance became my guide.

I found peace in the verses of the Bible and unexpected encounters that shaped me into the woman I am today. Each experience, every trial, led me closer to understanding my self-worth and the powerful love of God.

As you read my story, I hope God's love will restore you in your dark places, replacing your fears with hope and joy. The process and struggles are worth the miracle God has in store for you. Broken can be beautiful, and being broken will never negate being beloved.

> But you are a chosen people, a royal priesthood, a holy nation, God's special possession, that you may declare the praises of him who called you out of darkness into His wonderful light (1 Peter 2:9 NIV).

My brother and I were both "only children," but our circumstances were quite different. He was born when our mother was only 18 years old, while I came along when she was 49. At the time, my brother was in the military, serving in Korea. He was shocked and embarrassed to hear that our mother was pregnant at her age, and it took him some time to accept the fact that I was here to stay.

My father was overjoyed at the news. At 62 years old, I was his first and only child, and he couldn't have been happier. Our mother, however, had a much harder time coming to terms with an unexpected pregnancy. She went to the doctor for a stomach ache and came home with the shocking news that she was pregnant at 49. She cried all the way home, but after prayer and reflection, she accepted the situation.

As a family with limited financial resources, our mother prayed constantly for me to be either pretty or smart. She always had a feeling that I would be a girl, and she hoped that I would be able to succeed in life no matter what. With time, our family adjusted to the idea of a new addition and learned to survive the changes that came with my arrival. At the time of my birth, there were doubts about my potential for either brilliance or beauty. People whispered behind my mother's back, suggesting that I was proof of why older women should not have children. With my bald head and unannounced gender, I was a source of speculation for many.

My friends have horrific stories about abusive and unloving parents. The truth is that I received an abundance of love and care from my parents. The outside world was not always as kind. I was constantly reminded of my perceived inadequacies whenever I stepped outside our home. This led me to keep to myself, avoiding drawing attention to my presence. I felt isolated and friendless and was well aware of the rejection that would come due to my skin conditions: eczema, alopecia, and vitiligo. Other parents wanted to protect their children from me, fearing my conditions were contagious.

My experiences in kindergarten and elementary school were difficult. I often found myself alone, trailing behind groups of laughing children on my way home. The judgment and rejection I faced from my peers reinforced my sense of alienation. It was a lonely and challenging time for me, and I struggled to find my place in a world that seemed determined to keep me on the outside of it.

During junior high school, I often walked to school alone and experienced various demeaning situations. One particular incident stands out in my memory. A very handsome junior high school guy approached me. He was older than me and approached me with a proposition. For 50 cents, he would pretend to ask me out in front of the kids in my class. I was so stunned I was speechless. We shared a long moment of silence before he realized I wasn't going to answer and walked away,

One of the greatest things my parents did for me was to introduce me to the path of faith and Jesus. It was definitely an introduction because the decisions were left up to me. They provided me with the courage, strength, and guidance I needed (and still need) to get through the hard times.

Growing up, I had limited reading material. I remember only one kiddie book, but there was always the Bible. My other would read to me daily from the Bible, and to this day, I am always amazed at how many chapters of Psalms flow like second nature for me, always from the King James Version. The foundation of my faith that my parents laid for me through their teachings continues to be a source of comfort and guidance even to this day.

When I was just four years old, my father passed away suddenly from a massive heart attack, leaving my mother, a domestic servant and cook, alone to work double time to keep our little family together. With her demanding work schedule, she had to rely on others to look after me. By the time I was six, I spent time with a kind woman named Miss Bess, who lived a couple of blocks away. Next door to Miss Bess, a family with three kids welcomed me to the neighborhood. Their daughter Mary became my first real friend. Every day after school, Mary would visit me or invite me over to her house, providing me with the friendship and support I needed at this time. Mary didn't seem to care that I wasn't pretty or that my skin was discolored from the vitiligo. With Mary, I could relax and not be on guard for the next catty remark or strange look. This was truly something new.

During our playtime at Mary's house, her oldest brother, who was 16, was generally absent, either working or playing basketball. Her younger brother, Joe, who was 14, would often join us. One day, they proposed a disturbing new game. Joe would experiment on me to show me about sex. At 6 years old, I was ignorant of the topic, but I trusted Mary's judgment and agreed to play the game.

The concept of sex was foreign to me, so when I was asked to remove my underwear, I was uneasy. It struck me as odd that I was the only one undressing, and I questioned Mary about it. She responded defensively, explaining that siblings couldn't play in such activities. Her reaction and the accompanying eye roll led me to believe that I should have already known this rule.

As Mary's brother Joe began to explore my body, I realized I was not enjoying this new game. Mary watched silently, offering no intervention. Once Joe had finished, we all exchanged glances and then silently left in different directions, the weight of the encounter hanging heavily in the air. This was not the last time during my early years that I would encounter people like Mary and Joe, but by 8 years old, I had found my voice and was able to weigh what friendship was actually worth.

Following that traumatic experience, I found myself without a best friend. Miss Bess later took in a new girl to look after. Caroline quickly became Mary's new best friend. Reflecting back on the incident, I regret not informing Caroline about the game that had occurred. This is the first time that I have shared this story with anyone. Shortly after, my mother relocated us to a different city, and I lost touch with that group of people.

The game and the subsequent loss of my only friend at the time left a lasting impact on me. It solidified the fact that I was not sufficient—not intelligent enough and not attractive enough. These feelings of inadequacy persisted until I reached the age of 16.

When Mom and I relocated, she introduced me to not just one but three different churches. Through these connections, I felt the love of the Lord reaffirmed in my life. Although I still preferred solitude, I considered myself a knowledgeable loner, thanks to my time reading books and the Bible.

But another force in my life was pulling in the opposite direction. When Mom and I moved, we went to live with her brother, a minister and a very prominent figure in his community.

My Mom adored her younger brother, and I looked forward to having a strong, loving male figure in my life. My father was that for me, but there had been no one to fill that role since he died.

My uncle was a charismatic figure that people flocked to. But I guess by the time he got home at the end of the day, he had no love and charisma left for a six-year-old. I tried everything I could to show I was worth loving, but nothing seemed to work,

One of my classmates started coming home with me after school for dinner and to hang out. There was no better place to be than at my mother's dinner table. She was one of the world's greatest cooks. My friend Stella was one of 14 children, and the special attention paid to her at the dinner table made me glad for her,

Stella was also one of the most beautiful children I had ever met; she had long curly hair, beautiful skin, and a sweet disposition. My uncle and his wife gravitated toward Stella. They were so taken by her that they started talking to Stella's mother about adopting her.

Once again, I was not enough. Not pretty enough, smart or lovable enough. At this point in my life, I was learning to cope with rejection pretty well.

Without my saying anything, my mother understood what was happening. She got a second job, saved up her money, and bought a house for the two of us without anyone else's knowledge.

I was 14 when we moved into the little house on 48th Street. It was small, but to me, it was a mansion and the start of a new life.

I was grateful to my mom for helping me in this way. Due to the reading and my classroom performance, I knew I was intelligent and capable. I told my mom that her prayers had finally been answered at last, though she initially seemed puzzled by my statement. I reminded her of her prayers during her pregnancy: if the child was not pretty, let her be smart. She smiled and told me she had always seen me as both smart and beautiful. In her eyes, God had answered her prayers from the very beginning.

Her words felt like a typical mother's response, but I could sense the sincerity behind them. She truly believed in my worth and the potential she saw in me. As a parent, she understood the importance of carrying a child through its darkest moments, even if it meant being a nuisance at times. Encouraging communications and offering support can alleviate the burdens that weigh heavily on a young child's soul. Children will believe about themselves what we pour into them.

I should have known that if anyone knew and understood what I was going through, it would be my mom. She was born in a rural farming community, the sixth of eleven children. She was different from her brothers and sisters. She was allergic to the poisons used to cure the tobacco they raised and could not work the fields. To help her earn her keep, at the age of 8, she was shipped off to live "on premises" with a wealthy family who had a young daughter. She was both a maid and companion to the young girl, Esther. Mom loved the classes she took more than Esther.

My mother blossomed with this experience. After two years, though, it was over. Mom was sent back to the farm and put in charge of her younger siblings since she could not work in the fields.

When Mom returned to the farm, she was even more isolated from her family. As a result of her time away, she spoke differently, dressed differently, and wanted different things in life. Everyone who met her saw the difference, labeled her as haughty, and steered clear of her.

But Mom enjoyed the isolation when she could get it. It gave her time to read and pray. The only books she owned were the Bible and two books she brought back from her time "on premises." (Those books often came up missing.)

At age 16, Mom was married off to an abusive man. After their first son was born, she ran. She started a new life for herself in a new city and eventually remarried. She also came to understand that while her brothers, sisters, aunts, and uncles teased and abused her, they also admired and respected her in a strange way,

To this day, Mom was the most articulate woman, steeped in the Lord, that I have ever known.

"For I know the plans I have for you," declares the Lord, "plans to prosper you and not to harm you, plans to give you a hope and a future" (Jeremiah 29:11 NIV).

My brother, Ray, and I never became as close as I had hoped and prayed for—not even as adults. Every only child longs for a big brother or sister.

Ray was career military, and he married three times. Each of his wives was tall, thin, and beautiful. I never fit the mold of a woman worthy of his attention. My mother bragged about my academic achievements to him, but that didn't matter. I was never thin and beautiful.

As adults, Ray's daughter and I became extremely close. Alecia did not fit his mold of classic beauty either, but it didn't matter. She had personality that ruled any room she entered. She was smart and funny and a joy to be around. Most important, she loved her father. As a result, I learned to love him too.

My brother, sister-in-law, and I all lived in Florida. Alecia went away to college in Virginia and never came home. When my brother and sister-in-law both became ill, Alecia and I developed a plan for their care. She made sure the bills were paid, and I worked with caregivers and others to help with their daily living, including scheduling and providing transportation to doctor's appointments. Alecia made it a point to fly in every two to three weeks. I lived 45 minutes away and would get there as often as possible.

Alecia had made a promise to her parents that she would never let them go to a nursing home, and I was determined to help her keep it.

I remember a special moment before my brother's passing when he gazed at me and posed a question that resonated with me deeply.

"When did you get to be pretty?"

What I heard was, "When did you get to be enough?'

I wanted to answer: "I've always been pretty and funny and caring and loving; you just never looked at me or saw any value in me."

But I heard God say, "You've always been enough." So I said nothing and just smiled.

Ray's inquiry about my perceived beauty felt like a broader inquiry into my worth and adequacy. While I yearned to respond with a declaration of my value, I was struck by a revelation. Instead of focusing on the external, I heard a message that I had always been enough, just as I am.

My brother passed away in July of 2017. Alecia and I supported each other in our grief and worked to give my brother the type of homegoing celebration he would want.

Then, I lost Alecia in October of 2018 to a fast-moving and inoperable brain cancer. Her mother, my sister-in-law, passed away in February of 2019.

The back-to-back losses were devastating. The kind of pain and emptiness only God can help you get through.

Today, as a mature woman, I am surrounded by genuine Christian friends, and I am blessed with a strong sense of self. God has graciously returned to me the childhood joy and wonder I had lost prematurely. In place of fear and doubt, I now have a deep love of the Lord, recognizing Him as a faithful and loyal friend. I have been renewed and guided onto the path that aligns with the Lord's will for me. I cannot claim to always know what that is, but I open my arms willingly to God's direction.

Never lose faith in yourself. Forgive yourself, and trust that you have a purpose in God's will. Perhaps it is God's plan for you to walk on the outside of the world. No matter where you are and what you are going through, take heart. God's plan for you is perfect. Even when we feel broken, we can trust that we are God's beloved,

> *He restores my soul. He leads me in the paths of righteousness for his name's sake* (Psalm 23:3 ESV).

Alisha McCarthy

Alisha McCarthy is a 27-year-old single mother of a three-year-old child. Passionate about makeup and writing, she finds joy in helping others feel good about themselves and cherishing moments with friends and her faith in Jesus.

Alisha is active in her community and has a rich history of community service that reflects her commitment to helping others. Currently working on her self-growth, Alisha is focused on her education and personal growth.

At this stage in her life, her most significant asset is her testimony, which she aims to share in order to spread awareness and inspire others. Alisha aspires to advocate not only for individuals with disabilities but also for single mothers and troubled teens. She believes that the scariest moments in life can lead to the most beautiful transformations when one surrenders to God.

"For I know the plans I have for you," declares the Lord, "plans to prosper you and not to harm you, plans to give you hope and a future" (Jeremiah 29:11 NIV).

Renewed Hope in the Unexpected

By Alisha McCarthy

The year 2020 marked a significant turning point in my life. At 23 years old, I found myself nine weeks pregnant and trapped in an abusive relationship. Then, my child's father was incarcerated, leaving me homeless and feeling alone. Finally, I experienced an unthinkable incident that permanently altered me physically.

Looking back, although I faced challenges from those closest to me—family, friends, and boyfriends—much of what I experienced resulted from my own choices. Still, I can't even begin to count the sleepless nights I endured or the countless days I spent questioning, "Why me?" By 23, I had already faced more challenges than many people experience in a lifetime.

However, the lessons I learned from all this were life-changing. I know now that we need to surrender every part of our lives to God, and He will fill us with joy. Not only will He bring us joy, but He can also turn what seems impossible into reality. All we have to do is trust in Him and let Jesus take the wheel.

I was born into a large Christian family; our lives revolved around church and church events. Many of my relatives were pastors who led their own congregations. As a child, I absolutely loved this environment. Being young, I cherished the worship, the sense of community with family and friends, the children's classes, and especially the outings we enjoyed afterward.

As a child, however, I always felt different from my peers. I was the goofy, loud kid who couldn't stop smiling and laughing. Now, I recognize that my outgoing personality has been one of the key factors in helping me get through life's obstacles. I've come to believe that having a positive outlook, even in the hard things, can take us further than we ever imagined.

I was a wonderful child until puberty hit, and then everything changed. I became rebellious, lost interest in going to church, and was drowning in anger. During this time, I faced bullying from my peers for being overweight and hairy. My grades began to slip, and I started skipping classes.

I was growing up with a single mother and a younger sister, and I went on a quest to find my father, which added to my struggles. I sent letters to addresses I could find, called various numbers, and even searched for him on Facebook. I was desperate to connect with him.

By the end of middle school, I found myself in therapy, anger management classes, and group sessions.

A few years later, I managed to locate my father through a mutual friend of my mom's. I began spending time with him and his family, but it was a complicated relationship. He showed me the letters I had sent him in the past, which left me feeling like he didn't want me around. I realized we needed to build a bond, but despite my efforts, I often felt unworthy of being his daughter.

It seemed my "daddy issues" triggered a cycle of unforgiveness within me. I held onto grudges for years, no matter the person or the situation. Even the smallest things, like someone looking at me a certain way, felt like a personal affront, leading me to believe they had some secret resentment towards me.

I became cold and bitter, harboring negative emotions toward others over

Restoration: God Brings Beauty from Ashes

the smallest things. Eventually, I lost myself and found myself in abusive relationships that left me feeling numb. These experiences sent me straight into traumatic events I genuinely wish I could erase from my memory. I went through physical, mental, and emotional abuse, struggled with addictions, and even faced time in jail.

My mindset was so distorted that I believed it was acceptable to surround myself with toxic people—thinking nothing could harm me as long as I had faith in God. I was convinced that my lifestyle and the people I surrounded myself with had no bearing on the struggle I was facing—it was all just bad karma.

I couldn't have been more wrong. But what I didn't recognize at the time is that, despite my struggles, God was with me.

The Lord is close to the brokenhearted and saves those who are crushed in spirit (Psalm 34:18 NIV).

With my mind set on not taking responsibility for the direction of my life, I entered an abusive relationship, which turned out to be a wild ride. He had his own troubled history, and during our time together, we found ourselves in jail three times, leaving me with a record that I can't escape.

When I got out the last time, I secured a good job working full-time and moved in with some close friends. However, I soon found myself back in that unhealthy relationship, and just a month later, I discovered I was pregnant.

I was incredibly excited to receive the news of a baby on the way, especially after having experienced a miscarriage in the past. All I ever wanted was to be a mom. My pregnancy was considered high-risk, so I reduced my workload. I envisioned this as our chance to start a family. It could be the turning point for us.

I hoped the baby would motivate my child's father to change. Unfortunately, he ended up back in jail, leaving me pregnant and filled with fear.

I didn't want to return to my mom's house, so I decided I needed to figure things out on my own. I thought that if all else failed, I could always reach out to her later. Looking back now, I realize I was being given signs to go home, but I was too focused on clinging to what could have been instead of acknowledging the reality right in front of me.

Little did I know, my life was about to take an even more dramatic turn. I never imagined I could find myself in a situation that would leave me not only pregnant but also in the hospital—pregnant and paralyzed from the neck down.

On December 22, 2020, I had a day off work when I received a call from a childhood friend inviting me to hang out. After I arrived, we spent some time catching up, and not long after, he received a phone call from another friend asking for a ride to see his son. I could never say no to a parent in need. Despite not knowing this individual, I agreed to drive him to see his son. My friend came with us. When we arrived at our destination, the son's mother greeted us. Then, a young man around my age, the son, came outside.

The father and son got into my car while the mother went inside. It was 12:30 in the afternoon on a Tuesday. I was with a friend and felt safe. I never imagined anything bad would happen.

While the guys were chatting, I was busy messaging another friend who needed a ride home from work. A few minutes later, I informed the men in my backseat that I had to leave and they couldn't come with me because there wouldn't be enough room for both them and my other friend in the car.

As soon as those words left my lips, the atmosphere shifted. It felt like the air became still as everything around me fell silent. I couldn't even hear my own breathing.

Then, when I looked up, I saw the father standing in front of my car, panicking. To my right, I noticed my friend taking his last breath. At that moment, it still hadn't registered that something terrible had happened to me.

My mind struggled to process the fact that I couldn't move. It wasn't until I looked to my left that I noticed I was bleeding. From the color of my blood, I immediately knew it had to be coming from an artery. I had been shot. My first instinct was to get someone's attention to stop the bleeding because I didn't want to lose my baby. I tried to lean forward to hit the horn, but nothing worked.

Eventually, I made eye contact with the father, and he came over. I told him to stop the bleeding, but he couldn't locate where it was coming from. I informed him that I was pregnant and urged him to calm down and call 911.

It felt like the paramedics arrived within seconds. They found the exit wound but struggled to locate the entrance, so I continued to bleed out. Surprisingly, I stayed calm and fully aware until they transported me to the hospital, where they had to sedate me to begin surgery.

They were able to contact my mom, so by the time I woke up, she was there by my side. She informed me that she had given her consent for a blood transfusion because of the significant blood loss I had experienced.

However, after surgery, when the doctor spoke with my mom, he revealed that I hadn't needed a single drop of blood. He said it was a miracle, as he had never encountered an injury like mine, let alone seen someone survive it.

My daughter—still in my womb—and I were stabilized, but there were concerns about her survival. Given the circumstances, the medical team suggested terminating my pregnancy, as they believed it could hinder my recovery.

When they suggested this, I told them absolutely no. I would not go through with the termination of my pregnancy. I believed that God had protected both my daughter and me through this ordeal, and I felt He had a greater purpose for both of us. I was certain our testimony would be powerful, and I refused to let the devil win. Even after they informed me that I was a quadriplegic, I was grateful to be alive.

> "So do not fear, for I am with you; do not be dismayed, for I am your God. I will strengthen you and help you; I will uphold you with my righteous right hand" (Isaiah 41:10 NIV).

Throughout the day, the obstetrician came in several times to check on the baby. Even with all the trauma and medications I was on, my daughter was active, awake, and thriving. Every time they came to check on her, she would respond by wiggling and moving, making it clear that she was perfectly fine.

I had no doubt she would be healthy because she was covered by the blood of Jesus.

Once they transferred me out of the intensive care unit, my aunt reached out to a cousin of ours and had him come to pray over me and the baby. At that moment, I wasn't even angry with the man who had done this to me. All I could do was pray for him and find it in my heart to forgive him. I realized there was nothing I or anyone else could do to change the situation, so why should I take matters into my own hands? All I could do was surrender it all to God.

God saved me from a situation I shouldn't have survived, and I saw it as a big part of my testimony. From that day forward, I knew that my daughter and I had a purpose far greater than I could have ever imagined.

While I didn't know our exact purpose, I recognized it was time for a fresh start. God blessed me with another chance at life— something few people receive.

Since that moment, I've committed myself to changing my life for the better. I was not wrong. God had incredible plans for me.

"For I know the plans I have for you," declares the Lord, "plans to prosper you and not to harm you, plans to give you hope and a future" (Jeremiah 29:11 NIV).

Today, I can honestly say I am the happiest I've ever been. God has transformed my life and given me something far better than I could have imagined.

The journey has not been easy; I have faced many battles along the way. The medical system has its challenges, but we've learned to make the most of it. We've had to fight for everything we have. There were times we nearly lost our house and we did lose our vehicles. Sadly, we endured the disappointment of many people walking away from us. But I believe that God had a purpose in all of it.

We have also been abundantly blessed. God has given us an incredible community. I am grateful to be involved with Hearts For Moms, who have supported me in becoming a better mother and provided me with the resources I need to achieve my goals.

Our church even blessed us with a van, helping me to attend therapy and doctor's appointments. Not only that, but they also helped make my dream of getting baptized a reality.

God transformed my life at the moment when I thought everything was lost. He renewed my spirit entirely. I've found the strength to forgive everyone, including myself, for everything I've experienced.

I am filled with a joy that only God can provide. I now have a renewed hope for life, along with goals and aspirations, and I am surrounded by people who are dedicated to helping me achieve them. This experience has taught me that what we perceive as an ending may actually be a new beginning.

> *Trust in the Lord with all your heart, and do not lean on your own understanding. In all your ways acknowledge Him, and He will make straight your paths* (Proverbs 3:5-6 ESV).

To any woman who has faced abuse or found herself in a situation where life feels hopeless, I want you to take my story to heart. Believe that God is good and faithful, and know that we can still find *renewed* hope in the unexpected. I had to endure unimaginable circumstances to truly realize that my hope is renewed in the One who created me.

Dear Heavenly Father,

I come before You with my heart wide open, lifting up every woman who feels trapped in despair or pain. Lord, I ask that You wrap Your loving arms around her and remind her that she is never alone. I pray she feels Your presence in her life, bringing comfort and healing to her brokenness.

Help her see that even in the darkest, hardest moments, You are working for her good. Open her heart to believe in Your goodness and faithfulness. Give her the courage to seek You and to trust in the hope that You offer.

I pray she will find strength in her struggles and renewal in her spirit as she turns to You. Lead her into a relationship with You, a relationship filled with love, support, and guidance. Show her that You are the Creator who desires to walk alongside her always and through everything!

In Jesus' name, I pray. Amen.

Please remember always—you are valued and cherished. Believe in the hope God has for you and know there is a beautiful purpose in all things.

> And we know that in all things God works for the good of those who love him, who have been called according to his purpose (Romans 8:28 NIV).

Restoring the Joy

By Kimberly Ann Hobbs

Some people are wandering this world, saying, "I'm just not happy anymore!" It's easy to get caught up in a fleeting desire for instant gratification and look for fulfillment in a feeling, thinking it's the end of the world when we do not experience it. It can help to understand that there is a difference between feeling happy and possessing true joy. As believers and followers of Jesus Christ, we should know that joy and happiness are not the same thing.

Happiness is a feeling. When things aren't going well for us, or we have a bad outlook on something particular, we experience sadness, feeling the opposite of happiness.

Joy, on the other hand, is a deep sense of knowing beyond a doubt that despite our feelings, everything will be OK. Joy is independent of our circumstances—it comes from a deep-rooted conviction that our confidence is in God alone; He brings us joy. A scripture that can help us identify this promise is: *So, we are convinced that every detail of our lives is continually woven together for good, for we are his lovers who have been called to fulfill his designed purpose* (Romans 8:28 TPT). God uses *every* circumstance, even our pain and suffering.

God promises that He will work everything together for the good when we love and trust Him. If we don't believe we have joy or when we feel we have lost it, we must remember that God can restore joy. God can cause our hearts to smile even when we feel our world is falling apart. How? If we trust Jesus as our personal Lord and Savior, God comes in and restores life to us. He delivers an eternity in heaven with Him, filling our hearts with joy. God's desire is that we would know His joy in our hearts every day and be willing to share it with others.

Restoration: God Brings Beauty from Ashes

You may already know God but have drifted away from your relationship with our Savior—that will diminish your joy. That was the situation for me at one point in my life. I had walked away from God, going deeper and deeper into my own selfish desires. Over years of heartache, I lost all my joy. Sure, I found moments of fleeting happiness, but those were just feelings that lasted only a short time. My inner joy disappeared more and more the further I got from my God. Finally, it was gone because the sin crept in and took over! True joy is found only in the presence of God, and God and sin cannot co-exist. If you recognize this pattern in your life, I beg you to find a way to confess your sin, turn from the wrong direction you are heading in, and draw close to God again by accepting His forgiveness. Let Him reveal the pathway you are to follow, and as you follow it, watch your joy return, just like I did.

> *You make known to me the path of life; in your presence there is fullness of joy; at your right hand are pleasures forevermore* (Psalm 16:11 ESV).

When our hearts are right with God and we are walking with Him with a clean and clear conscience, our joy begins to increase. His light shines on us when we obey His Word. Our joy can be restored when we take God's Word and hide it in our hearts. *Your testimonies are my heritage forever; for they are the joy of my heart* (Psalm 119:111ESV). *God* gives us wisdom, knowledge, and joy when we do what pleases Him.

Further, God desires that each one of us who walk with Him share life-giving power and wisdom from His Word with others; when we do this, it will bring joy to our lives. There is no greater blessing or joy to receive than to see another person's life changed by the power of God's Word.

When I wake up each day, I ask God to direct me to who I should speak to throughout the day. I have joy in my heart continuously because He answers that prayer and leads me to people who need to know Him. I open my mouth and share Jesus; the joy that floods my soul is immense when I can do this! If you develop a habit of anticipating that God will use you each day you live, you will have joy! *The prospect of the righteous is joy* (Proverbs 10:28 NIV).

I can't encourage you enough that if you want to restore the joy in your life, you need to walk with God. Joy is produced by the Holy Spirit; He tells us in Galatians 5:22 about the fruits of the spirit. Love, joy, peace, and so much more are included in the fruits He gives to those who walk with Him. If something is blocking the work of the Holy Spirit in you, you need to ask the Lord to reveal what it is. Please do not be hindered from a heart full of joy by avoiding a simple open request to God through prayer to help you understand what needs to be changed in your life. Then, when God shows you what needs to be changed, commit to doing something about it.

Joy comes when we trust the Lord. He loves you more than you can ever imagine or comprehend. He has promised to help you. Put your full trust in Him and prepare in your heart to do what He asks of you. When you do this, oh, the restoration of joy that will flood your heart! That restored joy is beyond anything you can imagine; you will never want to live without it again.

. . . .

Rebecca Figueroa

Rebecca Figueroa is a 45-year-old single mother of two beautiful daughters, aged 27 and 19, and a grandmother to a lovely 3-year-old. She enjoys being with her family and chasing God daily!

Rebecca has worked in property management for 20 years and has also engaged in various side businesses over the past 24 years, including residential and construction cleaning, personal assisting, and catering. Even in these areas of work, she finds ways to share about her loving God.

Her passion outside of her family and faith is in property management, and in 2018, she was thrilled to establish her business, Southern Hospitality of Palm Beach.

Rebecca's journey has been both interesting and rewarding; she acknowledges God has gotten her through many experiences, both good and hard. Currently, she is starting on an exciting new journey, trusting God! Due to life circumstances, she may not know exactly what He has in store for her, but she believes there is a purpose behind it all.

Rebecca hopes that by sharing her message, she inspires others and also advocates for various organizations that align with God's message.

Pieces of Faith

By Rebecca Figueroa

I am a single mother to two beautiful daughters who are my entire world. Throughout my life, I have experienced many different journeys with God, even times of being broken down and rebuilt. No matter where I've found myself, Jesus has always been by my side. Even when I chose the distractions of the world over Him, He was there, fighting for me and giving me pieces of faith.

> The Lord is close to the brokenhearted and saves those who are crushed in spirit (Psalm 34:18 NIV).

In my times of worldliness, I've made poor decisions. But God never gave up on me. As a single mom, I focused on raising my girls, juggling two or three jobs, and building my relationship with God. I became proud of the woman I was growing into—one who had control over her life and the circumstances around her.

As the girls matured, I truly loved where I was in life. I was actively involved in my church and dedicated to my family. That was what mattered most to me.

However, my pride and controlling nature began to take root. As a single mother, I had worked hard and was very proud of my achievements. I felt in control of everything around me and had no desire to return to my past struggles. That motivation and doing it all for my girls drove me forward. It may have taken me a while to get where I was, but I made it and was very proud.

My faith continued to grow stronger, and I felt genuinely happy and comfortable. But that's when I had to be especially cautious. The enemy seeks opportunities to attack, targeting our families, children, and everything dear to us when pride begins to creep in.

I always stayed involved in my girls' lives, even as I faced challenges, such as differences with my oldest daughter, ensuring they participated in church activities, after-school sports, camps, and volunteer programs.

I did my best with the resources I had. As the head of the household, I knew I had to be strong. Thankfully, I also had my parents and two older sisters for support. When my oldest daughter moved out, it was a tough transition, but I stayed strong in my faith. Even though she no longer lived with me, I remained involved in her daily life. I was managing everything.

I have always struggled with thinking that I am in control rather than relying fully on God—the great I AM. Because I believed I was in control, I felt safe and secure. I was a strong woman, holding my head high, and I had no intention of returning to my past.

Why would I want to risk everything I had worked so hard for—my daughters, home, career, family, and most importantly, my relationship with God?

Little by little, everything started to change, and I began to feel like I was missing out on something. These were new feelings. The enemy was always lurking, waiting for the perfect opportunity to strike me. I needed to focus on my daughter and be there for her, no matter what.

Restoration: God Brings Beauty from Ashes

I began seeing someone I knew wasn't God's intention for me, but I put blinders on. It was fun and fleeting, and that was all I could see. I convinced myself I could handle everything that came with it.

Slowly, my world began to shift, and I no longer recognized the person I was becoming.

I started making excuses to skip family events and began missing church more frequently. Bit by bit, I lost sight of what was truly in front of me. My life was slipping away, and I was losing myself. But I continued to work and fulfill my responsibilities—being there for my daughters and family.

As time passed, my oldest daughter faced her own relationship struggles, but we always managed to work through them. Right or wrong, she is my daughter, and no one could ever come between me and my girls.

And I continued to go through a lot in my relationship. Even though God sent me every sign, feeling, and thought, I kept making excuses to stay in the relationship. Before I knew it, I wasn't going to church, and I wasn't surrounding myself with my family or friends.

I stopped talking to some of my closest friends and distanced myself from business associates. I was becoming a completely different person without even realizing it.

Little by little, my spirit became more and more broken. My inner joy was absent, and my shine was gone. When I look back at pictures from that time, I can see it in my face. I was trying to be there for everyone around me while losing myself in the process. I didn't recognize it at the time. I wanted to help and see those connected to me happy and blessed.

I would often say, "God blessed me; let me pay it forward." However, I don't think He meant me to respond the way I did. I was doing more harm than good to myself.

> *So do not fear, for I am with you; do not be dismayed, for I am your God. I will strengthen you and help you; I will uphold you with my righteous right hand* (Isaiah 41:10 NIV).

My youngest daughter was in middle school and in a good place, but she was going through a lot through this as well. I didn't realize how this was affecting my family. It's crazy how, when God is not in the equation, your world can turn upside down in the blink of an eye.

I was so blinded to it all, even when God was placing all the signs before me. I believed I had control and that I was going to fix everything. It worked for a while until I began to realize what my life had become. I found myself so upset about where I was emotionally that I just played it off, telling myself everything was fine.

I trusted those around me—my friends and family. But I kept making excuses, trying to avoid facing reality.

My oldest was on her own roller coaster of life, and I was unhappy with the relationship she was in for many reasons. However, there wasn't much I could do at that moment except pray and hand it over to God.

Throughout all her struggles, I tried to always be there for her. I still hadn't fully turned back to God yet. I was clinging to the idea that I was in control, but I was slowly breaking down. I felt as if everything I had worked so hard for was slipping away, and my spirit was gradually dying.

No matter what I did, I felt like I was losing. I was not happy in my relationship or with my surroundings. I didn't feel like myself. My spirit felt hungry. I was missing something in my life. Being in the battle of differences made it hard to fill that void.

Nothing around me brought happiness. Through it all, I continued to try to be the best mother I could be.

Restoration: God Brings Beauty from Ashes

Fast forward to 2020, when my world really took a turn. I could never have imagined in a million years what was to come. Three days before Christmas, my mother received a call from hospital personnel who were looking for me. She called me at work to inform me of the call, saying they did not provide a reason they wanted to talk with me.

I reached out to the hospital and was told to get there as soon as possible. I wasn't given any more information over the phone. I thought maybe my oldest daughter was having issues with her asthma.

I arrived at the hospital after what felt like a lifetime of waiting. The doctor came out to talk to me. He first told me to sit, and that's when I knew something terrible had happened.

He proceeded to inform me that my daughter was a gunshot victim and that she had instantly become a quadriplegic.

She was on her day off and had gone to pick up her friend. They gave a ride to a neighbor to his stepson's house, and when they arrived at their destination, everything was fine until she was ready to leave.

It was 12:30 in the afternoon and there had been no altercations. Why would she worry? But then her world changed. The neighbor's stepson shot my daughter and her friend. Her friend passed away instantly. She did not realize what had happened and didn't know anyone else there besides her friend. They said she was in shock, and all she could think about was her baby.

My daughter had just found out the week prior that she was pregnant; she was supposed to be on bed rest. During a tough period of her life, expecting her first child was what kept her going and prevented her from giving up.

The doctor who spoke to me said my daughter needed to have surgery, and they were not sure if she would make it or if her baby would survive. I felt so alone. I wasn't talking to my family much at the time because of everything I was going through. I just stayed in the waiting room, praying and feeling isolated. I didn't even know who to call or what to say. I was in shock.

Soon after her surgery, my daughter was moved to trauma. By this time, it was evening, and I didn't know what to do. I felt lost. The surgeon sat down and spoke with me. He said he would normally never say this, "Your daughter had an angel watching over her."

He was amazed she even survived. She did not need a blood transfusion, which was hard to understand given all the blood she lost. And the baby was still strong.

In my head, I kept telling myself that it would all work out. My daughter is strong, and I know God has always protected her. We were in the hospital for a little over a month. I stayed with her almost seven days a week, only leaving her side to come home, pick up clothes, go to the office, and then quickly return to the hospital.

> "For I know the plans I have for you," declares the LORD, "plans to prosper you and not to harm you, plans to give you hope and a future" (Jeremiah 29:11 NIV).

I was still in shock during this time, but I always tried to keep my daughter's spirits up. I would tell her that God has a purpose in all this; we may not know what it is, but He does. The baby was what kept her going. I still did not fully realize what was to come. In my mind, I had control; I was going to overcome this, fix this. But I was not being honest with myself.

When my daughter was released from the hospital, I began to understand the complexities of the situation. I tried to take care of my oldest, still be a mom to my youngest, and manage my work and run my business. For the first six months, I was working partly from home.

At that time, anyone who was around started to disappear. At first, I did not understand why, but now I know it was part of God's plan. Then, the baby was born, which was amazing, especially when they didn't think she would even survive. She was so strong. Everyone was shocked that both my daughter and the baby had survived such a terrible trauma.

Now, both were in my care, and I had to choose between my home, my job, and my business. I chose my family; with the lack of help, I had no choice. At first, it was okay. I felt confident I would figure it out and that all would soon return to normal—whatever normal was.

With all I had been through and overcome in my past, I felt that I would make things alright. I still had the notion that I was in control. But slowly, my world started to unravel. I did not know what to do or how even to make sense of this whole situation. I was holding in so many emotions. With everything I had already gone through and the roller coaster of life I was experiencing, I still hadn't recovered emotionally, spiritually, or mentally.

Now, my daughter was going through this life-altering situation, and I was still trying to stay strong for those around me, not showing my true emotions. One thing I learned is that no matter what you are going through, you have to be 100% honest with yourself. You cannot make excuses for people's behavior or bury who you are to accommodate those around you. Doing this will cause you to spiral, especially when life is being sucked out of you.

So there I was, feeling all this and not knowing where to turn. Well, I knew who to turn to—God—but I was ashamed and emotionally not in the right place. The first year of caring for my daughter and the baby was a round-the-clock job. It was exhausting.

I had many moments when I felt like I would fail my girls. My youngest, through all this, was trying to deal with her own emotions. It was her first year in high school—that alone was hard. She had to be put on the back burner so many times. No matter how many attempts I made to make it work, it was just hard on everybody. The emotions in the house were chaotic. Imagine there were only women in the house... you can imagine.

Trying to stay strong while internally breaking down was not ideal. But I had to keep moving forward. And I did. We were now trying to figure out the healthcare system, learning as much as we could about my daughter's care.

Being a person with quadriplegia is not easy. I had to do everything for my daughter. And I was starting over with a baby in the house, trying to figure out our new life. I felt angry with God. Yet I recognized that I was the one who had walked away from Him. I was the one who made bad choices. So I was feeling guilty *and* very angry.

I felt like God had left me completely; I didn't know what He had in store for our journey. The round-the-clock care required me to rearrange everything we had known and start completely over. I was scared, not knowing what I would do once the money ran out. How was I going to care for my three girls?

> He says, "Be still, and know that I am God; I will be exalted among the nations, I will be exalted in the earth" (Psalm 46:10 NIV).

As I became my daughter's full-time caregiver, the first year was all about trying to figure it all out. It felt like being in a whole different world. Hearing people say they didn't believe she could get any better was disheartening. Those who left our side were probably doing us a favor; if they didn't believe in my children, why have them around? It was a lot to take in as I tried to figure myself out. I was so hurt; it felt like a dark cloud was over us.

We would move forward one step and then go back ten. I felt like I was going in constant circles until I reached a breaking point. Throughout it all, good or bad, I learned to be my authentic self with Jesus. All I could do was pray and give it over to God.

My mother passed in 2022. That was the straw that broke the camel's back. I just lost myself. We struggled. All I could do was pray. It took two more years

Restoration: God Brings Beauty from Ashes

of breaking down and rebuilding, but now God was being reintroduced to me like never before.

With all the prayer came blessings. With all the prayers came peace. With all the prayers came a strong spiritual family. What more could we ask for? Even though being a caregiver was not easy, I would go to the ends of the earth for my girls.

As a primary caregiver, I had to give up so much of myself to be there at all times, but together, we've made it work. And we keep going!

Since the day my daughter was admitted to the hospital, I've made sure we laughed. Even in our moments of doubt and confusion, we have always tried not to harden our hearts.

Going through all of this hand-in-hand with my daughter has taught us both the true meaning of empathy, compassion, and understanding. It has opened our eyes to see things in a different way.

In our time of solitude, God has shown us that we had to be broken down to be rebuilt with a bigger purpose. And that He alone is in control.

The year 2024 was a year of great blessings. Everything has felt like a puzzle that God is putting together one piece at a time, and I cannot wait to see what He has in store for the future.

What, then, shall we say in response to these things? If God is for us, who can be against us? (Romans 8:31 NIV).

> *Wait for the Lord; be strong and take heart and wait for the Lord* (Psalm 27:14 NIV).

When all we have are pieces of faith, we can give them to God and trust that He will make a beautiful whole.

Angela Ball

Angela Ball, originally from Colombia, South America, moved to the United States at the age of 15 during her high school years. She settled in North Palm Beach, Florida, where the support of family and friends helped her navigate her new surroundings. It was there that she met her husband, Ray, with whom she has shared 30 cherished years. Together, they are proud parents to Ashton, a 21-year-old basketball enthusiast and budding entrepreneur with his business, Ready Set Dump iT.

With over a decade of dedicated service to single mothers and their children, Angela's passion led her to establish Hearts for Moms in West Palm Beach, Florida, in 2017. As the CEO, Angela is committed to inspiring hope, fostering personal growth, and empowering women to break free from reliance on government assistance. Her mission is to help them pursue their dreams, become exceptional parents, and embrace a fulfilling and abundant life.

Angela is also an active member of the Christian business community. She serves as Vice President of the Christian Business Association and holds a position on the Leadership Advisory Council for the Association of Christian Business Women, further exemplifying her dedication to faith-driven leadership and service.

Restoring Beauty from Ashes

By Angela Ball

Writing this chapter is itself an act of restoration. I'm not naturally inclined to write; in fact, it intimidates me. I enjoy journaling privately, free from the fear of criticism. Many have encouraged me to write a book, noting the stories of restoration and blessings witnessed through Hearts for Moms, the non-profit I founded in Florida. Finally, I trusted that the Lord would guide my thoughts and hands to share my story. Now, I'm writing my story and a devotional for the ministry. This process has been unexpectedly enjoyable, and I hope my testimony will inspire others, especially women seeking healing and purpose.

RESTORING MY LIFE

Before I can share any of my stories, it is essential to start with the one decision I made when I was 39 years old. Without this one decision, my life would have turned out very differently. It was the most important decision I ever made, radically transforming and restoring my life.

I grew up Catholic, and as I got older, I felt a gap. I couldn't quite understand why I felt that way. I was married to an amazing man, Ray (we have now been married for 29 years). Our son, Ashton, was 7 years old, and I was a stay-at-home mom with two cute Westies. Life was good, yet something was missing.

As I started seeking answers, I realized we were the perfect CEOs— "Christmas and Easter Only" church attendees. We did not have a church to call home. Feeling a new pull, I began searching for where God would have us worship Him, intent on leaving all my judgments outside the church's doors and being open to what He had for me.

I remember the first day I stepped into one of the biggest non-denominational churches in our area. It was very different from my Catholic upbringing, yet I sought to discover what this church community was all about. That was the beginning of God filling the gap within me. Every time I attended, so many emotions surfaced. The worship music spoke loudly; I often cried for joy, for I had found what had been missing most of my life.

Although I wished I had stepped into this church family much sooner, I knew I could trust God's perfect timing. I was ready for more!

For the first time, I started reading the Bible. What a new concept that was for me. At first, I had trouble understanding, but I quickly learned that the Bible translation you read matters. The "thou shalls" of the King James Version were not a match for me. I needed plain English, please! The New Living Translation was where I landed, and I finally could understand it. It spoke to me. But I wanted more.

Ashton attended a small, private Christian school, and slowly but surely, the Lord surrounded me with strong Christians. My friend Belkis was one of them. Our conversations became more meaningful and purposeful. She invited me to join her Bible study group, and although I was hesitant, something kept nudging me to be a part of it. I finally decided to join her. It felt strange at first. It was out of my comfort zone.

One day, while spending time with Belkis out on her patio, she prayed over me and asked me the most important question someone could ever ask. "Angela, are you ready to receive Christ in your heart?"

"YES, YES, YES!" I cried.

Everything changed after that moment. It is hard to explain the joy I felt. I was different. My views became different. I wanted them to be contagious. My heart was on fire for the Lord. Belkis saw me spiritually growing, and she clapped her hands and chanted, "Hercules, Hercules!" She wanted everyone she led to Christ to run like Forest Gump did—to go for it and keep going with nothing stopping them. I felt the same way.

As time passed, I realized I had a bigger purpose in my life. I began seeking how best to serve God. Let's be clear about one thing: All I wanted was to volunteer and serve in a small capacity. LOL! I asked Jesus daily to use me and show me what I needed to do. Yes, life as a housewife was great, and spending time with our son was precious. Taking care of my family will always be my first ministry, but my deeper purpose was still missing. I knew I had a calling in my life I needed to fulfill, and the Lord took care of that, too!

As I started serving by coming alongside non-profits, the Lord surrounded me with single moms. I had no idea how difficult life was for them and their children. My heart ached for them. I found my passion! From that day, my life was restored as God led me in a direction I could not have imagined. It was like a fresh new start. I was ready to do whatever it took to please my heavenly Father.

Before I tell you more about fulfilling my life's purpose, I first need to share another story of restoration that led me to serve single moms and their children. It is a story that only a few women feel comfortable talking about. It took me a while to heal from it, but I am now able to share it on a public stage or in individual conversations. Without the proper healing, there is no way I could serve others effectively.

RESTORING ME FROM PAIN AND SHAME

This story is heavy and may trigger you. As I share, please know that no matter our wrongdoings and sins, when we give our lives to Christ, He offers us complete healing and forgiveness. I pray that if you and I share the same story, any shame or guilt that harnesses you will be broken today, in the name of Jesus! As you enter a season of healing, allow the Lord to speak to you and set you on the path of your calling. I desire this the most for you. I understand the feelings and emotions of guilt we can be burdened with, but as you read my account, you will see that, with God, there can be such beauty at the end of our stories. Although my world was turned upside down, God helped me find my purpose. Mine is a story of restoration as God gave me a crown of beauty for ashes (Isaiah 61:3). God also has a beautiful crown fashioned for you from your ashes. With Him, you, too, can find the healing and purpose you have been yearning for.

> *To all who mourn in Israel, he will give a crown of beauty for ashes, a joyous blessing instead of mourning, festive praise instead of despair. In their righteousness, they will be like great oaks that the Lord has planted for his own glory* (Isaiah 61:3 NLT).

When I was 19 years old, my now husband and I decided to abort our child. I wish I had known God's Word, love, and promises to us back then. It was a hard decision, and I did it despite having no peace. Deep inside, I knew it was wrong, but I justified it all. It is a moment in time I wish I could take back. I have regretted this decision for many years.

I shared how it rocked my world when I gave my life to Christ at 39 years old. Soon after, my healing began. Only after I became thirsty for God's Word did I desire to read life-giving books—which made a monumental difference in my life.

The book *Heaven Is for Real* by Todd Burpo is a true, miraculous story about his young son, Colton, being taken to heaven while he lay dying in the hospital. While in heaven, Colton met his sister, a girl with brown hair and no name. As Colton later shared that story with his mom, Sonja, she told him he only had one sister, Casie. Little Colton pressed on. His mom then realized Colton was referring to the child she had miscarried long ago; she had never shared with her children about the miscarriage.

As I read Burpo's account, I sank to my knees, crying uncontrollably. I prayed for forgiveness for aborting my child, who God graciously shared with me, is now in heaven. I am so grateful for God's grace and gentleness. My healing began at that moment. It was a process that took time for me to work through. One of the most difficult aspects was allowing myself to receive God's healing and forgiveness—that was the last thing the enemy wanted. The devil works to keep us shackled with shame and guilt, knowing that they will hold us in bondage to him. But I knew God was working. He was fighting the devil; if I let go, God would do the rest.

I soon realized that my babies had no names. Yes, I did say babies. When Ashton, our earthly son, was three years old, Ray and I wanted more children. We miscarried twice. It was awful, a pain I don't wish on anyone. I cried out angrily to God, "Why is this happening? Is this a punishment for my previous choice to abort my child?"

That was the first time I experienced depression. I couldn't escape it; my days felt like years.

One day, the Lord spoke clearly, breaking through my woes. "But I gave you Ashton."

Although I couldn't understand why we couldn't have a larger family, I knew the Lord had blessed us with the most amazing son. I had to rejoice and be grateful for that blessing. My mindset shifted, and more healing took place.

I share all of this as I believe many women must bravely embark on a journey to heal from their abortions and/or miscarriages. Often, when I share my story, I start by saying we have one son, Ashton, who is now 20 years old.

But, in fact, we have four children.

After reading *Heaven Is for Real,* I knew I had to name our babies—they could no longer remain nameless. I prayed to God to drop in my spirit if they were boys or girls. I felt strongly that we had two more boys and a girl. It brings me great joy to tell the whole world about my other children, whom I will see and be reunited with in heaven one day. I will finally be able to embrace and love on them. I will see their faces and smiles. I can't wait for that day.

Allow me to introduce them to you in the order of their birth. Our firstborn is Jonathan, the son we aborted. I named him after reading the Bible's story of David and Jonathan. Ashton, our earthly son, is now 21 years old. He is the perfect mix of Ray and me. Ashley is our only heavenly daughter. She is only three years younger than Ash. Before Ashton was born, Ray and I had picked two names, as we didn't know whether Ashton was a boy or a girl. Hence, this is the reason why our little girl inherited her name. And then there is the baby of the family, David. We have three boys and a girl!

Every time I share this, it brings many tears to my eyes. With every part of my being, I know the Lord will use my story to bring healing to many. I pray this is the case for you. I am here for you and encourage you to pray and bring your pain to the throne of grace. Let your healing begin. If you feel led, I encourage you to read the book and name your baby or babies. Surround yourself and talk about it with your sisters in Christ to help you walk through it. Don't carry guilt anymore. Let go, let God, and let restoration begin!

RESTORING MY PURPOSE

It is amazing how God uses our mess and turns it into His message! Little did I know that after my healing and restoration from abortion, I would found a non-profit organization. Earlier in my life, I would have laughed at that thought. My plans were completely different as I wanted to do interior design and volunteer to help others in a small capacity. Keyword "small".

But clearly, the Lord had other plans for me. Jeremiah 29:11 says, *"For I know the plans I have for you, declares the Lord, "plans to prosper you and not to harm you, plans to give you hope and a future"* (NIV). But this hope and future were not only for me—they also included a plan for single moms and their children God surrounded me with. I have never been a single mom, and honestly, I was clueless about all the challenges they and their children face daily. However the more I understood their challenging journey, the more I wanted to be there for them.

I wanted to champion the women who said YES to life! Women who have been much braver than I was at 19. Women who, despite their life challenges and lack of financial and family support, chose life. That was my catalyst to serving single moms in different capacities and with other non-profits. I learned what mommas needed and realized that support and resources would help them succeed and be amazing parents—help them go from surviving to thriving and enable them to live the abundant life God has for them.

Then, in 2017, the Lord opened the doors for me to start a non-profit organization. That was not what I had prayed for or even wanted. Remember, I prayed to God to allow me to serve Him in a "small" capacity! Well, this was a lot bigger. But I knew this was His perfect plan, and I had to surrender all my fears in obedience to His call.

But how was I supposed to do that? I didn't feel qualified to lead in that capacity. I just wanted to come alongside others and help them grow their mission. But clearly, the Lord had bigger plans for my life and the lives that will be served through His ministry. After all, He is our CEO, and I couldn't say no to Him, for I fear the Lord more than man.

I had to relinquish all my fears and do it afraid. I had to trust that God would establish my steps and make the impossible possible. It has not been an easy journey, but it has been one of the most rewarding things I have accomplished. And I give all the glory to God!

In 2024, we celebrated seven years of ministry. Hearts for Moms is a ministry that has touched many lives, including mine. I often ponder that moment when I could have chosen to say YES or NO to God. I was a stay-at-home wife living comfortably, caring for our son and home. If my fears and comfortable lifestyle had led me to say no, I would have missed out on so many blessings, miracle stories, and seeing lives restored. Today, I can't imagine not doing what I do.

If only people knew what a privilege it is to serve our God and help those He surrounds us with who are in need. Serving brings so much joy and makes life look different. Suddenly, my life was no longer about me and my to-do list—it was about helping restore the lives of single moms and their precious children in our community and beyond.

I pray you will allow the Lord to grab hold of your heart and ignite a fire in you to do what He created you for. It may even be something you never imagined or thought was impossible. When we let go and let God, everything changes for the good.

I leave you with my life verse. Romans 8:28 says, *And we know that God causes everything to work together for the good of those who love God and are called according to His purpose for them* (NLT). Every part of my journey brings me back to this verse—from the moment I accepted Christ as my Savior to the forgiveness and healing from my abortion and saying "yes" to starting Hearts for Moms, a non-profit that was not on my bucket list. I know, beyond a shadow of a doubt, that God worked it all together for my good and the good of others.

The journey has not been easy. Along the way, there have been many heartaches. I had to leave my comfort zone and allow Him to stretch me, learning new things to help me become a better leader. I had to become bolder, more courageous, and more aware to shut down the voice of the enemy constantly, as his purpose is to kill, steal, and destroy the plans God has for me. I had to increase my faith and belief and lean on God every day. I have had to trust God, even when things didn't make sense.

As I reflect on the woman I was, I am grateful to God for the woman I have become. It all started with restoration. The ironic part is that my own restoration story has led to bringing restoration through Hearts for Moms to the lives of so many single moms, their children, and the community.

I implore you to let YOUR journey of restoration begin! You will be shocked by the story you will one day pen and speak off. And as God works in your life, let me encourage you not to keep it to yourself. Your story, like mine, is meant to bring restoration to others, for such a time as this (Esther 4:14). All glory to God.

Restoring Your Walk with God

By Kimberly Anne Kahn

Do you remember?

Do you remember when God's presence wrapped around you like a warm embrace? When His voice whispered in the stillness, and every breath felt like a sacred moment with Him? You walked in His love, were bathed in His peace, and found strength in His promises. But then—something changed.

One day, you woke up, and it felt different. A distance. A silence. Life happened. The demands of work, family, ministry, and responsibilities crept in, pulling you in a thousand directions. Little by little, your quiet moments with Him became shorter until they became infrequent, then nearly nonexistent. You told yourself, *Tomorrow, Lord. Tomorrow, I will make time for You.*

But tomorrow never came.

And now, when the world finally pauses in those rare quiet moments, you feel the ache in your soul—a longing for what once was.

But here's the beautiful truth: God never moved. He never left. He has been there, waiting, watching, whispering—not in anger or condemnation, but in love. A love so deep, patient, and relentless that even when we drift away, He never stops calling us home—to Him, our first love.

RECOGNIZING THE DISTANCE

Not long ago, I found myself in that very place—a place of silence. I had let life's distractions consume me, and before I even realized it, I felt so far from God. I wanted to return to Him, but the enemy whispered, "It will take months before God will accept you back."

That was a lie!

The enemy will always try to deceive you, making you believe you've gone too far, that you've been away too long, that God is disappointed in you. But the truth?

The truth is that you are a child of God.

God's love for you has never wavered. He is not waiting for you with a list of your mistakes. He is waiting with open arms.

THE FIRST STEP BACK

So, how did I restore my walk with God?

First, I had to acknowledge where I was. Perhaps, like me, you have let distractions pull you away from God's presence. Or maybe you are running on empty spiritually. Recognizing the distance between you and God is the first step to closing the gap.

Recognizing my position, I repented. Repentance means we simply turn back to God. With a heart of sorrow, I cried out to Him, asking for forgiveness. He had not abandoned me; I had let the world's noise drown out His voice.

Here's the most powerful truth of all: Returning to God does not take months or years—it takes a moment. Right now, in this very moment, you can whisper His name, and He is already there, drawing you close.

I will never leave you nor forsake you (Hebrews 13:5 NKJV).

God is not waiting for you to earn your way back. His love is already yours. The minute you turn from the distractions and back to Him, He is there.

WALKING IN RESTORATION

Although you can restore your walk with God in a single decision—maintaining that restoration is a daily commitment. God wants to shower you with the joy of His presence every hour of every day! And because He is always walking beside us, you and I have the privilege of looking to and communicating with Him daily. You can start with these simple steps:

- Intentionally make time for Him. Pray, read His Word, and sit in His presence.

- Worship Him with all your heart. Let God's love fill the spaces where doubt once lived.

- Journal your journey. Write what He speaks to you, and remind yourself of His faithfulness.

- Seek Him first in all things. Keep Him at the center of your life.

God's love for you has never changed. If you feel you have put God on the sidelines, listen for His voice—He is calling you back, not with a voice of condemnation, but with love. Taking that first step back to Him takes just a moment.

Will you take that step today? I invite you to pause right now and invite God back in. Then, make a plan to pray, read scripture, and worship Him. You've made a great start by picking up this book! Keep reading!

Jessica Prukner

Jessica Prukner is a devoted mother of three teenagers and a passionate homeschool mom with over ten years of experience nurturing her children's education at home. She writes the "A Beautiful Mess" column in *Voice of Truth* Magazine, where she writes about faith, family, personal growth, and finding beauty in the imperfections of everyday life.

A committed follower of Jesus, Jessica strives to live out her faith in every area of life. Her relationship with Christ shapes her perspective and motivates her to share His love with others in her work and personal life.

In addition to her writing, Jessica is a professional speaker and influencer in the marketplace community, empowering others to pursue their passions with purpose and authenticity. Her personal growth journey, including therapy and inner child work, has helped her heal, develop resilience, and live with greater intentionality.

When she's not working, Jessica enjoys spending time with her kids, husband Ian, and their dogs in the sunshine of Florida. She loves being outdoors and witnessing God's handiwork in nature. Above all, she is passionate about sharing the love of Jesus and encouraging others to experience the hope and peace that comes from a relationship with Him.

Finding Light in the Darkness

By Jessica Prukner

I remember the day like it was yesterday. I was standing in a cold shower, hoping the cascade of frigid water pouring over my head would make me feel something. Anything. It was a temporary place of escape. I stepped out and caught a glimpse of myself in the mirror—nothing. All I could see were two completely empty brown eyes staring back at me. My heart started racing in my chest as my mind filled with questions.

How did I get here?

Why am I in such a dark mindset despite all the blessings and goodness surrounding me?

How am I so devoid of tears and emotions?

Looking into those sad, lonely eyes, I attempted to calm my racing heartbeat with breathing techniques. The world around me felt suffocating, and an overwhelming burden pressed down on me, making me feel like I was failing and the world was collapsing around me.

I had everything I could ever wish for—a loving family, a devoted husband, three wonderful children, a beautiful winter home in Florida, a stunning estate in Michigan, and a thriving business that ensured money was never a concern. Yet there I was, feeling lost, alone, and empty.

As a Christian, I read my daily Bible devotional, attended church every Sunday, and had worship music playing around the clock. I could even quote scripture relevant to any situation. But still, I found myself trapped in a lonely, dark pit of despair.

Nothing seemed to make sense anymore.

As I lingered there, lost in thought and grappling with those heavy questions, my supportive husband, Ian, walked in and asked how I was doing. I couldn't find the words; I had to muster every bit of strength to manage a casual smile for him. I felt totally empty, unable to articulate my feelings.

Each day began to blur into the next as I went through the motions—completing chores, caring for the kids, and trying to appear happy. But once the doors were closed and the lights were off, even Ian could sense my emptiness.

After a few weeks of that routine, I noticed Ian's concern deepening; he seemed increasingly sad for me. He struggled to understand how I could be devoid of words, emotions, and any desire for life. Watching him hurt for me broke my heart even more, adding to the overwhelming weight I already felt inside.

Despite the many positive aspects of our lives—some might even say incredible aspects—there were areas that left me feeling utterly hopeless and filled with despair. Our son Zachary had recently been diagnosed with Ulcerative Colitis. One day, my fun-loving and energetic 9-year-old began noticing blood. After numerous doctor visits and tests requiring us to travel back and forth from Florida to Michigan, we received the devastating news. It was an autoimmune disease, one that I was all too familiar with, having been diagnosed with a similar condition—Crohn's—when I was just 15.

Restoration: God Brings Beauty from Ashes

How can this be happening?

At first, I received the news with strong faith and a positive outlook. Having lived for twenty years with few complications from my own illness, I believed in God's promises of total healing. We found a specialist and began an aggressive treatment plan, but to our shock, it wasn't effective. Zachary's condition deteriorated. He reached a point where he could hardly eat, spent most of his time near the bathroom, and slept more than he played. I tried holistic methods and diets that had previously helped me, but nothing seemed to improve his situation. My adventurous little boy was now confined to the couch, growing pale and gray before my eyes.

I felt utterly helpless.

I spent my days caring for Zachary, remaining positive and encouraging while simultaneously battling with doctors' offices and insurance companies to secure the best care and answers for him. I was relentless in my search for new approaches, plans, treatments, or diets that might lead to his recovery. My obsession with finding a solution consumed me. There we were, living what should have been the dream—beautiful home, lovely weather, nice possessions, and time to spend with the kids—but I felt powerless to help our son.

Things continued to deteriorate. We began trying biologic medications that promised remission, yet Zachary kept failing those treatments and getting worse. We found ourselves visiting the doctor almost weekly. During one of those appointments, the same physician who had treated me as a teenager looked at us with grave concern. He informed us that Zachary had a 24-hour window to show improvement, or he would lose his colon. My once-active, vibrant 11-year-old son was facing the possibility of needing a colostomy bag for the rest of his life. I couldn't believe this was happening; I struggled to process the words coming from the doctor's mouth.

It felt like I was in a slow-motion movie scene and had been dealt a gut punch that took my breath away.

Hearing the doctor's words echo the same words my mom had heard when I was hospitalized at 15 triggered my own personal trauma.

How did we end up in this situation?

How could God allow this to happen?

My mind began to spin, my heart raced, and my body felt heavy and hot as the reality of the news sank in.

Ian and I immediately brought Zachary home and surrounded him with prayer, reaching out to friends, our church, and social media to share our prayer requests. We gathered prayer warriors from around the world to lift Zachary up in their prayers.

This just can't be happening.

I went to war with God, feeling like Jacob as he wrestled God. I was so angry and crushed that we had ended up in such a hopeless place after all the prayers and medical interventions we had tried.

Why, God? Why?

I cried, sobbed, and screamed into pillows during my prayer time; I was a complete mess at the feet of Jesus. After I laid all my emotions at His feet, I gave the entire situation to God and went to bed feeling depleted and exhausted.

The following day, we took Zachary back to the doctor's office and received miraculous news: his symptoms had improved enough to avoid surgery. I felt an overwhelming sense of gratitude in that moment, but I knew that while we won that battle, the war for my son's health was still far from over. Fortunately, he had stabilized enough on high, albeit unhealthy, doses of prednisone to start a new biologic infusion medication.

The doctor kept reminding us that recovery would take time and nothing would happen immediately. Little by little, Zachary began to improve, and my mama's heart was filled with gratitude for the progress. Yet it was also heavy with concern over the adverse effects the high doses of medication might have on my son's small body. Ian and I remained positive and encouraging. We kept Zachary engaged with Lego sets and even found a sweet, emotional support Australian Shepherd puppy named Sky to brighten his days.

The road was long, but thankfully, there had been many small improvements over the weeks, and Zachary was getting better. I continued to have him on a special nutritious paleo diet, keep him active, positive, and engaged, and manage his medical care. My phone calls to doctors, home nurses, hospitals, blood lab centers, and insurance companies seemed to become my full-time job.

Each day was a battle.

I showed up, homeschooled our three kids, provided medical care for Zachary, and continued to be a mom. Slowly, this began to take a toll on me; I could only be strong for so long. Thankfully, Zachary continued to improve over time, but as I started to focus on things beyond his health, I began to realize how much I had neglected our other two kids while concentrating so heavily on Zachary.

Our oldest daughter, Kayley, was now entering the pre-teen phase of adolescence and began to struggle. I started to notice how watching her younger brother battle his health issues was impacting her. The days and nights I spent consumed searching for answers for Zachary and caring for him were deeply felt by our little girl transitioning into a teenager. She often felt all alone while my husband and I were directing most of our attention toward her sick brother.

As mentioned, we lived a complex life, splitting our time between Michigan and Florida, and for a social pre-teen, the constant coming and going of her friend groups became increasingly difficult. One night, Ian and I were in bed when Kayley came in, physically shaking with fear from a noise outside or a car passing by. This was completely out of character for her, and it was unusual for her to feel this way, especially since we lived on 19 acres at the end of a dead-end street. Despite reassuring her multiple times that there was nothing to fear, night after night, she continued to experience these bewildering episodes that we couldn't quite understand.

We began seeking help for her at our church, first having her speak with her children's pastor and then the counseling pastor, but no one seemed able to assist her beyond simply labeling her with anxiety. The more we sought help, the worse she seemed to get. There were days when nothing made sense.

As her mother, I felt completely at a loss and helpless while trying to support my daughter. I started to question where I might have gone wrong. My kids attended church on Sundays, participated in AWANA on Wednesdays, memorized Bible verses, were homeschooled, watched only certain shows, and had limited exposure to negative influences. It felt as though my daughter was under attack. I began fighting again, praying life over her, teaching her Bible verses to recite when she felt fearful, exploring supplements, arranging counseling, changing her diet—whatever it took.

I battled for my little girl.

Months passed as we tried various approaches, but Kayley seemed increasingly unresponsive and disconnected. One sunny day in Florida, I discovered her sitting fully clothed on the floor of her shower, soaked and crying uncontrollably. I felt helpless, unsure of how to fix what she was going through. My husband and I exhausted all our resources, even taking her to clinics for brain scans in hopes of understanding the reasons behind her struggles. Thankfully, they were able to provide us with some answers, hope, and direction.

Depression and anxiety were the struggles she faced, and we did our best to help her fight them. As a family, we made significant changes and realized that living a life split between Michigan and Florida was too difficult for teenagers. We made the tough decision to sell our dream estate and all of our barn animals to relocate to a single location in Florida. This meant selling three homes simultaneously to move into a Florida house that would accommodate our family year-round. This added another layer of stress for me that felt almost too much to bear.

So there I was on that fateful day, stepping out of the shower, staring at my empty eyes in the mirror, wrestling with God over so many difficult questions after facing battle after battle with the people I love most. I was exhausted and in my own state of depression.

How did I end up here?

Life seemed to keep beating me down, and despite my best efforts, I felt like I was losing the internal fight. Thankfully, God continued to win the wars. Zachary's health was improving and stabilizing, Kayley was discovering joy with new friends, a new school, and dancing. All three of our houses sold simultaneously, bringing us great blessings. God was clearly present in all these wonderful outcomes, yet I still felt empty.

Our new home in Florida was situated in an area with significant public exposure. The location had a history of legal issues and prior media attention, and being the new residents brought a whole new set of challenges we hadn't anticipated. One morning, we woke up to find news reporters on our property, taking pictures of my youngest daughter in our backyard and attempting to talk to her. The media distorted the story to fit their narrative and published it.

Before we knew it, Ian and I were receiving death threats via phone calls and social media messages due to an inaccurate news story. I began to spiral downward, feeling fearful even to step outside. I found a personal protection service dog to accompany me at all times and sought counseling. I had officially hit rock bottom.

I was scared, empty, and living a nightmare in what should have been paradise, completely overwhelmed with depression and anxiety.

Thankfully, my weekly counseling sessions began to uncover the roots of my issues and provide me with tools to address some of the surface problems. Had life thrown a lot at me? Absolutely! But through those sessions and by delving deep into my heart and past, I started to understand where some of these deeper issues originated. I had grown up in a household marked by trauma, with a verbally abusive alcoholic father who created an environment that felt unsafe for a child seeking security and love.

After 18 months of weekly counseling, I began my healing journey. I started understanding how to mend the hurt and uncover the underlying issues. My dog became my angel without wings, helping me emotionally through this difficult time. Through extensive therapy and hard work, I was able to overcome my depression and manage my anxiety.

There was hope. I knew I could find light in the darkness!

> Now to him who is able to do immeasurably more than all we ask or imagine, according to his power that is at work within us (Ephesians 3:20 NIV).

Five years have passed since the day I first saw the emptiness in my eyes in the mirror. I wish I could say that every day is filled with joy and happiness, but that's not the case. However, each day is infused with the joy of the Lord, which is my strength.

I continue to engage in deeper levels of therapy and inner child work. I am a work in progress, learning to express my feelings to my husband and those I love most, communicate my heart's desires, and be honest with God about my struggles.

While I want to say that everything is perfect, life simply isn't perfect—it's life on earth. I've come to realize that perfection is not attainable until we reach our final home in heaven. Life exists in the balance of both. I choose to dwell in a space filled with God's goodness, blessings, protection, healing, favor, and grace while also acknowledging I live in a complicated world filled with difficult circumstances, fights, and battles.

Life is a landscape that can be both beautiful and ugly on the same day. It is a place filled with hope, light, and blessing in one direction while harboring darkness, evil, and uncertainty in the other.

Every day, we must choose what to see and where to focus our attention.

My son still has Ulcerative Colitis and receives biologic infusions and blood tests every six weeks, yet he is also thriving—healthy, active, happy, and on the path to healing.

My daughter continues to navigate the challenging seasons of teenage years in a confusing world, and I'm here to guide her through it, showing God's grace, patience, and goodness along the way.

I recognize that I am a work in progress, and each day, God is at work in me and through me.

Philippians 1:6 reminds me, *He who began a good work in you will carry it on to completion until the day of Christ Jesus* (NIV).

When I look back and reflect on all God has done for me, I realize He has accomplished far more than I could have ever asked or imagined. He has transformed my messes into masterpieces and my tests into testimonies. He has created beauty from ashes.

> *To bestow on them a crown of beauty instead of ashes*
> (Isaiah 61:3 NIV).

This is what I choose to focus on every single day!

I am profoundly grateful that even when I walk through the valley of the shadow of death, the Lord is always with me. He orchestrates everything I experience in my life for His good. Like Paul in the Bible, I recognize that I am a work in progress, with a plan and purpose greater than I can comprehend, and God is in complete control of my days. He has never left me or forsaken me, and He never will. His promises sustain me through my struggles, and they are all I need. His promises and presence are sufficient to help us weather life's storms.

> *And we know that in all things God works for the good of those who love him, who have been called according to his purpose* (Romans 8:28 NIV).

I gave my heart to Jesus when I was 12; it was the best decision I ever made. Through that choice, I received everything I could ever want: the promise of a perfect, eternal life with Him in heaven, along with a Savior and Friend who walks with me and carries me through the highs and lows of life here on earth until it's my time to go home. I am certain I have everything I could ever need and will ever need.

You can have that blessing as well. Give your heart to Jesus and trust Him with your highs and lows. He will always be with you; He will never let you down.

This I know for sure.

> *"The thief comes only to steal and kill and destroy; I have come that they may have life, and have it to the full"* (John 10:10 NIV).

Maria Dabe

Maria Dabe's journey from São Paulo, Brazil, to the US at 21 was the start of a life filled with transformation. After 27 years in the fast-paced streets of New York City, she found peace and purpose in the sunny embrace of Boca Raton, Florida, where she enjoys beach walks, kayaking, paddleboarding, and hiking with her husband, Brett.

In 2015, Maria experienced a profound awakening when she surrendered her fears and disappointments to Jesus, who healed her heart and gave her life new meaning. This transformation ignited a passion within her to help others find their true purpose.

As co-owner of EBT Experts, she empowers small business owners to thrive, and through the Ready Set Go Experience—a ministry she co-founded—Maria helps singles align their desires with God's plan for covenant marriage. Driven by faith and a desire to see others flourish, Maria's mission is to inspire and uplift as she walks alongside those seeking fulfillment in both business and life.

Maria can be reached at maria@readysetgoexp.com

Letting Go

By Maria Dabe

The song lyrics from "Let It Go" filled the dark movie theater, shining a massive light on the weight I had been carrying for decades. The message was undeniable: I had spent my life trying to be the "good girl," hiding my feelings, and keeping up appearances so no one could see the real me. But something deep inside me shifted—I could no longer suppress the truth of who I was. It was time to release everything I had been holding back.

Much like the transformation of Queen Elsa in *Frozen*, I had been trapped by fear for far too long. At 41 years old, I was at a critical turning point, realizing that the time had come to break free from those self-imposed chains. Little did I know, this moment would begin a ten-year journey that would completely reshape my identity and redefine what truly mattered in my life.

My life began in a remote, impoverished neighborhood in São Paulo, Brazil. I was born in a tiny two-room home where I lived with my parents and two older siblings. Our house was at the bottom of a hill, surrounded by dirt roads that turned into muddy streams whenever it rained. My parents eventually added a second bedroom and a proper bathroom, but we remained impoverished throughout my childhood.

Although I was born to a functional, alcoholic father and a mother who had finished only second grade, I always felt destined for something more. My father's drinking led to violent outbursts, and my mother, despite her hard work, couldn't shield us from the chaos. I attended catechism at a catholic church, where I learned a little about Jesus. The pressure to be a "good girl" and the abuse I witnessed at home made me tough and resilient. I vowed to rise above my circumstances.

At ten years old, I realized my parents couldn't help me; I would have to make things happen independently to get out of the slums. My determination grew as I entered my teenage years. At 14, I started working full-time during the day and going to school in the evening. Seeking answers, I turned to a religion called spiritism, which taught me that my sufferings would end at death and that I could redeem myself through reincarnation. My heart grew colder and became filled with unforgiveness toward my father.

While I was still in high school, I met a much older, successful man who I had my first sexual relationship with. I thought he would love me and offer the escape from poverty I desperately craved. When I discovered he was seeing other women, I made a vow to myself to treat men the same way he had treated me. This choice led me down a dark path. I sought attention and validation from men (married and unmarried), treating sex as a cheap commodity rather than the precious jewel it was intended to be. Bad decisions and a deepening sense of loneliness marked this period of my life.

I met my first husband shortly after graduating high school. Michael was an auditor and US citizen from an American company in São Paulo. Desperate to escape my oppressive home, I forged my boss's signature to get an American visa and visit Michael in New York City. Our connection was immediate, and he proposed shortly after. However, from the beginning, our marriage was strained due to my unresolved resentment, guilt, and shame. After two years, the pressure of learning English and working full-time along with our mutual immaturity, separated us.

During that tumultuous time after my first marriage, I met my second husband, Tom, a successful New York City doctor. He seemed to understand me more than Michael had. Tom and I got engaged after two years and were married four years later. However, after two years of marriage, our relationship fell apart due to my infidelity. I was very broken but did not know why. I had everything and more that a girl from the slums could desire, but I sabotaged it all and fell deeper into a lost state. More empty male encounters began the next year as I tried to fill the void in my heart.

Around the same time, my brother and sister-in-law in Brazil gave their lives to Jesus and began praying for our family. Their prayers, combined with the grace of God, started to work in my life. I took a course to learn how to forgive my father. Miraculously, I was able to release complete forgiveness. However, I was still searching for a "savior" without realizing it.

Years later, I met Chris, a man in his early thirties. Despite the fun and attention he gave me, I felt unsettled. Our relationship, however, continued for several years because I was comfortable enough not to leave. Until I wasn't. That was when I found myself in that dark movie theater with Chris, watching *Frozen*. The main character, Elsa, created a monster to protect herself from rejection. Somehow, I connected to her pain, and at the end of the movie, I ran to the bathroom to cry my heart out. I felt as if God was saying: "Let it go! Let it go! Let go of this relationship and come to Me." Chris had no idea what was going on, but I knew. I felt deeply convinced that my relationship with Chris needed to end, and God was calling me to turn my life over to Him.

After all the pain I had experienced, I was unable to muster up the courage to break up. Chris was attentive, young, fun, and loved me! Why was I not satisfied with that? Being in NYC with a large homosexual and lesbian community, I had moments when I started thinking that men may not be for me. Perhaps I should go to the other side since I was not good with men? As I considered that, something happened that forced a change. Chris's lease was up, and he proposed that we move in together or get married. He was in love with me and wanted whatever I wanted. Although I was afraid to end it, I knew I had to. Once again, I was about to hurt another man. I knew Chris's heart would be crushed.

I genuinely needed God.

On the day of the breakup, I was on my way home, and the church door across the street from where I lived happened to be open. I had never seen that door open on a weeknight, and something led me to enter. The church was empty except for a piano player practicing at the altar. I knelt, cried, and prayed, "God, I don't know what this is, but I need You. This hurts a lot. Please lead me to where You want me to go." I felt God was there and would take me on a long journey. I was right.

Even though I had that moment with God, I was still who I had been for many years. I didn't know how to be alone or take some time off after a breakup. All my breakups in the past had been filled with other men shortly after. This time was no exception. My best friend from work was separated from his wife; the alcohol and festive environment at the company Christmas party was all it took. That evening, we began a secret affair.

A few weeks later, I traveled to Brazil to visit my family for Christmas and New Year's. My Christian sister-in-law was relieved when I told her Chris and I had broken up. I, of course, did not tell her I started a side affair with my work colleague. I was afraid she would judge me. She said she had been praying for me to let go of Chris and let God transform my life. She knew my emotions were corrupted, and they needed to be healed by Jesus. I told her I was considering attending a church but had no idea what church to attend. She encouraged me to look online for churches and try some in my neighborhood. Although I did look, I was overwhelmed and decided to keep an eye and ear open for an opportunity.

In May 2015, a miracle happened. After drinking his entire adult life, my dad suffered a mild heart attack and was firmly instructed by the doctor to stop drinking. And he did. Just like that. 100%. I could not believe it. I knew that only God could have made that happen. A year before, my brother told me his church was praying for Dad and his drinking. This miracle cracked my heart open, and I was getting ready for a complete surrender to the Holy Spirit, even though I had no idea what that meant at the time.

God had put out the bait for my heart—He just needed to hook and reel me into a relationship with Him. In September 2015, while I was still having a secret affair with my co-worker, I went on a Christian dating website, somehow thinking I would find what I needed. I met a guy who suggested having our first date at a Sunday service at Hillsong Church in NYC. I remember thinking, *This is perfect since I have been thinking about how to find a church.*

We met at the church. Upon entering, I was in awe of how many young people were praising and worshiping the Lord. I didn't understand why their arms were lifted high when the worship began. I kept my arms down since I thought it was weird to raise them, but as the music continued and penetrated my soul, I began to cry. I was self-conscious about what my date would think, so I tried to contain myself.

It was Sunday, September 13, 2015, and on that day, I became aware that Jesus was with me in my mess. I was broken, but He was there. He had always been with me. I had no idea how to follow Him. He unconditionally loved me.

My date and I left the church and went to have brunch. At brunch, he was very enthusiastic and started to quote the Bible and tell me many things. I was clueless. I had never read the Bible before, so I told him to slow down, and he realized I was immature in my faith. Though I never saw him again, I know God moved him to take me to a church so I could experience the Holy Spirit.

From that day forward, I went to church on Sundays and gradually felt God's work in and around me. Although I was still in my hidden relationship with the co-worker, God began to peel away the fear and get to the root of my problems.

In December 2015, I went to Brazil for the first time as a Christian. I was invited to give my testimony at the small church that had prayed for me for almost four years. I did not know what a testimony was, but I quickly learned.

I didn't want to stand in front of strangers, but my sister-in-law said that when God changes our lives, we need to share His grace. She told me my obedience would produce blessings from God. So, I stood up and shared my story. After my testimony, the guest pastor picked me out of the crowd and said, "God will bring that husband that your heart desires, but in the meantime, He wants you to learn everything about Him, seek Him, and serve Him."

I naively thought that the co-worker friend I was having an affair with could be that husband God promised. I did not understand, however, that God never breaks a marriage to create another. I didn't know that God was calling me to go through the fire to remove the impurities, flaws, lies, and deceptions from my soul and sanctify me for the marriage He had promised. I also had yet to learn that the pastor's prophecy would take seven years to be fulfilled.

Once back in NYC, I invited my friend to church. He said he was Catholic, but he was not practicing his faith. I told him if we were to get married, I wanted my husband to go to church with me every Sunday. He said we could compromise by attending Catholic mass one week and attending my church the next. That did not make sense to me, mainly because the Holy Spirit had begun teaching me about covenant marriage. I started to understand what being "equally yoked" in a relationship would look like.

For the upcoming year of 2016, we had two significant trips planned for the Spring and Summer that he was paying for. Although our relationship continued, and we went on the trips, I started to pick on him for nothing, and we fought most of the time. I knew deep inside the relationship was not of God, and the Holy Spirit was convicting me for having relations with a man who was not yet divorced. My spirit was uneasy every time we met.

The breaking point happened after I went to a worship conference. During the event, the Lord rocked my heart deeply. The next day, I called and ended the affair. He called me a hypocrite, and I said, "Yes, I am a hypocrite." He was correct, but I was finally determined to let go of him and surrender my body to Jesus.

From then on, I decided to take a year off dating, hooking up, or anything related to men and instead focus on learning and listening to the Holy Spirit inside me. It was an amazing time of thanking God for His love and mercy. In the process of sanctification, the Holy Spirit helped me learn about and respect Jesus as my Lord and Savior. It was challenging to change and renew my mind, but I knew it was my only option.

As I walked with Jesus and learned many things from the Bible, the Holy Spirit inspired me to get baptized in April 2017. After that, my relationship with the Father, Son, and Holy Spirit intensified. Many truths from the Bible were revealed to me. For example, I knew that one of my core sins had been related to sex, so I resolved to not have sex until I was married. The Bible became more alive to me than ever.

At the end of 2017, I went to an online dating site again, convinced I was ready to meet God's promised husband. After the first couple of days, I met Mark, a man from Harrisburg, Pennsylvania; we quickly started a long-term relationship with clear upfront intentions of getting married. We were both committed to waiting for sex before marriage. I thought he must be from God since I believed finding a man to agree to that would be challenging.

After a couple of months, he traveled internationally and broke up with me over the phone. I was distraught and thought it was strange; however, three days later, he called me crying, apologizing, and asking to get back together. In hindsight, I should have realized something did not line up.

In August 2018, he broke up with me again, saying he had received a "prophetic word" that we were not meant to be together. I didn't know how to seek God and get an answer for myself at that time, so it was tough to swallow. I was outraged, devastated, and utterly confused. On the day of the breakup, I called my sister-in-law, and God gave me a word:

All things work together for good to those who love God, to those who are the called according to His purpose (Romans 8:28 NKJV).

Although I had broken many hearts, this was the first time someone had broken mine. I felt the pain that the significant men in my life had felt when I had broken their hearts. The breakup with Mark gave me a different perspective that woke me up to the pain I had caused. I felt that the Lord wanted to teach me something, and His grace helped me through it as I continued to grow in His Word.

Nearly two and a half years later, I met a couple from a church I had started attending who had found each other later in life. They inspired me with this truth from the Bible:

> *But seek first His kingdom and his righteousness, and all these things will be given to you as well* (Matthew 6:33 NIV).

I turned the search for my future husband over to the Lord. I did not know how or when, but I trusted God knew who I needed and when; He would provide the husband He had for me.

In May of 2022, my prayers were answered. I began conversations with a man who had endured struggles and battles in life. And, like me, he had turned his search for a wife over to God. He also wanted a covenant marriage and was committed to not settling for anything less than God desired. We got to know each other over two months, began dating in July 2022, he proposed in October, and we were married on February 27, 2023. I cannot fully describe the miracle of what a covenant marriage has done for my life. Everything has changed and was not what I could have ever imagined. My husband Brett and I serve the Lord in our ministry, helping Christians prepare to have covenant marriages.

Throughout my life, the Lord has never left or forsaken me. Even when I disobeyed, He remained faithful. His love and grace transformed my life, bringing beauty from ashes. I am eternally grateful for the life and salvation

He has given me through Jesus Christ, my Savior. My past is a testament to His power to redeem and restore, and my future is secure in His hands.

Looking back, I see how every trial, every tear, and every joy has shaped me into the person I am today. My story is one of resilience, forgiveness, and unwavering faith in the One who unconditionally loves me. And He loves you unconditionally, too.

Restoration in the Community of Christ

By Kimberly Ann Hobbs

When we are isolated from the body of Christ, the very community we are supposed to call family and friends, we may feel discouraged, alone, abandoned, and sometimes rejected. Our isolation and pain hurts the heart of God. God set up the church because He knew we needed community to be edified. He knew there would be power in a community of believers gathered in His name who are all on a journey of sanctification. But because we are human, keeping the community of Christ healthy takes work and, at times, requires restoration.

We can look to God's Word, specifically in the book of Nehemiah in the Old Testament, for an example of how God can bring restoration to His people. Nehemiah was a great leader who was burdened for the brokenness in his homeland. He cried out to God in prayer and fasting, admitting the need for supernatural intervention, knowing that fulfilling his calling to work to restore the Jewish people and their land would take much prayer and personal involvement on his part. Then, he personally got involved in many ways in the restoration process.

God is calling every one of us to be active for Him in the body of believers, too.

We can each bring restoration to the body of Christ if we actively engage one another through encouragement from God's Word and commit to transparent fellowship by intentionally reaching out to the community He has given us.

Restoration: God Brings Beauty from Ashes

Be enthusiastic to serve the Lord, keeping your passion toward him boiling hot! Radiate with the glow of the Holy Spirit and let him fill you with excitement as you serve him. Let this hope burst forth within you, releasing a continual joy. Don't give up in a time of trouble, but commune with God at all times. Take a constant interest in the needs of God's beloved people and respond by helping them. And eagerly welcome people as guests into your home (Romans 12:11-13 TPT).

If we each strive to emphasize values from God's Word by being peacemakers while promoting strong leadership, we will spur one another onto active personal spiritual growth. This is a functioning way we can each be used by God to advance restoration in the body of Christ.

God's Word speaks of deep fellowship among His followers, which strengthens any restoration process as it brings people together for a purpose. We can facilitate fellowship by gathering in small groups that promote strong relationships with members of the community of Christ. If we passionately include young and old, not leaving anyone out or excluding people based on our differences, then we are obeying God's commandment to love everyone!

"So I give you now a new commandment: love each other just as much as I have loved you. For when you demonstrate the same love I have for you by loving one another, everyone will know that you are my true followers" (John 13:34-35 TPT).

We can also promote restoration by identifying local needs and actively serving in the community where God has placed us. When we voluntarily use the gifts He has imparted to us, we can be assured that others will clearly see the example we are showing within the body of Christ. The Bible tells us that just as the human body has many parts all working together to sustain life for the individual, so the church is made up of different individuals with various gifts, all meant to function as one body in Christ. We must function well to be fully restored.

Partnering with other ministries also shows the world that we embrace one another for a greater restoration purpose. By taking action, we are obedient to what God has instructed us to do.

> Just as the human body is one though it has many parts that together form one body, so too is Christ. For by one spirit we all were immersed and mingled into one single body. And no matter our status—whether we are Jews or non-Jews, oppressed or free—we are all privileged to drink deeply of the same Holy Spirit (1 Corinthians 12:12-13 TPT).

To bring about restoration in our Christian community, we need to promote a peace to the world that emulates God working in us. A peace that passes all understanding. We must encourage members to be active and make a change to promote peace with strength and conviction rather than sowing seeds of discord, clinging to the waves of emotion of fleeting issues. By being busy about God's business and actively obedient to His Word, we will develop strong, effective leaders in all areas of our church body who will promote the proper influence of a peaceful environment. When we see division among the body of God's believers, we should lovingly identify the areas that need improvement. Amidst heartache and chaos, God empowers his people to be instruments of His grace and renewal. By addressing any conflict and taking the initiative to follow the steps taught in God's Word, He will work within you to bring hope and restoration to His people, just like He did with Nehemiah.

May we all look to be servants in God's community to bring about restoration within His church and, one by one, restore the community of Christ.

. . . .

Beverly Bray

Beverly Bray is a Christ follower and lover of the Word. She is a devoted wife to Gene, to whom she has been married for 33 years. Beverly has a son, daughter, and stepson. Together, she and Gene have five amazing grandchildren and six great-grandchildren. Although Beverly holds a Bachelor's degree in science, she is currently a retired Catastrophic Insurance Adjuster and is actively pursuing God's calling on her life as an artist.

After extensive travel around the US with her husband working storms, she settled down in Oklahoma and loves ministering with her artwork to churches and other outreaches. Beverly's primary purpose for this season of life is to use her talent as an artist to glorify God. Her goal is that her art reflects God's creation, communicates biblical truths, and shares the message of Jesus Christ. Art brings her closer to God, deepening her relationship as she uses it as a form of worship. Ultimately, her goal as a Christian artist is to align herself with God's calling on her life.

You can view Beverly's artwork at bev-bray-artwork.com

God's Divine Canvas

By Beverly Bray

Scripture says in Ephesians 2:10 that we are God's masterpiece, His work of art, and His workmanship. We were created with purpose and destiny. Our identity in Christ is vital and should provide us with a profound sense of purpose, belonging, and security. Although I was raised in a church, this destiny was not imparted to me. I didn't know that I was loved unconditionally.

Before Christ captured my heart, my life had no rhyme or reason. Chaos guided me! I was always searching for my identity, looking for something to give me confidence. Looking back, I realize this lack of understanding shaped my actions and decisions.

I learned from my father that achievements were paramount and failure was unacceptable. Without a solid foundation that was not achievement-based, I did not develop a sense of self-worth to stand on in times of trouble. My inability to handle my father's negativity became a big problem. Compounding the issue, I didn't understand the basis for his beliefs and attitudes.

My father was raised in a very strict family. Grandpa and Grandma were wealthy, high-society people, so outward appearances and status were critical. Dad was always expected to be perfect in everything and suffered mental abuse. His upbringing caused him to constantly strive for acceptance based on his performance and actions, leaving him highly judgmental and negative. My father unwittingly carried into my life the rigorous elements he received from his role model. Mother always told me my dad was proud of me, but I never saw or heard it from him. My failures became my identity. Eventually, I had very little confidence in anything I did.

Life under constant scrutiny was difficult. I was never in any way physically abused, but the continuous conflict bewildered and confused me. I began making up my own rules that I could live with and lying about everything. I avoided home as much as possible. I found acceptance through my many friends at school. However, I was not particularly smart, or so I was told. Consequently, I struggled with poor grades. The sense of constant failure wore me out.

Early in high school, I discovered a particular group of people who accepted me, no matter how messed up I felt. They didn't care if I was perfect. Hanging out with those friends supplied something that was missing. Meanwhile, conflict at home encouraged my bad behavior. Alcohol, drugs, and immoral sexual behaviors served as coping mechanisms to alleviate my emotional stress and poor self-image.

My mother was an artist, and we created art together. Mom would encourage me. I loved art and worked diligently to become good at it. Conversely, Dad wanted me to do something that made money, not art. "It's just a hobby," he would say, making that point over and over again.

After high school graduation, I convinced my parents to let me attend college for art training. I chose to study at a college close to home, not knowing it was not the best place to get art training. I hated it and failed, setting myself up for another disappointment in life. Perhaps Dad was right. I was not an artist, after all. After a while, I grew tired of the struggle and put my art supplies away in a box. I didn't open the box for many years.

Soon after I left college, I got married. Honestly, I just wanted to get away from home, so I married for all the wrong reasons. For sure, my husband was very different from my father, but I was miserable for twelve years. Yes, you guessed it—our marriage failed, and we divorced. We had two beautiful children; they were the one great result of our union. But I couldn't help but wonder how I was going to raise my children alone. How could I raise children when I couldn't even make sense of my own life? I started drinking more and doing drugs regularly to hide my emotions.

After a party one night, I had an auto accident. I got out, fell to my knees, and prayed, "Lord, bring someone to help me. I can't do this alone."

Before long, I met Gene, my future husband, who told me about Jesus. Gene and I got married a year later.

And you will seek Me and find Me, when you search for Me with all your heart (Jeremiah 29:13 NKJV).

Gene was a cowboy from Texas who, like every other cowboy, loved the outdoors, horses, cows, and all other animals. We started our dairy calf grow yard. At full capacity, we ran a 2000-calf herd and farm in Idaho. This was a very labor-intensive, large business; after 12 years of raising calves, we sold our farm and moved to Texas. With the proceeds from the sale, we bought a herd of goats. Gene planned to raise goats while pursuing his passion for Team Roping. Life with a Christian cowboy was undoubtedly very different.

Although I was often alone, I settled into my role as a "Goat Lady." I struggled trying to fit into the small Texas community. Churches were not friendly, and we were not accepted. I had no close friends to confide in. I was alone frequently, tending 300 head of goats and kids. They became my new family. They all had names. Once again, I had found a group of friends that accepted me unconditionally. Still, I slowly slipped downward into depression and loneliness.

Although I had given my life to Christ and was happily married, I was still very much a work in progress. My attitude towards marriage and men still needed to change. Marriage counseling helped, but years of dysfunction had to be undone. I had no accountability partner, and I desperately needed one.

Gene and I took our responsibility as goat herders very seriously. Goats need shelter from the rain. We had set up a system recommended by locals of putting old metal cotton trailers close together in the pens, enabling the goats to crawl under the trailers during a storm. One night, a terrible storm created more lightning than I had ever seen, with cloud-to-ground strikes everywhere.

The next morning, I got up as usual to feed grain. The goats usually all came running to be fed, but hardly any goats came up. I looked for a hole in the fence, but there was no damage. Then I remembered the metal/steel trailers and the lightning; I immediately knew what had happened.

I walked over to the trailers and found my entire family all dead. Lightning had struck the trailers and killed all but about 50 goats. In a moment, I lost my babies and friends. I fell to my knees and cried out, asking, "Lord, how do I deal with a season like this, and why did You let this happen?"

Where was that solid foundation to help me get through troubled times? My foundation was so cracked that I was speechless. I drove to town to get Gene and give him the news.

The next day, we returned to the field to take care of cleaning up the carnage. Gene has a crippled leg, which prevented him from getting down under the trailers to pull out the goats. So, I crawled under the trailers and recovered each goat. In tears, I pulled out each mamma and her kids, whom I had named. We piled the goats up in a heap and set them on fire. The stench was horrific. I can still smell it to this day when I think about it.

We watched our financial livelihood go up in smoke, and I felt my purpose slip away. *Where is God?* I wondered as the fire burned for what seemed like an eternity. I was at the end of myself, and I did not know how to deal with this tragedy. I knew it was the enemy, not God, who had destroyed our goat herd.

> *My brethren, count it all joy when you fall into various trials, knowing that the testing of your faith produces patience. But let patience have its perfect work, that you may be perfect and complete, lacking nothing* (James 1:2-4 NKJV).

This scripture says God permits testing to strengthen faith and character. It has to be true, right? Was this a test from God? Scripture also says God does not allow us to be tempted beyond our ability to endure and overcome. But why could I not overcome this? Were we being punished for something? I struggled with this.

The enemy was after me now, reminding me of all my past failures, all the conversations with my father, and my failed marriage. I could not overcome my feelings of inadequacy and fear, so I pulled away from God. I questioned everything. After about two weeks of misery, I snapped. Gene had taken a job at a feedlot far from home, and I was left alone for hours at a time. I knew God was there. I could feel him nudge me, trying to get my attention. But though I prayed constantly, I could only hear my negative thoughts as I slipped farther and farther into depression.

> *You prepare a table before me in the presence of my enemies;*
> *You anoint my head with oil; My cup runs over* (Psalm 23:5 NKJV).

God was trying to show me all He had for me, but I could not hear past the tumult of the enemy's voice. I couldn't focus on God's goodness or understand what was right in front of me. God wanted me to see He would get me through this if I just let Him, but I kept thinking of how much I failed at everything. I kept hearing, "You're just not good enough, work harder." I was reminded of all the times I had tried to do it my way and messed it up.

I left the house with a handgun and sat on an old trampoline in the backyard that had been left there by the landlord. I sat there for hours while Gene was gone to work. Crying, I pleaded, "God, please just speak to me and tell me what I am good for. Who am I? What is my purpose?" I yelled until I could not yell anymore.

I finally got very still and began thinking about my family. What would my children do? How would my family get through if I died?

Then, there He was—that still small voice not heard in the wind or earthquake or fire. When I got completely still, I heard Him say, "You used to love to draw."

What? I knew it was God speaking.

Then He said again, "You used to love to draw."

God drew me back inside the house. I pulled out the box of art supplies I'd packed away so many years ago. To me, that box represented all my past disappointments. It was old and covered with yellowed tape, just like my dreams.

Surrounded by Western materials, I began to draw a saddle.

Gene came home while I was drawing and wondered what I was doing. I told him I felt the Lord tell me to draw as therapy to help deal with my depression. Gene had no idea I could draw. He wept as he looked at my work, saying, "You should have been drawing all along, not feeding goats or calves."

A new chapter opened in my life as I began to pursue art. I called Mom and Dad soon after God spoke to me about my art. I announced that I had decided to be an artist.

Of course, Dad was very unsupportive. "What makes you think you can compete with all the other outstanding artists?"

I declared, "Because God says I can."

In conjunction with my drawing, I would read the Bible, sometimes for hours. I began to understand who God is and why Jesus had died for me. The Lord spent much time teaching me to be His daughter. He taught me to value Him for who He is, not what He could do for me. My upbringing had taught me that I determined success by my attitude. That box represented both my wilderness and my failures. All this time, I had been fighting against the enemy of my soul to reach my destiny.

> But seek first the kingdom of God and His righteousness, and all these things shall be added to you (Matthew 6:33 NKJV).

I watched God's hand move in front of me, guiding me.

God provided a teacher for me. He brought a young man Gene knew to live with us and work with Gene. It just so happened that he was a very good artist.

God also provided a new community when He had me join the local art guild.

Over the course of two years, every art piece I made sold. My art became my opportunity to minister to others. God showed me a vision of myself drawing Jesus in live settings, enabling me to minister to church groups and youth outreaches. Soon, Gene and I gave videos of this ministry to people we met while traveling.

Then, we moved to a foster family ranch in Oklahoma as volunteer grandparents, where God allowed me to speak prophetically to the children while drawing their portraits. It was my joy to address congregations and children about Jesus.

As I traveled to churches to draw my Jesus portraits, I hoped my father would be proud of me, and he was, in his own way. But he was disappointed that I was not making money with this art venture. My father's disappointment stung me deeply; I was so sad. I questioned whether I would ever really understand him and whether I had forgiven him the same way Jesus forgave me. This doubt lingered with me for a long time.

I challenged God, asking why He made my father that way.

God replied, "I didn't. His father did, and his father before him did." Generational curses of fear, failure, and rejection had driven my father.

Mom used to say, "He doesn't mean what he says." Maybe she was right.

Years have gone by. I'm now 70 years old. I never totally stopped art, although at times I struggled; still, the question of forgiveness kept coming up. Our pastor talked one day in church recently about generational curses. I asked myself, *Have I forgiven? Am I just like my father, operating in generational fears and rejection?*

I asked the Lord to forgive me of my unforgiveness if it was still there and help me see my father through His eyes. Finally, after all those years, I was released. Oh, how I wish it hadn't taken so long.

My father has now passed away. My first thoughts when he died were not only thoughts of grief but that my father was finally free of that horrible torment. Maybe for the first time ever, He was truly at rest. My father knew Jesus intimately, but he never entered into His rest during his lifetime.

Artists only sometimes prosper financially. There are hard times, as there are in any profession, possibly due to the economy or other circumstances. I go through dry spells. Still, I work really hard at what I do to glorify God through my gifting. Through seasons of good and abundance and seasons of little financial gain, I am learning to rest in God's presence. I am no longer anxious or afraid of failure.

In this morning's prayer time, God reminded me of His divine sovereignty. Divine sovereignty is that which God exercises—His universal loving control over all things. Everything that has happened to me in my life was allowed through God's permissive will.

> And we know that all things work together for good to those who love God, to those who are the called according to His purpose (Romans 8:28 NKJV).

The Lord's mercy and grace pulled me through tough times, even though I did not recognize it at the time. Like the disciples on the road to Emmaus, I was unaware of God's presence.

It's so different to be at rest, not constantly striving. I'm newly retired from my job and fully believe the Lord will continue to guide me in my gifting. He will complete the work that he started in me. I'm at rest because I know God is sovereign. I can't mess it up as I stay submitted to Him.

If I create the best artwork ever, God is sovereign.

If I create the best artwork ever and nobody likes it, God is sovereign.

If I do a bad job at creating art and even fail, God is still sovereign.

How can I not believe in a sovereign God who is working all things to my good when my life was so messed up and I came this far? He has my story.

God, the Master Artist, is drawing my life story on His divine canvas. He took my life choices and the choices of those around me and created my story. He also knows all the people who need to hear *this* story. He has prepared everything that I need. That's what His sovereignty means. I can't mess it up.

I love what C.H. Spurgeon said: "The sovereignty of God is the pillow upon which the child of God rests his head at night, giving perfect peace."[1]

You, too, can trust that God is orchestrating your story. From the moment you were born until you pass into eternity, you are God's divine canvas. You are His masterpiece.

---

[1] https://theology-and-life.com/2024/05/30/should-the-sovereignty-of-god-be-controversial/

Cindy Edgett

Cindy Edgett is a wife, mother, teacher, and author of *Hear God's Voice Everyday*. Over the past forty years, she has served the Lord in multiple ministries, including the worship team, women's Bible studies, small group Bible studies, inner healing prayer ministry, intercessory prayer, and children and youth ministries.

Cindy has a heart for this generation to know God intimately and have a relationship with Him. She is passionate about teaching people to hear the voice of God. She loves to facilitate workshops and help train others to hear God's voice for themselves.

Quote: "Give a man a word from the Lord, and he will be edified; teach a man to hear God's voice, and he will have faith that produces hope for a lifetime."

Cindy and her husband, Curtis, currently reside in beautiful South Florida, along with her four adult children and their spouses.

Contact Cindy to schedule a workshop at cdedgett@gmail.com.

To purchase a copy of her book, *Hear God's Voice Everyday,* go to keepingtheedge.com

Only God Can Restore Like This

By Cindy Edgett

My story starts in Knoxville, Tennessee, where I was born. When I was three, my family moved to Palm Beach Gardens, Florida. I grew up there and eventually met my husband, Curtis, whom I married in 1982.

Curtis and I bought a home and had three sons, all born in Palm Beach Gardens, where we lived for 14 years. It was a fantastic place to live; however, as the boys grew older, we found that there wasn't much space for them to play outside. Their toys became larger, and their strength and energy levels matched the size of their toys. When our 2-year-old began hitting the ball over the fence, we realized it was time to find a bigger place. Our business was about 30 minutes from our house, and Curtis was commuting daily, so moving closer to our business would also be an advantage.

An employee who had been searching for a new home discovered one just five minutes from our cabinetry shop. He and his wife visited the property and were thrilled about the possibility of owning it. However, after navigating the financing process, things didn't work out for them, and they suggested that my husband and I check out the house since it was so near to the business.

Curtis went to see the property first, and he was thrilled! The home had three bedrooms and two bathrooms and was situated on a half-acre lot. The property appeared to have everything we wanted and needed at the time—ample space for the boys to enjoy the outdoors and more room for us. My husband was especially excited about the idea of no longer commuting 30 minutes to work each day. Yet he still questioned if we could actually afford this beautiful home.

I, however, wasn't quite as happy about the house. I didn't want to move. I was reluctant to leave my friends, the ministry I was involved in, and everything I had at that moment. As a result, I found myself arguing with the Lord about the move. I trusted God, but I also wanted what I desired.

One day, I received a call from a close friend. She told me that her sister-in-law had tragically passed away while on vacation. She had been preparing lunch for her family when she suffered an aneurysm and died instantly. We were both left in shock. After hanging up the phone, I immediately heard the Lord speak to me: "I've been trying to tell you that time is short, there are many souls to be saved, and you're wasting My time. You're putting stock in material things."

I knew what the material things were—friends, the comfort of our home, and our lifestyle and ministries.

After the phone call, I felt a sense of peace about moving. I knew it was time—God was calling us to a new area. He had presented us with a new house and a new town just seventeen miles away from where I lived and where my children had grown up. All I could say was yes.

After my conversation with the Lord (with Him clearly winning), my husband and I were ready to put our house on the market and purchase the new one. Curtis was eager to put up a for-sale sign in front of the house, and since we hadn't yet made it to the store to buy one of those big, bright signs, he came up with a creative solution. My husband wrote the necessary information on a piece of cardboard and attached it to the light post in our front yard.

Restoration: God Brings Beauty from Ashes

Naturally, I couldn't help but tease him about the sign since it was made of cardboard and didn't look very appealing! I learned a valuable lesson: be careful what you joke about because it might just come back to bite you.

The day after the sign went up, we received a call from someone who had driven by the property and wanted to see but was home sick with the flu. We exchanged information and decided to keep showing the house to other potential buyers over the next few days.

When the woman recovered, she called again and told us she was ready to see the house. However, we were down with the flu at that point, so we had to postpone. A day or so later, she reached out again and, not having seen the house yet, offered the asking price. By the following day, her deposit was in escrow. That evening, we made an offer on the new house.

The owner informed us he had several people interested in the property, but all their offers and agreements had fallen through, and he wasn't sure why. We communicated our financial limits clearly and placed an offer that was actually below what the owner had originally paid for the house. To our amazement, our offer was accepted. The closings for both houses were scheduled one hour apart on the same day—three weeks after the money was in escrow and five weeks from when Curtis put the handmade cardboard sign in our front yard. This transaction was a financial miracle; we knew God was helping us! We didn't know He was setting us up for two restoration miracles we would never have imagined—one involving our peace and even material possessions, the other involving something far more precious.

We lived in our new home for over nine years, feeling secure and at ease. However, in 2008, our house was broken into and robbed. At that time, I was working from home, handling the bookkeeping for our business. On that particular day, my husband insisted that I accompany him to drop off cabinetry at a job site because he wanted me to see the home.

In the 20 years we had owned the business, my husband had never asked me to go with him on deliveries, but that morning, he was quite insistent that I join him. Our teenagers had left for a church youth camp the day before, and my oldest son was working with my husband, leaving no one home when the break-in occurred.

Our neighbors recognized the odd activity but initially thought someone was checking out the house for sale on the corner. Then they noticed that they stayed for only about ten minutes. As I was driving home from the shop, I approached my house and saw that a window was broken and the door was ajar.

I called my husband first and then the police—they were there within five minutes. The thieves had been watching our home and other properties around us. We were the first of many homes in our neighborhood to be robbed that year by a professional ring run out of Miami.

My husband's father had just died a couple of months earlier, and his diamond ring was in a little safe we had tucked away. An heirloom double string of pearls from my great aunt that I wore for my wedding and a few other heirloom pieces were also in that safe. The safe was stolen, and the thieves made off with 28 years' worth of jewelry I had collected, laptops, and a few other items. I had always enjoyed switching out my jewelry, so everything was stored in a jewelry box, which the robbers took with them. The only pieces I had left were what I was wearing and one item that was caught in a piece of clothing.

The next two days were filled with sadness and a sense of violation. On the second night after the robbery, I was in my bedroom watching TV when Jentezen Franklin came on. While he usually preached, that night, he played the saxophone. As he played, I began to feel the presence of the Lord; it was incredibly calming. I sat there, listening and eating ice cream—my comfort food, of course—when I suddenly heard these words very clearly: "Mourning is over." In that moment, something shifted in my heart. The sadness and depression lifted as peace was restored.

I got up, told my husband what happened, and changed my mindset. I became grateful that only material items were taken and no one was hurt. I reassured myself, saying, "It's okay; it's just stuff." What mattered most was that my family was safe. The Lord had protected all of us.

After the robbery, jewelry didn't have the same appeal as before, but God cared for my heart in a beautiful way.

One of my favorite pieces taken was a sea turtle on a rope chain Curtis gave me. It was lovely—I received compliments from people about that turtle pendant all the time. Later, when Curtis and I went away for our 25th anniversary, he wanted to give me something to replace what was stolen. We went to a jeweler in Sanibel, where we were vacationing, and found an estate piece I loved—a new turtle, even bigger than the previous one. Curtis bought it for me, along with a new rope chain.

As I'm writing this now, the turtle is hanging around my neck. It is a reminder of God's restoration in my life. When God restores, He doesn't just return what you lost; He gives you something even greater. I liked the first turtle pendant, but I really love the second one! I would have never bought such an expensive piece myself, but the Lord used my husband to bless me. That is the God that I serve, a God of restoration! He cares about the big and little things in my life—every detail. The Lord knows I love jewelry, so He spoke my jewelry language (Haha). He blessed me with something greater than I had previously. He restored my peace, gave me joy, and filled me with gratitude.

> *Beloved, I pray that you may prosper in all things and be in health, just as your soul prospers* (3 John 1:2 NKJV).

The original Greek meaning of the word "prosper," used in the above verse, refers specifically to financial prosperity. But God is concerned about every aspect of our lives—finances, health, and, of utmost significance, our souls.

And He is in the *restoration* business, but not just restoring the material things in life. You see, God loves to restore beyond our wildest expectations. And the greatest restoration was yet to come.

God restored my relationship with my mom before he brought her home to heaven.

When I was growing up, my mom, a single parent, worked a lot. My grandparents moved to live next door. They were the safe haven I could turn to when I needed support—God protected me through them. As I write, I don't want to be dishonorable to my family, but at the same time, I want to be transparent to let you know that, like many people, my life was not perfect.

Things went on in our home that caused me to find solutions to soothe the pain I experienced. Later, when Jesus came into my life, I no longer needed outside solutions, recognizing that He was the solution, but as a child, I hadn't yet learned that.

When I was 10, my mother remarried. A year later, she and my stepfather had a son named Chris. I loved my brother, Chris, and helped take care of him. My stepfather and I did not agree about certain things he would do as Chris' father. It was hard for me to watch, so when my mom got home from work, I would tell her what was going on.

As a result, fights and arguments often ensued at 2 o'clock in the morning. It was very ugly. One night, when Chris was about four, I woke up to the yelling, got out of bed, and walked to the other side of the house to see what was going on.

I peered around the corner and realized the fight was because of something I had shared with my mom. I stood there watching, completely numb. I vowed that from that moment on, I wouldn't share anything important with my mom; I would take care of myself and keep everything to myself, and that's exactly what I did.

Restoration: God Brings Beauty from Ashes

The years passed, and my relationship with my mom grew increasingly distant; I always placed the blame on her. It wasn't until recently that I recognized my vow prevented me from having a close relationship with my mom. Looking back now, I can see how He was always working to restore my relationship with my mom.

When we don't yield to God's wisdom and strength, the outcome of our vows can actually create the opposite of what is good and fruitful. Despite the mistakes I made, God did something miraculous towards the end of my mom's life.

In 2020, my mom lived in an assisted living facility when she fell and was taken to the hospital and then to a rehabilitation facility. Prior to her fall, I had not seen her for six months because I was not allowed to visit her due to COVID-19.

By the time I could finally see my mom, I discovered she had developed dementia—and it was not just in its early stages. At that point, I knew I couldn't allow her to return to a place that I felt wouldn't properly care for her and would confine her according to the standards set by the medical community. So, she came to live with us. I'll be honest, I was not prepared for that. I had to deal with a lot of lies I had come to believe about my mom and my relationship with her. But our time together was one of the best things that could have ever happened.

As God began healing my heart through inner healing, I began to have such a strong, intense love for my mom that I never had in my life. I am crying as I write this because *God is so good!* I lost so many years when I could have had a great relationship with her.

I had prayed for restoration for my family for years, and God, in His faithfulness, restored my relationship with my mom before she passed away.

We took care of Mom as long as we could—until the dementia and her physical needs were beyond our capabilities of care. I became very protective of her, just like I was with my kids as they were growing up.

When the last stages of dementia set in and my mom could no longer take care of herself or make decisions, the Lord helped me find a small assisted living facility that was a dementia care facility. The staff was amazing! They watched over her so well that I was able to leave peacefully, knowing that she was cared for and safe.

The Lord blessed me during the time Mom was in our home. Do not misunderstand me; I have always loved my mom, but during that time, God gave me a greater love for her that hadn't been there before. When I finally broke the vow I had made to never share anything important with her, it seemed easy to love her. If you knew my mom, she was easy to love. She didn't have a mean bone in her body. I was the one who had withheld love.

God wanted to restore our love before my mom passed from this earth, and I'm so grateful! Not everyone gets a second chance, but I'm glad I did.

Looking back, I can see God had been working for years.

When God provided our new home back in 1999, He knew that my mom would be coming to live with us over 20 years later, and He prepared a home that would be safe and big enough for her in her last days. God gave us time together, restored my love for her, and left me with lasting memories of her.

After the break-in back in 2008, God restored my peace and even the jewelry that had been stolen—that was miraculous! But God also restored what He knew I needed most in my life besides Him—my heart and my relationship with my mom.

I don't get to take jewelry with me to heaven, but I do get to take other people with me. People are what's most important in life! My mom was a believer in Jesus Christ, and she knew where she was going when she died. I know I will see her again—because heaven is for eternity.

> He has made everything beautiful in its time. Also, He has put eternity in their hearts (Ecclesiastes 3:11 NKJV).

Restoration: God Brings Beauty from Ashes

God has set eternity in every man's heart, whether you recognize it or not. Eternity—that longing for something you can't find and can't see—is actually a longing to be with God. If you ask Jesus to dwell in your heart, that longing will be filled.

And one day, you'll spend eternity in heaven with Him; my mom and I will see you there!

Restoring Our Love for God

By Kimberly Anne Kahn

Reading through some of my old journals recently reminded me of some of the beautiful conversations I've had with Jesus. In those precious moments, as I wrote to Him, I felt His love deeply. He whispered His plans for me, painting glimpses of my future filled with purpose and hope. Every vision He gave me has unfolded in time; as I walked closely with Him, His promises came to life. Those moments were more than just words on a page; they were intimate exchanges, reminders that I was never alone. His love for me poured out daily as I wrote; it was our sacred time together.

> *"For I know the plans I have for you," declares the Lord, "plans to prosper you and not to harm you, plans to give you hope and a future"* (Jeremiah 29:11 NIV).

As I re-read those personal writings, I felt an ache in my heart. I missed those conversations. I longed for the intimacy I once had with the Lord. Then, God reminded me of a vision He gave me years ago. I saw a plain white canvas and heard Him say, "We will be painting this canvas with beautiful colors together." Each stroke of color would represent the work of His ministry and the purpose He had set before me. It wasn't just a painting. It was a journey, a partnership, an unfolding masterpiece of His love and grace.

Standing before that blank canvas, joy and love washed over me. His presence reassured me I was never alone; my life was meant to be a canvas painted with the beauty of His purpose—each color representing something meaningful: faith, passion, and the unwavering light of His love.

> Love is patient and kind; love does not envy or boast; it is not arrogant or rude. It does not insist on its own way; it is not irritable or resentful; it does not rejoice at wrongdoing but rejoices with the truth. Love bears all things, believes all things, hopes all things, endures all things. Love never ends (1 Corinthians 13:4-8 ESV).

God's unwavering love is so beautiful. Included in His love is one of the most precious gifts He presents us: the gift of choice. God does not insist on His way but gently calls us, waiting for us to choose Him. He will never pressure us into doing what He wants, even though He longs for us to walk in alignment with Him.

Yet, how often do we place other loves before God? These other loves become idols, capturing our devotion and worship. It could be a spouse, a career that consumes our thoughts and time, social media that we turn to for comfort, or even fitness that we prioritize over spiritual health. Without realizing it, we even idolize our self-image rather than prioritizing our relationship with God.

> "You shall have no other gods before me" (Exodus 20:3 ESV).

Idolatry doesn't always look like a golden statue; sometimes, it is the hours we spend scrolling through our phones instead of spending time in prayer. It is placing our identity in things that will fade instead of in the eternal love of our Creator. But the beauty of God's love is that He always welcomes us back. He invites us to pick up the brush again, allowing Him to guide our hands and paint a masterpiece together.

Restoring our love for Him isn't about guilt or condemnation but grace. It is about realizing that no matter how far we have wandered, He still waits for us with open arms, ready to forgive and accept us. *Draw near to God, and He will draw near to you* (James 4:8 NKJV). You are His child, and He desires to paint a masterpiece with your life, one filled with His love, purpose, and presence.

Do you still have the same love for God you once did? He loves you as He always has. What things in your life have become idols, causing you to love them more than your first love, Jesus? What dream or vision did the Lord give you? Are you fulfilling it, or has it been set aside?

I want to encourage you today to step back into the vision or dream God has given you. Pick up your paintbrush and paint with Him. Let go of the idols you have put before God and allow Him to fill your canvas with the beautiful colors of His love and purpose.

· ·

Janet Berrong

Janet Berrong is a board member and founding member of Women World Leaders. She also serves on the Florida Faith Alliance Board of Directors, united to fight sex trafficking.

As a business owner with a heart to serve God, Janet focuses on serving the community of women through her God-given gifts of intuition, compassion, and empathy. She has been a licensed health and wellness professional for 28 years, helping others be the best version of themselves physically, emotionally, and spiritually.

Janet is the Chief Operating Officer and Co-Founder of Rainbow of Love, a ministry that focuses on being the hands and feet of Jesus. In addition, she has created a new enterprise, The House of Berrong, dedicated to bringing elegance and tranquility into lives with a higher divine purpose by incorporating products and messaging that inspire and uplift others with the love of Jesus. She is motivated every day to share joy and love with the world, as each day is a beautiful day and an opportunity to establish a legacy.

Janet is a bestselling author in the United States and internationally who thrives upon her love of family and traveling the world.

HouseofBerrong.com

His Grace Set Me Free

By Janet Berrong

Restoration is a process that does not happen overnight. In fact, for me, it took decades. However, it is vital to know that restoration is possible and very much doable! Some essential elements of successful renewal include confronting the underlying issues and forgiving yourself, regardless of how daunting the task is. I pray that sharing my journey will provide you encouragement and, ultimately, enable you to be the person you were meant to be—free of guilt, fully committed to Jesus, and fully restored.

To experience renewal, we must delve deeply, seeking to understand how and why we experience feelings that prevent our wounds of the past from healing. Having personally gone through this process, I now realize it was necessary to achieve inner healing as well as spiritual healing to get my mental capacity back. Being emotionally and spiritually healthy is vital to sustaining a balanced and thriving life.

Why is it so important to have our very core healed to experience total health? My own experiences have led me to envision our well-being as a wheel with three spokes: emotional health, physical health, and spiritual health. It takes all three spokes being solid and steady to ensure the wheel—our lives—can function properly.

My story began when I was nineteen years old. That was when I met my boss, Kevin[1], although I had been around him since I was seventeen. He was a real "schmoozer" and sweet talker. As a pillar in the community, Kevin was intelligent, charismatic, and always had the correct answers. I admired him. He was sixteen years my senior and was married with two children. Thus began our on-and-off relationship that endured for years, nearly destroyed the core of who God made me to be, and would require me to seek restoration in my life.

I was single and loving life—a child right out of high school. I was a good Christian who was walking with the Lord. However, though I knew the Lord, He was not the center of my universe.

As time went on, my boss had his eye on me. He sought to woo me, preying upon my insecurities and building me up with manipulation. Before I knew it, I was sucked into Kevin's world, wanting to be close to him constantly and compromising everything that I knew to be true and right. I was lured into his arms and seduced.

> *You love him even though you have never seen him. Though you do not see him now, you trust him; and you rejoice with glorious, inexpressible joy* (1 Peter 1:8 NLT).

Kevin was obsessed with me. He would not stop short of anything to have me. At the time, I was young and naïve and not grounded in God's Word.

I succumbed to a full-fledged affair with Kevin, which led to my misery. God tried to get my attention—I knew I was doing wrong. Unfortunately, because of Kevin's obsessive behavior, the only voice that I heard was his as he spoke into my ear daily, professing his love. I often asked myself, *How did I get here?*

Kevin started giving me money to put away for our future together. He also bought me jewelry. His wife found an item intended for me in the glove compartment of his car, which led her to call me directly! As a result, my life

Restoration: God Brings Beauty from Ashes

became an entangled web of deceit, guilt, shame, and pain. I was young and bore the weight of so much heaviness at a time in my life when I should have been free and joyful and searching for what God had in mind for my future.

> *"For I know the plans I have for you," says the Lord. "They are plans for good and not for disaster, to give you a future and a hope"* (Jeremiah 29:11 NLT).

I tried to break up with Kevin, but he excelled at mind manipulation, telling me he could not live without me. I believed every lie, including his seemingly sincere expression that things were going to get better. Once again, I would find myself back in his arms. It was a vicious cycle that felt never-ending. I felt like I was on a hamster wheel, trying to keep up with his promises. Just when I would gather the strength to get off the wheel, I would soon be convinced to get back on. It was exhausting as I ran and ran on that wheel faster and faster, envisioning the moment I would collapse.

I finally went to the doctor because my nerves were shot. They told me it was as if my body had endured being electrically shocked. My blood cells were jumping, and my nerves were overstimulated to the point of a nervous breakdown.

Unfortunately, I did NOT surrender to God at that moment, although I should have. Traumatically, there was so much more to come.

I suffered in silence.

I went on a ski trip with my uncle and a platonic friend, which caused havoc. When I returned to work, Kevin erupted with venom and tried to fire me on the spot. He had sold his business to a corporation; therefore, I was sent to another location. As an impressionable 20-year-old, my world was shaken. The job I loved so much would no longer exist. I could not comprehend how someone who professed his undying love could be so vicious and hurtful.

Whatever security I might have felt was destroyed. Despite the situation, he proceeded to show up at my new office to pursue me further.

My idea of love became skewed, which impacted me for many years. My thinking and clarity became severely clouded as I wondered, *What is true love?* The situation I was in conditioned me to believe that oppressive attention, control, and empty promises were what comprised love. I was being programmed. Yet all that was becoming ingrained in me did not set well as I vaguely remembered my expectations of the notion of love—and this was not what I ever expected it to be.

> Love is patient, love is kind. It does not envy, it does not boast, it is not proud. It does not dishonor others, it is not self-seeking, it is not easily angered, it keeps no record of wrongs. Love does not delight in evil but rejoices with the truth. It always protects, always trusts, always hopes, always perseveres (1 Corinthians 13:4-7 NIV).

I tried to move on with my life and erase Kevin from my mind. I buried the guilt, shame, and pain that exhausted me, but I never addressed the core issue of what I had done to my life. Meanwhile, Kevin continued to pursue me by interfering with any new boyfriends or relationships I tried to have. That added to my confusion. *Does he really love me?* There was a new trauma bond forming that would span many years of my life.

On and off over the years, Kevin wanted me to believe he loved me. Anytime I began a relationship, I would wonder if he would come back around, this time to really solidify a loving relationship. Although always filled with emptiness, his jealous spirit over me was confusing. The fact is that he wanted the control—to allow no one else to have me. He never knew what love was. Kevin played with my heart and emotions for years upon years. The toll it took on me was brutal, devastating my character—who I am as God's creation. I am a child of God, but during that time, I felt I was a prisoner, one of Kevin's selfish possessions.

*We have become his poetry, a re-created people that will fulfill
the destiny he has given each of us, for we are joined to Jesus,
the Anointed One. Even before we were born, God planned in
advance our destiny and the good works we would do to fulfill it!*
(Ephesians 2:10 TPT).

As I continued to process this twenty years later, I began to understand that Kevin did love me, but with an empty love. He did not want anyone else to have me. I knew I needed to make a change, but I was not yet strong enough to do it on my own. God led me to a group of women who would pour love, life, and truth into my heart and give me the confidence I needed as a Christ follower. Near the time I found Women World Leaders, Kevin popped back into my life. I was establishing my relationship with God and moving in the most positive direction when I was sucked back into his web.

*Stay alert! Watch out for your great enemy, the devil. He prowls like
a roaring lion, looking for someone to devour* (1 Peter 5:8 NLT).

Like a spider seeking his prey, my enemy Kevin was hoping to devour my soul again. He said all the good things I wanted to hear, and he and I were feeling so strongly about the future at this particular time because so much time had passed, and we were starting anew.

Unfortunately, I did not know scripture enough to understand the truth. I was fooled by a leopard who hadn't changed his spots. Kevin was disguised again. As the same leopard, he was stepping up his game.

If I had a closer relationship with the Lord and had allowed Him to heal my brokenness, I would have been less likely to be fooled again by someone falsely representing himself. But the devil is tricky and sinister and weasels into getting his way if we are not on guard.

Kevin was now a single man, a prominent elected official in the community with extraordinary power and prestige. He asked me to dinner. I accepted and went. The devil wanted me to align my life with him and, therefore, deviously worked to suck me back into emotional lies and empty promises. He strategically placed Kevin in my path to help with some of the needs that arose in my life at that time. Within months, I found myself in the clenches of the enemy as I misidentified evil for what mattered most to me—God.

> Therefore, each one must answer for himself and give a personal account of his life before God (Romans 14:12 TPT).

As our relationship intensified and I spent time in and out of Kevin's home, a major storm was brewing in my life. Hurricane Dorian destroyed my mom's home in the Bahamas, uprooting her, and before I knew it, I was caught up in my own whirlwind. The father of lies deceived me into following his plan, keeping me in bondage without my even realizing it.

I felt I needed a place to live and a place to offer my mother. It seemed so natural to just move in with Kevin. But that idea was really the enemy influencing me with his lies and distractions, keeping me away from God's purpose for my life. There would be a heavy price to pay for my decision. I began enduring the worst trauma I would ever experience in my entire existence; the torturer came behind closed doors.

I endured emotional abuse, stonewalling, and more lies. It was a twisted barrage of trauma. Kevin persisted in telling lies in the form of constantly expressing his undying love, repeatedly stating, "I love you. I love you. I love you more than life." Yet, his words and actions were contradictory. I held onto the words in desperate hope of alleviating my pain and feeling better. But his words burned up quickly into a pile of ashes as his actions of abandonment, disrespect, emotional abuse, and unwarranted criticism pummeled me.

I was living in a world of hurt with nowhere to turn. I began to constantly ask, "How do I get out of this?" I knew I had to break free of the invisible ties of this trauma bond that prevented me from moving towards the abundant life God wanted to restore to me. But how was I to do that?

I needed to renounce any connection with the enemy of my soul and turn and run to God with open arms, trusting Him to save and restore me!

> So, humble yourselves before God. Resist the devil, and he will flee from you (James 4:7 NLT).

That is exactly what I did. This step is what enabled me to begin to stand firm in my relationship with God.

I needed to repent of any known sin that was going on in my life and return to God, submitting my toxic existence with Kevin and reclaiming all it had torn away from me.

> My old self has been crucified with Christ. It is no longer I who live, but Christ lives in me. So, I live in this earthly body by trusting in the Son of God, who loved me and gave himself for me (Galatians 2:20 NLT).

Through a miracle of strength bestowed upon me, I ran to God, begging Him to free me from that destructive relationship, determined to flee any temptation that pounded on my door.

The temptations in your life may feel overwhelming. And while the devil works hard to tempt us each in our weakest area, we can stand firm against every temptation, knowing that nothing can overcome our God. God is always faithful to protect us when we turn to Him.

> *He will not allow the temptations to be more than you can stand.*
> *When you are tempted, He will show you a way out so you can endure*
> *(1 Corinthians 10:13 NLT).*

As I trusted Him, God provided a home for me—a beautiful, serene place where I could heal with Him. He freed me, renewed my sense of purpose, and instantly brought the support of friends and loved ones around me. God helped me break the chains that had held me captive for so long, and He restored to me the joy of my salvation. Nothing could squelch the expression of the contentment bursting out of me after three years of seeking restoration in God. He healed my mind, body, and spirit inwardly as I daily saturated my mind with the Word of God.

> *Your word is a lamp to guide my feet and the light for my path*
> *(Psalm 119:105 NLT).*

My prayer life became a constant commune with God.

> *Never stop praying (1 Thessalonians 5:17 NLT).*

I surrounded myself with a community of believers so I could be accountable to and grow in the Lord.

> *Let us not neglect our meeting together, as some people do, but*
> *encourage one another, especially now that the day of his return*
> *is drawing near (Hebrews 10:25 NLT).*

As I encourage you with my story, please know that no matter what you have gone through, restoration can occur in your life, too. You can live the good life, the best life, the only life that God desires for you—if you seek Him first. Just as God healed me, He desires to heal you and deeply influence you with His love and mercies, which are new every day! They will flow out of you like rivers of living waters when you surrender your whole life, including your insecurities, doubts, and disbeliefs about yourself. Stop believing the lies this world and the devil throw at you and, instead, counter them with the truth spoken from God's Word.

I am healed. I have attained inner healing—a spiritual healing that God has blessed me with. I now have the mental capacity to overcome adversity and sustain my everyday life. Each day is beautiful and filled with joy and happiness. These are days I can share with others the promise that Jesus loves them and that they are not alone or forgotten. By simply asking God, you, too, can receive and experience all the extraordinary things God has planned for you.

This is the day the Lord has made. We will rejoice and be glad in it (Psalm 118:24 NLT).

Forgiveness! Forgiveness is such a BIG word! This process of restoration could not have unfolded until I forgave myself for all I had participated in, the lies I believed, and the voices I listened to that were not God's voice. I was not able to move forward until I fully surrendered to God and recognized His voice, only then being able to release and forgive myself for all past issues. Forgiving myself allowed me the freedom to trust God and hear His voice through scripture and inner peace.

Perhaps you can identify with some part of my story. If you can, please know that your journey of restoration begins with forgiveness. Just as God has forgiven you, you must forgive yourself. Release any shame or guilt you harbor. Our God will always forgive and restore us when we turn to Him!

I'm free now to serve God with my best potential. I'm free to follow the desires of my heart He has placed within me. Because I now live in freedom, God gives me the vision to pursue those desires and dreams. He has brought me opportunities to use my gifts and talents for Him.

I am now pouring back into the community of women to help them receive restoration and freedom in Christ—emotionally, physically, and spiritually.

God truly brought beauty from the ashes of my life. I am now a strong, beautiful woman in Christ—walking out the purpose God gave when He created me long ago.

[1] Names have been changed.

Tewannah Aman

Tewannah Aman has been executive director of Broward Right to Life in Fort Lauderdale, Florida, for over 25 years. She ministers to women in unplanned pregnancies, providing resources and counseling, enabling them to choose life for their unborn baby. She also ministers to those who have had abortions, guiding them on the same path of healing and restoration she experienced, so they can experience true freedom in Christ.

Tewannah tells how she broke free from a cycle of unhealthy relationships in her book, *Guard Your Heart – don't give it away* (Amazon). The GYH ministry equips teens and women to live for Jesus and put Him first in all their relationships. Check out her YouTube channel and website: guardyourheart.net.

Tewannah is also a biblical counselor, fitness instructor, and jail ministry leader through her local church.

Her prayer is that God will use her story to touch many hearts and for the Holy Spirit to empower and enable others to share their own inspiring God stories. She proclaims, "He only is worthy of praise. He gets all the glory for my redemption story!!!"

Called for Such a Time as This

By Tewannah Aman

I heard the roar of the motorcycles coming around the corner. Most of the guys were my friends, except for one. *Who is this new guy?* As he came closer, my heart began to race. I felt faint. When our eyes met, I couldn't see straight. I had never felt this way before. Sure, I'd had crushes, but nothing compared to this. *This must be love,* I thought. I had no understanding of boundaries, infatuation, or what true love really is.

He poured on the compliments. I soaked up the charm. "Have you ever been on a motorcycle?" he asked. "Do you want to take a ride on mine?"

What do you think I said? I wasn't questioning who he was or where he came from. It didn't matter; I didn't care. The love bug had bitten me. I couldn't wait for him to come knocking on my door. It felt like I was floating on air. I couldn't believe he—the charming man on the motorcycle—wanted to go out with me!

My dad, alarmed by all the excitement, tried to rein me in. He put his foot down, "You aren't going anywhere!"

What was he talking about? I was oblivious to how temptation works.

Or how my heart could be so easily swept away. I told my father he was overreacting—it was just a motorcycle ride.

But, within a week, we were inseparable. I was a foolish and immature 14-year-old girl.

In the beginning, everything seemed perfect. But as the months went by, my heartthrob became controlling, wanting every moment of my time. The manipulation was slow but profound. I was being smothered and didn't even know it. I was flattered by all the attention.

Things quickly changed. Like the sun fading into the horizon, so were his feelings for me. My friends alerted me to his wandering eye. It took much convincing to realize he was seeing other girls. And then he broke up with me.

I was taunted by thoughts that I wasn't good enough. I couldn't accept the rejection. The once charming man had tossed my heart aside and didn't even look back. I felt so empty and alone. The pain was too much to bear as I fell deeper into despair. Desperate to rekindle the relationship, I reached out, hoping he'd return. He told me to leave him alone and slammed down the phone.

One night, I crawled out of bed and stumbled to the bathroom. I didn't want to kill myself; I just wanted relief from the devastation caused by the rejection. I took the sleeping pills out of my parent's medicine cabinet. Looking at the bottle, I pleaded with God, begging Him for help. I desperately wanted to break free from the darkness that had consumed me.

What happened next was simply miraculous. In the twinkling of an eye, my feelings of despair were gone. *What am I doing?* I asked myself. *Why am I wasting my time?* You might say that God opened the eyes of the blind.

The Lord answered my prayers—He revived my heart and brought me back to life. I walked into the bathroom, crumbling under the weight of despair. I walked out, healed of the brokenness and ready to start over. Praise God for

Restoration: God Brings Beauty from Ashes

His faithfulness. Even though I wasn't seeking Him with my whole heart, He still had His hand of protection on me.

> *"Call upon me in the day of trouble; I will deliver you, and you shall glorify me"* (Psalm 50:15 ESV).

After that first painful breakup, I wish I could say I never got into another toxic relationship, but the cycle would later continue.

I had accepted Jesus just a few years before. My friends at school invited me to a Bible study where I heard the good news that Jesus died on the cross for my sins, that He sacrificed His life for me. I can't put into words the joy that filled my soul.

I attended church events three times a week, but changes came that rocked my world. There was a shake-up at my church, and the van no longer came by to pick me up. Just like that, my source of spiritual support had been cut. I entered a spiritual vacuum, and the enemy brought a good-looking guy to fill the godly void in my life.

Again, I thought I'd met "the one." It wasn't long before the same dysfunctional scenario began to unfold. I couldn't handle another breakup, so I decided to stay in an unhealthy relationship rather than be alone.

I continued to hang on, hoping things would work out. We had been together for a year when I started having constant bouts of nausea. One evening, It felt like the walls were caving in on me. And then, I fainted. Coming to, I thought, *Can I be pregnant?*

It was the 80s! There weren't pregnancy tests that gave quick results. I went to the local pregnancy center. I was so nervous as I entered the building. I saw this stack of brochures that had beautiful images of unborn babies in the womb; they left me breathless. We truly are fearfully and wonderfully made (Psalm 139:13-16).

What will the results be? I was chomping at the bit.

The nurse called me back to the examination room. "The results are positive," she said with enthusiasm. "You're having a baby!"

I was thrilled! She asked what I was going to do. And then she asked again.

Surprised and confused, I responded, "I am having a baby!"

I already knew the first person I'd tell. When I got to the house, I shouted, "I am a mom!"

My friend's response broke my heart. "Oh no, you're not," she boldly proclaimed. "You are only eighteen. What is wrong with you?"

As the tears streamed down my face, I asked, "Why would you say that to me?"

She said abortion was the only option for me.

I had no idea what she was talking about. She began rattling off the many reasons why it wasn't the right time for me to have a baby. I was too young and immature. I lived at home and worked part-time. She reminded me of the connection I'd have with the father for the rest of my life. That thought shook me to my core. She convinced me that abortion was the "right" thing to do. She made an appointment for the next day. She assured me that I'd have more children... one day.

A wave of fear washed over me as I entered the abortion facility. I didn't like going to the doctor, to begin with. And surgery? I was petrified! The woman who checked me in gave me a release form and instructed me to sign on the dotted line.

As tears filled my eyes, she said, "I've seen many women struggle, but you've made the right choice. It will be over soon."

I felt trapped, with nowhere to turn.

Afterward, I didn't feel regret. I had been brainwashed into believing it was for the best. I continued in my toxic relationship for several more years, even though it created deep feelings of insecurity and inadequacy. But God did not abandon me. I was in for a mighty rescue from a relentless Savior who never lost sight of me.

The Holy Spirit began stirring my heart. I started reading the Bible and wanting to go back to church. God gave me the strength to move out of my live-in relationship. I told the guy that Jesus had to be first in my life. And then it dawned on me: *He needs the Lord!* I was relentless in my efforts to pray and read the Bible to him, but he never wanted to seek God on his own. After months of trying to get him to church, I fell to my knees. "God, I don't know what to do. If this person isn't the one, please make it clear. If you tell me to go, I will leave."

God answered my prayers. A few days later, I ran into a pastor at church. He asked how I was doing. I responded, "I have been praying for clarity about something."

The pastor kindly invited me into his office and listened as I shared details of the ungodly, sinful relationship I'd been stuck in. And then he told me that I needed to answer four questions.

"Sure," I replied.

"FIRST QUESTION: Does he love Jesus?"

"SECOND QUESTION: Does he study God's Word?"

"THIRD QUESTION: Does he seek God in prayer?"

"FOURTH QUESTION: Does he go to church and serve in ministry?"

All my answers were a resounding "No!"

The pastor said I had to make a choice. I could return to the relationship or put Jesus first and make Him the priority of my life. I had spent too much time with someone who wasn't walking with the Lord. The Bible was clear: I needed to walk away. He said that the Lord would bring me a godly man and a spiritual leader. He had something better for me. He encouraged me to let go of the ungodly relationship so I could fulfill my God-given destiny.

Thanking God, I heeded the pastor's—and God's—guidance and fully left the relationship. God had answered my prayer for clarity.

I dove into ministry and warded off dating. I believed that I would meet my husband in ministry. I was willing to wait. Many guys tried to convince me that dating was something I needed to do, but I'd gone that route before. I decided to let God write my love story and trusted He would.

Seven years later, it happened! I was in evangelism classes when I met my husband. We were friends and did ministry together. It was just like the pastor had said. We dated with intention, not like my other relationships. Eighteen months later, the church bells rang, and we said, "I do."

We had only been married six months when we found out we were pregnant. It is difficult to put into words the happiness I felt inside. My heart was bursting with joy! I had longed to be a mom, and now, that dream was finally coming true.

And then came the ultrasound, "It's a boy!" I imagined all the many things we'd do together: walks on the beach, trips to the museums and aquariums, and so much more. I couldn't wait to be a stay-at-home mom! We were determined to raise our child in the admonition of the Lord. With each passing day, the love for my son grew. I couldn't wait to hold him in my arms.

The pregnancy was going well. And then, on a dark Saturday afternoon, I felt feverish. I knew something was seriously wrong. On the phone, the doctor reassured me that contractions were normal at this stage of pregnancy. It was only a few minutes later that my water broke!

The cramping was getting worse as we raced to the hospital. They rushed

Restoration: God Brings Beauty from Ashes

me into triage. Everyone seemed to be moving in fast motion. I could hear the heartbeat on the monitor as I begged the Lord to let our baby live.

As I lay in the hospital bed, the doctor slowly made his way to me. You could see the sadness in his eyes as he shared, "He is too young. His lungs aren't developed. Your baby boy is going to die."

Those words, *he is going to die,* just kept reverberating again and again in my head. And then, I thought I would drown in a river of tears. The pain was like a knife that had been thrust through my heart. I was frozen in time, unable to move. Everything I'd hoped for had just evaporated into thin air.

We named our son David Nathan. He lived three short hours, and then he passed away. In the blink of an eye, our precious baby boy was gone. I was lost. My husband and I took time off from ministry; now, what was I going to do? *What is my purpose in life?* My dream was to be a mother. That's all I ever wanted.

I was angry at God. I wish I could say I pulled out my Bible and started quoting Scripture, but I couldn't stop wondering why God let it happen. It just didn't make any sense to me.

If not for my husband, I wouldn't have gone to church. Even during worship, I found it impossible to praise the Lord. The enemy wanted me to believe that God had given me a gift and then snatched it away. He wanted me to believe that I couldn't trust the Lord. But God's faithfulness will always be revealed if we continue to seek Him and depend on Him.

I began to want answers as to why I lost the baby. I cried out to God for understanding. I started searching the Word of God for comfort and strength. The fog began to lift. My trust in God started to grow. And clarity began to come.

I read everything I could on pregnancy loss. In the book *What to Expect When You Are Expecting,* I learned that women can be at risk of a premature delivery if they have had a prior abortion. It was as if someone had flipped on a light switch. *Could my prior abortion have any connection to the loss of David Nathan?*

I had to know what happened to me. I was able to get my file from the abortion facility. What I read caused anger and confusion. The abortionist stated he'd given me all the information regarding the procedure—risks, complications, and psychological effects that could occur. The release form even stated that there was a possibility I could be sterile from the abortion.

The woman who gave me the release form—the only person I talked to—never shared any of the above information. I had not been told of the potential risks to my maternal health. I wanted women to understand the harm that abortion can cause—to protect others from suffering a similar loss. I wanted God to take what I'd gone through and bring good out of it. Instead of *Why me?*, my thoughts became, *Please redeem what I have done.* I didn't know what He'd do, but I wanted Him to move.

My husband, John, who volunteered as president of a pro-life organization, knew I needed to talk to Michelle, who worked with him in ministry. She had experienced an abortion in her own life. I poured my heart out and shared the trauma I'd been through. She was a great source of comfort and encouragement.

At the time, doctors were not required to give women detailed information before performing an abortion. As a result, many, like me, knew nothing about the loss they would experience or the devastating heartbreak they would face. The Florida legislature was introducing a bill to ensure that women receive vital facts about the many abortion-related risks.

John was organizing a press conference about the legislation known as the Woman's Right to Know. On the morning of the event, Michelle—who was going to share her abortion testimony—called to say she could not attend, but a representative must be there to speak on behalf of women. God had awakened her in the middle of the night with my name emblazoned upon her heart. She urged me to tell my story. Initially, I said no! I didn't want my

Restoration: God Brings Beauty from Ashes

family, friends, or the kids I had taught in Sunday school to know what I'd done.

"God has called you for such a time as this," Michelle proclaimed. I couldn't deny the painful truth of how I had gotten the file and learned about the after-effects of abortion. I knew I had to obey what God was calling me to do. Through all these things that were happening, God was moving me into position to reveal the truth that abortion hurts women and takes the life of an unborn child.

I was nervous as I stepped before the reporters, but then a calm swept over me. I knew the Holy Spirit was with me. While the cameras were rolling, I shared that I would never have had the abortion if I'd known just how dangerous it could be. As I started speaking out, women began sharing their heartbreaking stories with me. I met many who had suffered devastating trauma from their abortion. Through those speaking opportunities, God led me into ministry.

God began to use me to counsel women in unplanned pregnancies. Several years ago, a woman introduced herself to me after a church event. She wanted me to meet her beautiful 16-year-old daughter. I had counseled the mother years before but was unaware she had kept her baby. The mother and I wept on each other's shoulders as she whispered in my ear, "This is my only child. Thank you." It's overwhelming to think that God used me to save a life. Praise God, there are many more testimonies like hers.

I began leading post-abortion Bible studies, helping women understand the love and forgiveness of Jesus Christ. As we seek Him and His Word, He brings healing and restoration to their souls. Almost three decades later, I am still doing this amazing work. Even though my husband and I never had more children, I know that the two I have lost are in heaven, and we will be reunited one day.

The tragic and painful loss of my children has not been in vain. I speak for all those who are unable to speak for themselves. By God's grace, I am their voice.

Thank you, Lord, for taking what the enemy meant for evil and working it together for good. You had a plan even when I didn't understand. You brought purpose out of my pain and life out of my loss. You, Father, get all the glory for my redemption story.

Restoration of the Heart

By Kimberly Anne Kahn

After the procedure, I awoke in tears, my heart wrenching with the loss of a life that had been growing within me, "My baby. I want my baby."

I had been misled. I was told a lie that my baby was just a blob of tissue with no heartbeat, a lie that my baby wouldn't feel a thing. Lies! I had believed these lies propagated by the media, television, billboards, and movies. They all seemed to say it was acceptable to end the life within me. And I, in my vulnerability and confusion, fell for their deception.

But deep in my heart, I knew something was wrong. I knew Jesus was the author of life, including the one I had ended. That truth haunted me for many years. The pain I tried to suppress would surface in quiet moments and on the anniversary of the day I killed my child. I had hidden this dark secret for decades, not telling a soul—not even my children. What would they think of their mother, who loves them so much? Would they think I didn't love the life inside of me and wonder why I had done such a thing? Would they disown me and never talk to me again?

I had carried the shame and heartache for decades and could no longer do so. It was time to release this to the One who loves me and died for my sins. In my surrender, I cried out to Jesus:

"Jesus, help! Restore my heart! Take this shame and guilt I've hidden for so long! Forgive me for taking the life of a precious child You gave life to. I know in Your forgiveness, I can find healing and restoration. Your love is more significant than my sin, and I trust You to heal my heart."

Like me, many of us walk this world carrying the weight of our sin. We mask our pain, terrified that someone will find out. We smile on the outside, but

Restoration: God Brings Beauty from Ashes

inside, we are tormented by regret, hoping no one will ever know what we did. We haven't told anyone of our dark past for fear of what others might think or say.

Sin is a heavy burden to carry. I want you to know that your struggle is real and you're not alone.

No matter what sin you harbor, nothing is greater than God's love for you, and He longs to restore your heart! There is restoration in Jesus! He came to heal the brokenhearted and to set the captives free.

> The Spirit of the Lord God is upon Me Because the Lord has anointed Me To preach good tidings to the poor; He has sent Me to heal the brokenhearted, To proclaim liberty to the captives, And the opening of the prison to those who are bound (Isaiah 61:1 NKJV).

We are free! We can walk in freedom because Jesus has set us free by shedding His blood for us on the cross.

For God so loved the world that He gave His only begotten Son, that whoever believes in Him should not perish but have everlasting life (John 3:16 NKJV).

On the cross, Jesus paid the cost of every sin you've committed or will commit. He paid our debt once and for all. Jesus loves each of us so much that He died for you and me. Because of His redemption, our fear of wrath and the shame from our pasts are removed. Thank You, Jesus!

> Do not fear, for you will not be ashamed; Neither be disgraced, for you will not be put to shame; For you will forget the shame of your youth And will not remember the reproach of your widowhood anymore (Isaiah 54:4 NKJV).

This scripture truly encourages me and lifts me up. If I let Him, God will restore my heart so completely that I will no longer remember the shame I have been carrying.

There is restoration in Jesus. There is healing in His name. There is love that is greater than any mistake I've ever made. No more hiding. No more shame. Jesus is waiting with His arms open wide for me and for you.

Will you come to Him today?

I encourage you to say this with me:

> *I repent of my sins and trust Your healing power, God. I now walk in the freedom of Jesus' grace, no longer bound by the sin I once thought defined me. I am free from the chains that kept me captive. Jesus, I claim the restoration You paid for on the cross. You have restored my heart and restored me to our Father in heaven. I have a testimony, a story of redemption. Thank you, Jesus!*

Kim Mayberry

Kim Mayberry was born in Southern California and spent most of her childhood growing up in Northwest Arkansas. She has now lived in Oklahoma for the past 42 years. Kim was widowed in 2022, losing her husband of 28 years, John. She is the mother of three and the proud grandmother of six.

Kim's journey is a powerful testament to love and unwavering faith in God. When her son Christian, her youngest, faced a tragedy that started with an accident and turned into a crime that left him disabled. Kim refused to accept despair.

Her story of forgiveness will encourage others to know the power of forgiving, to know just how key this is! Her story will encourage you to have hope no matter what "they" say!

Kim and Christian travel to churches, schools, and other events, sharing the miracles of God. Christian loves to share his testimony, no matter if he's at the grocery store, the gas station, or the gym. If you get within a few feet of him, you're going to hear his story!

Contact them at prayformayberry.com or on Facebook at *Pray for Mayberry.*

A Mother's Journey of Forgiveness and Miracles

By Kim Mayberry

The long-awaited day had arrived—my 50th birthday. Knowing my love for the ocean, my daughter Mia had planned a special celebration—a trip to the beautiful beaches of Cancun, Mexico. It would be our first mother-daughter trip.

I had already said goodbye to my 16-year-old son Christian, expressing my love and reassurance. However, before leaving for Mia's, an overwhelming urge compelled me to stop by the fieldhouse where Christian was practicing football to share one final goodbye. My son was a typical teenager in many aspects, and he held a deep affection for his mama. I knew he would miss me during my trip, and I couldn't resist getting one last hug, which he didn't mind at all, even in the presence of his football teammates.

I asked the Lord to please bring me safely home to my son, telling Him that Christian needed me. An uneasy feeling lingered within me during the drive to Mia's. Little did I know that the prayers I offered for my safe return would soon turn into prayers for Christian. That goodbye on August 30, 2013, marked the beginning of a chapter I never saw coming.

Mia and I landed in breathtaking Cancun. The beach's beauty, with its turquoise waters and pristine white sands, left me awe-struck. The hotel was also gorgeous. The reality of visiting such a stunning place with my daughter was a dream come true. We spent the following day enjoying the typical beach activities, soaking in the sun and sea. Little did we know, that day marked the end of life as we had known it.

The next morning, as I lay in bed excitedly thinking about what the day would bring, the ringing phone shattered the tranquility. Mia's husband was on the line. She answered, and distress quickly crept into her voice. My heart began racing at the mention of an accident involving Christian. The news unfolded; Christian had been airlifted to Tulsa. Panic and disbelief gripped me as a gut-wrenching cry to the heavens, pleading for my son's safety, escaped from within me.

I rolled out of the bed, hitting my knees, crying out, "Not Christian, not my Christian! Jesus, Jesus, no, not Christian!"

Struggling to lift myself off the floor, I swiftly began packing my belongings into the suitcase, convinced that we would soon be heading to the airport. However, despite Mia's and the hotel's best efforts, there was no way we could fly out that day.

I spoke with my husband, who told me Christian was unconscious and had suffered a brain injury. A wave of fear washed over me. I had limited knowledge about brain injuries, but I was keenly aware that they were among the most severe traumas. While I knew broken bones and internal damage would have a good chance of healing, I also understood that a brain injury often has more severe and long-lasting consequences.

Mia secured a flight for us that would leave the following morning at 6 AM. It was now afternoon; Mia turned to me and said, "Mom, we can't just stay cooped up in this hotel room all day."

I nodded in agreement, asking her, "But what should we do?"

She suggested, "Let's take a walk on the beach."

The beach has always held a special place in my heart, so I agreed.

As we left the hotel and set foot on the sandy shore, I almost stepped on a small blue cross nestled in the sand. Startled, I asked Mia, "What's this?" Deep down, I knew it was a special message, a sign that God was watching over us. That tiny blue cross could have been anywhere on that vast expanse of beach, yet it appeared right in my path, right where I couldn't miss it. It was the first of many miracles the Lord provided, showing He was by our side and guiding us through this journey.

And then, we saw the most beautiful sight—a single set of footprints imprinted in the sand. As a storm brewed on the horizon and our own personal storm was also brewing, we knew God was with us.

Mia captured the moment by snapping a picture of the blue cross in the sand alongside the set of solitary footprints, with the storm on the horizon in the background. We didn't even realize what she had captured until several weeks later when she and my mom were looking at photos. These images served as a gentle reminder from the Lord, telling us He was by our side. I still hold these photos dear—proudly displaying them on our living room wall, and the blue cross is in my jewelry box. These symbols remind me of the Lord's constant presence in our lives from the very start.

Before we even landed in the United States, my son Blake had already pieced together the puzzle with some investigators, uncovering the truth about that night. Receiving Blake's urgent phone call while I was at the Dallas airport left me on edge.

"Mom, you need to sit down. I have something to tell you," he said.

Despite my initial fear, I braced myself for a shocking revelation.

"Mom, Christian is alive, but I need to tell you what happened to him," Blake said.

I couldn't fathom anything worse than the current situation, but I prepared myself for the unexpected news.

Blake recounted that Christian had been on an ATV that crashed. What was shocking was that a very drunk adult woman had been driving the ATV that Christian was a passenger of. And instead of seeking help for Christian after the accident, the woman abandoned him in a ditch without offering any assistance.

I found the story hard to believe. I told Blake that such a thing couldn't possibly be true. However, as he revealed more details, it became clear that the unthinkable had indeed occurred. We initially assumed that the incident at the river involving Christian and his football teammate was just a harmless ATV mishap. Little did we know, it was a far more serious and deliberate act.

After arriving in Tulsa, I walked down the hall of the Intensive Care Unit at St. John's Hospital, feeling like my legs could give out at any moment. When I reached the doorway, I found myself unable to move any further. I stood there, paralyzed, at the sight before me: my baby lying in the hospital bed, unconscious and surrounded by tubes and machines, hooked up to a breathing tube. It was a scene that would be a nightmare for any parent.

Even after seeing my motionless 16-year-old son in bed, with no signs of movement, I refused to focus on the medical reports. I had to remain strong in my faith and be stronger than ever before. This was the ultimate test of my personal journey with the Lord.

A week after his injury, at a critical moment for Christian's survival, the doctors delivered horrifying news. If they didn't perform an immediate bilateral craniotomy to reduce brain swelling, we would lose him then and there. The risky surgery involved removing two large pieces of skull on both sides of his head, each the size of a grapefruit. The doctors warned us that Christian might not make it through the operation, and even if he did, his chances of survival afterward were uncertain.

As the gravity of the situation hit me, I fled the room in a panic, dropping to my knees in the hallway and pleading with God once again to spare my son. My daughter Mia caught up to me, urging me to stay strong and have

Restoration: God Brings Beauty from Ashes

faith. She reminded me I had always taught her to believe in God's care and protection. "You have to believe, Mom," she insisted.

At that moment, I made a firm decision that no doctor would ever speak a negative report over my son again without my objection. I refused to let those words "he might not make it" ever be uttered in his presence! They informed me that even if he pulled through the surgery, the prognosis was bleak—he most likely would never walk, talk, or lead a normal life. I made it clear to multiple doctors on numerous occasions to remember the name *Christian Mayberry*. I proclaimed the goodness of the Lord and declared with faith that Christian would not only survive, he would thrive. I was determined my son would return to me whole and healthy.

For we walk by faith, not by sight (2 Corinthians 5:7 NKJV).

I spoke only words of *life* over my son, knowing that *Death and life are in the power of the tongue* (Proverbs 18:21 NKJV).

Reciting Psalm 118:17, *I shall not die, but live, and declare the works of the Lord* (NKJV), I held onto that promise for my son. I was resolute in my belief that Christian would survive and share his miracle story with the world. Little did I know how true this vision would turn out to be.

Thank you, Jesus!

We faced so many challenges and went through almost impossible situations. One of the greatest hurdles was the realization that, as a Christ-follower, I could not harbor hatred toward the woman responsible for the pain inflicted upon my son, my family, and myself. I had to understand that forgiveness was essential to my prayers being answered for my son's healing. Despite learning that Christian had actually died while he lay there in that ditch uncared for by human hands, I had to release any feelings of hate towards her. It was impossible to cling to resentment while begging God for help.

The teachings in Matthew 6:14-15 were a constant reminder that forgiveness is paramount.

> *For if you forgive other people when they sin against you, your heavenly Father will also forgive you. But if you do not forgive others their sins, your Father will not forgive your sins* (Matthew 6:14-15 NIV).

I knew I had to forgive the woman who had caused such significant loss. Christian was robbed of the chance to graduate from high school, obtain the cherished truck he longed for, and work the job he had pursued for six months—which he finally landed just a month before his injury. He was stripped of his friendships and other possible relationships. His pain, suffering, anger, fear, sadness, and depression were overwhelming. How could I possibly forget and forgive all of this?

The answer was simple: *BUT GOD!*

Without the intervention of Jesus, I am certain I would have spiraled into darkness. Anger, bitterness, and resentment would have consumed me if I had allowed it. I couldn't afford to let that happen. Every moment of every day was dedicated to advocating for my son, tending to his needs, and tirelessly seeking the next rehabilitation opportunity. If I had succumbed to the negativity and challenges that the enemy hurled my way, I wouldn't have been able to effectively support my son. This was a full-time commitment, one that I couldn't have managed alone.

Facing the difficult task of finding a facility that would accept Christian for rehabilitation was just one of the many struggles we encountered. After exhausting all options in Oklahoma, we were left with only two choices, according to Oklahoma Medicaid—bring him home or place him in a nursing home. That was all they were willing to cover. Sending him out of state for the vital rehab he desperately needed was not an option they were willing to consider.

Now at 17, Christian's situation was not looking good. Stuck in a nursing home, he was deteriorating rapidly. I refused to accept this as our reality. Despite countless days, weeks, and even months filled with pleading and searching, I continued to be met with dead ends at every turn. It was clear that we needed a miracle. Miraculously, one came our way.

Reaching out to our State Representative, John Bennett, turned out to be the saving grace we needed. With a message guiding him, he took up Christian's cause and, along with Senator Mark Allen, managed to sway Oklahoma Medicaid to approve out-of-state rehabilitation for Christian. Julie Weintraub, the founder of Hands Across The Bay in Tampa, also joined our fight and provided assistance.

It was a battle. But with God on our side, we knew we would be ok. Thanks to the support of these three individuals, we were soon on a medical flight to Florida, where Christian received the life-changing rehabilitation he needed. The impact of their intervention cannot be overstated; we will forever be grateful for their role in turning our situation around. *Another miracle!*

My husband, John, with his boundless energy, would stay by Christian's side every night, regardless of the hospital, rehab, or nursing home we found ourselves in. During the days I was there with Christian. My mother was a constant source of support, always lending a helping hand and doing whatever was necessary. I owe her such a debt of gratitude for her love and support. My family was always there doing whatever it took, whether it was researching the next rehabilitation facility for Christian or sitting by his side while I made urgent phone calls to secure his placement.

After just five months of Christian's hospitalization, the stress took a toll on John's health, leading to his first heart attack, which occurred in the middle of the night even as he was caring for Christian in his hospital room. John had been in good health, but the combination of stress and restless nights in the hospital room proved to be too much for him to bear.

Around 2 1/2 years after Christian's injury, after three heart attacks and three strokes, John had to be admitted to a nursing home. This period was incredibly difficult for all of us. John remained in the nursing home for over six years, adding to the already heavy burden we were carrying.

And then... he was gone.

The loss of John in 2022 was a heartbreaking blow, and I knew in my heart that his decline was linked to Christian's ordeal. Once again, I found myself faced with the need to forgive the woman driving for the pain she had brought upon our family. Yet, through it all, I held onto faith, knowing that with God's grace, we would find the strength to keep going.

Despite everything we have faced and even lost over the past nearly 11 years, God has given many beautiful miracles and gifts to Christian and our family. The blessings and miracles we have experienced are too vast to capture fully in this chapter. God has graced us with so many blessings. While Christian still struggles with moments of depression, he remains one of the most joyful, sociable, and loving young men you could encounter. His resilience and spirit are truly a testament to the power of faith and the ability to *KEEP GOING!*

Months into his recovery, Christian revealed to us that as he lay without breath or a physical heartbeat in that ditch, he found himself in heaven in the arms of Jesus. There, he met his three grandparents for the first time, as well as his sister Vanessa, who had been stillborn. He described the moment as beyond perfect, filled with love and beauty everywhere.

Christian struggled to find the words to explain the overwhelming sense of love and peace he had felt. He recounted how the Lord had told him to "just breathe" and assured him that he would return to earth with a purpose and a platform to bring thousands to Christ. While I had heard of near-death experiences before, it was truly incredible that this had happened to our Christian.

God has fulfilled His promise to Christian. Now, everywhere we go, people are instantly drawn to him. Whether we're at a grocery store, gas station, or restaurant, individuals are naturally attracted to him. They approach him, eager to engage in conversation. Christian seizes these opportunities to share his story of what the Lord has done for him and how deeply God loves them. He offers everyone a warm hug—those Christian Mayberry embraces are cherished by all who receive them. The light of Christ shines through Christian and is evident from the moment you meet him. I have heard this repeatedly from people throughout these last 10+ years.

It is clear to all that Christian carries the love of Jesus within him. The Holy Spirit radiates from him, captivating those around him. It's as if they are drawn to him for a hug from Jesus Himself.

Jesus told Christian that he would have a platform and would lead thousands to Him. Today, Christian has a substantial platform on Facebook with a huge following whom he uplifts and encourages daily. He is proud to tell people he is a professional speaker, using his experiences to inspire and bring hope to others. He loves to tell people that "they said I would probably never walk or talk again, but let me tell you 'bout my Jesus. He'll make a way where there ain't no way."

Christian and I travel together to churches, schools, and any place where we are invited to share Christian's miracle story. He is a co-author in the number one best-selling books *Navigating Your Storm* and *Fit 2 Fight*— momentous achievements that have brought him so much joy and pride. We are grateful to Ken Hobbs for these wonderful opportunities and blessings.

I am keenly aware that others are experiencing pain and hurt. I hope and pray that by offering a glimpse into our lives, this chapter may serve as a guide to help others through their pain and, if necessary, toward forgiveness. Understanding the power of forgiveness is crucial. It holds the key to healing and moving forward. For those who share my faith as a Christ follower, forgiveness is not just a choice but a necessity.

The transforming power of forgiveness can bring about healing and restoration, allowing us to cling to a future filled with hope and peace.

Have faith, shine bright, and KEEP GOING!

Tammy A. McCrory

Tammy A. McCrory has a 23-year career as a Nationally Registered Paramedic. She works in the Emergency Department of a large hospital in Western North Carolina.

Tammy is proud to boast that she is, first, a follower of Jesus Christ and, second, a proud mother of four adult children/spouses and seven grandchildren. Her love for her family is a beautiful earthly love that has not always been perfect. However, the love of God is perfect and unconditional.

Tammy's identity is in Christ alone; she is learning to live and accept herself for who God says she is, and *that* has made all the difference in her life journey.

Tammy has felt the call to share her story for quite some time, and writing this chapter has been a great step of faith and obedience. This story only gives a brief snapshot of the events she lived during this season, and she hopes all who read it will see the love, forgiveness, and restoration power of Jesus Christ.

Pride & Shame to Joy & Restoration

By Tammy A. McCrory

> *"For I know the plans I have for you," declares the LORD, "plans to prosper you and not to harm you, plans to give you hope and a future. Then you will call on me and come and pray to me, and I will listen to you. You will seek me and find me when you seek me with all your heart. I will be found by you," declares the LORD, "and will bring you back from captivity. I will gather you from all the nations and places where I have banished you," declares the LORD, "and will bring you back to the place from which I carried you into exile"* (Jeremiah 29:11-14 NIV).

I found myself in a season of social and spiritual controversy, entangled in feelings and circumstances that are "taboo" and unacceptable by much of society. I deeply questioned my moral and Christian beliefs and compromised my own standards that were deeply rooted in the Word of God. I was cheered on by some and shunned by others.

I wrestled with my loneliness, questioned my identity, and attempted, with relationships, to fill a deep void in my heart that I would later discover only

Jesus could fill. I was divorced, had a daughter out of wedlock with a man I lived with, and then began living a lifestyle that was at a legal and societal crossroads—I found myself in a homosexual relationship.

> For the word of God is alive and active. Sharper than any double-edged sword, it penetrates even to dividing soul and spirit, joints and marrow; it judges the thoughts and attitudes of the heart (Hebrew 4:12 NIV).

Conversations and relationships that were historically hidden and scarcely spoken of are now debated as acceptable and are legal publicly and politically at local, state, and federal levels. Isn't it ironic that Satan has a cunning way of making what is scripturally unacceptable seem acceptable? By not following God and what I knew to be scriptural truths, I stepped away from the foot of the cross, and I walked right into a living hell and a spiritual drought of my own making.

My choices created a season that was long, hard, and life-changing. I selfishly and willingly chose my flesh and the pressure of the world's views over my relationship with Jesus Christ. On that day, I once again did what I often do. I made a choice; I charted my own course and deviated from God's will and plan for my life.

> Elijah went before the people and said, "How long will you waver between two opinions? If the LORD is God, follow him; but if Baal is God, follow him." But the people said nothing (1 Kings 18:21 NIV).

My husband and I got married in 1983. Our relationship lasted thirteen years, and we were blessed with three amazing sons. For the duration of our marriage, we attended and served faithfully in our church, but our story ended in divorce.

Restoration: God Brings Beauty from Ashes

I then met and fell in love with a wonderful man; we did not get married, as God ordains, but we had a beautiful daughter together. We lived together for a few years after our daughter was born, ultimately deciding we were not compatible for a long-term relationship. We mutually agreed to end the living arrangement but remained committed to working out a way to mutually raise our daughter in separate, healthy, stable environments. That was, until I shook the foundation and confidence in those who loved and knew me, including him.

In early May 2008, a seemingly innocent ride home from work led to so much more than I could have ever predicted, much less imagined for myself. It was the beginning of a newfound relationship with a woman—yet another attempt to fill that emptiness inside that became nearly crippling to everyone around me. Little did I realize it would cripple me too, but our merciful God had victory waiting for me on the other end—I just had to choose Him.

> They exchanged the truth about God for a lie and worshipped and served created things rather than the Creator—who is forever praised. Amen. Because of this, God gave them over to shameful lusts. Even their women exchanged natural sexual relations for unnatural ones (Romans 1:25-26 NIV).

Our text messages and phone calls seemed harmless at first. My new friend was a lesbian who was currently in a 9-year relationship. She offered me attention that was very flattering and exciting but, at the same time, confusing. She knew I was "straight"—I had four children, ages 24, 23, 19, and 10, and twin grandchildren on the way. But soon, it was clear she was interested in me, a heterosexual woman with children who was soon to be a grandmother. From the beginning of May 2008 to August 2008, our feelings for each other grew quickly; we were convinced we were in love with each other.

On my daughter's first day of fifth grade, her father and I accompanied her to school. As we pulled into the driveway after dropping her off, I told him that I had met someone—a woman—and I was in love with her.

I remember the moment so clearly; I was so proud and confident. But I will never forget the hurt and disbelief on his face. If I hadn't been so full of myself in that moment, I might have allowed the truth he spoke to bring me back to the reality of the situation. He was desperate for me to change my mind. He was scared for me but was exceedingly worried about how this would affect our daughter and my sons. I didn't know it at the time, but I had just marched right into Satan's trap.

Hindsight is always 20/20. Looking back, it is very clear: I took my eyes off God; it was as simple as that. I was divorced and single again. I was seeking acceptance, security, and love, and I thought I found it with another woman. I had lost my identity somewhere along the way and was already in a sinful posture; now, this seemed to be the unsolicited answer. There was a void and loneliness I was trying to fill, and it truly "felt right" yet also so wrong. I knew better. When this confident and persistent woman showed up and began filling the emptiness in my life, I was blindsided and compromised everything I knew and believed.

I do have to sincerely express that the five months leading up to the marriage were not without spiritual warfare. God was trying to get my attention, and He gave me multiple opportunities to escape the deception of this darkness. I succumbed to the lies of the flesh and this world. If I'm being honest, my heart was fully invested in all that I was feeling. No one was going to change my mind; I was all in. It was exciting, and I was feeling things I had not felt in a very long time. Someone loved me and wanted me, and it felt right.

> *No temptation has overtaken you except what is common to mankind. And God is faithful; he will not let you be tempted beyond what you can bear. But when you are tempted, he will also provide a way out so that you can endure it* (1 Corinthians 10:13 NIV).

I honestly felt like God had placed this woman in my life to show the world that same-sex relationships/marriages were to be accepted. I just knew this was God's plan… and boy, was I deceived.

I was not prepared; my armor was nowhere to be found. I was not careful, and I did not guard my heart. I compromised the cross and all that Jesus did for me there.

> *Therefore put on the full armor of God, so that when the day of evil comes, you may be able to stand your ground, and after you have done everything, to stand* (Ephesians 6:13 NIV).

As our relationship progressed, the news media was full of debates about the legality of same-sex marriage. There were only a few states at the time that had legalized same-sex marriage, California being one of them. However, Proposition 8 would soon be on the ballot in California; if passed, it would ban same-sex marriages. So, we made plans.

We decided to get married while it was still legal. We were going to be part of history! We would fly to San Diego, California, where my middle son was stationed at Camp Pendleton in the Marine Corps. He and my daughter-in-law agreed to be present for the ceremony for support as our witnesses.

We told our families our plans for marriage. There was a lot of head shaking, questions, and concern. But, overall, almost everyone wished us happiness. My kids and parents genuinely just wanted me to be happy.

My daughter, however, was at the vulnerable age of 10. This relationship caused her great concern, anxiety, and embarrassment. It upset her so badly that she ended up suffering from shingles. The stress of the changes in her young life were very unsettling and confusing to her and all she knew to be true in her life to that point. I had raised her one way, and now I was going against everything I had ever said I believed in.

I tried my best to ensure that my daughter felt safe and secure during all the changes taking place around her. I did not feel worthy of taking her to church, but I was so thankful she had godly grandparents who taught her the love of Jesus and took her to church in my place. She would need this strong foundation as we leaned on each other through the ups and downs of the next 12 years.

> O God, do not remain silent; do not turn a deaf ear, do not stand aloof, O God. See how your enemies growl, how your foes rear their heads. With cunning they conspire against your people; they plot against those you cherish (Psalm 83:1-3 NIV).

Our marriage was difficult. Marriage is hard under the best of circumstances, but when things were difficult, I knew my disobedience was a factor and that there would be long-term consequences.

Even though I was living in sin and disobedience, God loved me and wanted what was best for me. He never left me. He heard my cries and knew my heart. Once we took our vows and the marriage was legal, it was as if Satan stepped back, grinned, and said, "Thank you for playing. You are on your own now!" I was the victim of a cruel game that I took full responsibility for participating in. I was empty, ashamed, and felt more pain and loneliness than I had ever felt in my life.

> For everything in the world—the lust of the flesh, the lust of the eyes, and the pride of life—comes not from the Father but from the world (1 John 2:16 NIV).

When we returned from California, my daughter and I moved into my wife's apartment. My daughter split time between her father and me, just as before, but now with an added stepmother dynamic. I intentionally and unintentionally sabotaged our marriage from the very beginning. We were both very independent, strong-willed, and stubborn. This union was toxic. Arguments would begin over the smallest things and quickly escalate into coldness, bitterness, and resentment. Communication, as it was, was always twisted and manipulated.

My daughter and I left my wife in the middle of a family vacation in June of 2012. I rented a car and, leaving my wife with her family at Myrtle Beach, I rushed home, packed my necessities, and put the rest of my daughter and my belongings in storage. My daughter's father graciously allowed me to stay in his spare bedroom for a month while a rental was being made ready to move into. I stayed in the rental for a few months—until Satan once again preyed on my weakness, and I moved back in with my wife to try again.

There is a misconception that sex is the driving factor in homosexual/ lesbian relationships. In my situation, our relationship began as an unnatural attraction between two women, which led to the progression and expectation of the act of sex. I can only speak of my relationship, but the act of sex was not a regular part of our marriage. I did not welcome the intimacy when she made the attempts. Looking back, I know the Holy Spirit was convicting me that I was not on the path God had for me.

> *The law is made not for the righteous but for the lawbreakers and rebels, the ungodly and sinful, the unholy and religious, for those who kill their fathers or mothers, for murderers, for the sexually immoral, for those practicing homosexuality, for slave traders and liars and perjurers—and for whatever else is contrary to the sound doctrine that conforms to the gospel concerning the blessed God* (1 Timothy 1:8-10 NIV).

The foundation of my faith had been established, but as I wrote this story, the Holy Spirit so beautifully revealed the difference between my faith then and my faith now. My growth at that time was horizontal and shallow, with no tangible root systems to prepare me for the times the winds would blow and the storms would come against me. I was easily swayed and treading on dangerous ground.

Oh, but God! In His mercy and grace, He responded to my many prayers to be delivered from my sin and shame. God heard me, but some of our messes take time, and God had a lot of work to do in and around me. I had to be patient; it was going to take a while for Him to work through the entanglements I created by trying to fill the void in my spirit with three different relationships I orchestrated on my own instead of submitting to what God wanted for me. I believed, trusted, and knew how to pray—and I needed God to hear me. But all I heard was silence, or so I thought.

> *I sought the LORD, and he answered me; he delivered me from all my fears* (Psalm 34:4 NIV).

Those who know your name trust in you, for you, LORD, have never forsaken those who seek you (Psalm 9:10 NIV).

God's unconditional love has beautiful timing.

One of the many ways God worked so beautifully is that there were no family estrangements throughout all of this. No one walked away from me, and there were no family arguments or confrontations. My children, my parents, and my siblings and their families loved and supported me. So many families cannot see past the sin and love the sinner. I was fortunate. God's grace was immensely evident in all aspects of the crazy mess I created.

Events took place and doors opened that could only be explained by the orchestration of God's hands. Toward the end of 2019, my new life began. I left the marriage and repented of the sexual sin and disobedience that had held me prisoner for 12 years.

I now attend and faithfully serve at a church that God told me I would attend even while I was deep in the sin of my same-sex marriage years earlier. My healing, clarity, and growth in Christ have taken time. It was certainly not immediate. But my first steps of turning my life and heart back to Jesus brought peace and fullness that only He could provide.

Then they cried to the LORD in their trouble, and he saved them from their distress. He brought them out of darkness, the utter darkness, and broke away their chains. Let them give thanks to the LORD for his unfailing love and his wonderful deeds for mankind (Psalm 107:13-15 NIV).

I filed for divorce. My life since that beautiful day of freedom has been nothing short of miraculous. I once again have joy, security, and purpose in Jesus Christ, my Lord and Savior. He alone filled the void I sought to fill on my own for so many years. Now, I have peace and contentment in my singleness. I have truly been redeemed and restored; He has brought beauty from ashes in such a complete and healing way.

Satan continues to try to lay shame on me, but the more I tell my story, the freer I become! God continues to give me opportunities to share my story with others who are trying to fill the Jesus void in their lives with false security.

When I began seeking after God with all my heart, my healing began. I intentionally go to the foot of the cross every day to nurture my relationship with Jesus. I never again want to be found unprepared. The love of God now fills me and has made me whole. I am loved, forgiven, accepted, and restored!

To appoint unto them that mourn in Zion, to give unto them beauty for ashes, the oil of joy for mourning, the garment of praise for the spirit of heaviness; that they might be called trees of righteousness, the planting of the LORD, that he might be glorified (Isaiah 61:3 KJV).

Being confident of this, that he who began a good work in you will carry it on to completion until the day of Christ Jesus (1 Philippians 1:6 NIV).

Restoring and Maintaining Spiritual Health

By Kimberly Anne Kahn

People are constantly searching for ways to improve their health. Advertisements regularly bombard us, making us keenly aware of new diet theories, exercise methods, supplement options, and wellness routines. Every year, fitness centers promote New Year's resolution sales to entice people to join their gym to improve the look of their bodies. And while seeking to improve our physical health is important, our well-being goes beyond the physical; it also encompasses the mind and spirit.

The Bible says that man shouldn't live by bread alone. Jesus answered, *"It is written: 'Man shall not live on bread alone, but on every word that comes from the mouth of God'"* (Matthew 4:4 NIV). Just as our bodies need proper food to survive, our spirits need nourishment from God's Word to flourish. Without it, we may become weary, anxious, or spiritually drained, even if we are physically strong.

A couple of years ago, I was taking a counseling course on healing the inner child. The instructor handed each of us a piece of paper with a simple drawing of a glass. "This glass represents you," she said. "Now, divide it into three sections—physical, emotional, and spiritual—and mark your levels."

I stared at the blank image before me with my pen. How full was I? I started with my physical level, drawing a line about three-quarters of the way up. I was eating well and getting rest—at least on the outside, I seemed fine. Then came my emotional level—I hesitated before drawing a much lower line, realizing how drained and weary I felt. But when I reached my spiritual

Restoration: God Brings Beauty from Ashes

level, my pen stayed frozen. I couldn't deny the truth—I had been running on empty. I was taking care of myself physically, but I was not adequately caring for my spirit. Pausing, I drew a line just above the bottom of the glass. I was spiritually empty. I was in the red zone, needing to be fed the living Word.

Our physical, emotional, and spiritual lives must be equally balanced for us to be healthy and whole. Our bodies can only be aligned when we are spiritually fed by the Word of God. Scripture is more than words on a page—it is living, powerful, and life-giving.

> *My son, pay attention to what I say; turn your ear to my words.*
> *Do not let them out of your sight, keep them within your heart; for*
> *they are life to those who find them and health to one's whole body*
> (Proverbs 4:20-22 NIV).

I'd love to share the Glass Levels exercise with you and encourage you to take a moment to reflect on where you are right now. How are you truly feeling? Are you mentally exhausted or emotionally drained? Do your emotions feel like a rollercoaster?

Think back over the past few days—have you been running around nonstop, feeling overwhelmed? Or have you been intentional about resting, recharging, and spending time in God's Word?

Once you've taken a moment to reflect, complete the exercise. It's a powerful way to check in with yourself and see where you might need to be refilled and restored.

1. Draw a Simple Glass
    - You can sketch a basic outline of a drinking glass.
    - This glass represents your whole being—physical, emotional, and spiritual health.

2. Divide the Glass Into Three Sections
   - Physical Health (bottom portion): Your energy, health, rest, and physical well-being.
   - Emotional Health (middle portion): Your heart, relationships, peace, and joy.
   - Spiritual Health (top portion): Your connection to God, faith, prayer life, and time spent in the Word.

3. Mark Your Current Levels
   - Shade or color in where you feel "full" or "empty" in each section.
   - Are you spiritually overflowing but emotionally drained?
   - Are you physically healthy but spiritually malnourished?

4. Reflect on Your Balance
   - *Am I feeding my spirit daily with the Word of God?*
   - *What is draining me emotionally?*
   - *Am I caring for my physical health with rest and nourishment?*

5. Use Scripture to Fill the Glass
   - Physical: *Do you not know that your body is a temple of the Holy Spirit?* (1 Corinthians 6:19 NIV).
   - Emotional: *"Come to me, all you who are weary and burdened, and I will give you rest"* (Matthew 11:28 NIV)
   - Spiritual: *"Whoever drinks the water I give them will never thirst"* (John 4:14 NIV).

Just as we make time to eat daily meals, we must also prioritize consuming God's Word daily to restore us spiritually. This is not just about reading the Bible occasionally but meditating on it, declaring its promises, and allowing it to transform us from the inside out.

Consider setting aside a specific time each day for scripture reading and reflection. You can use tools like devotionals and Bible reading plans to guide your daily reading. Even as you read this book, take time to pause and focus on the scripture, asking God what He wants you to learn.

As you seek to restore or maintain your health, remember to nourish yourself wholly: body, mind, and spirit.

. . . .

Tina Rains

Tina Rains is a bestselling author, speaker, and consultant with a passion for empowering women to unlock their full potential. With over 30 years of experience as a business leader and strategist, she helps women break free from limitations, achieve their goals, and step into their God-given purpose. Tina also helps ministries and nonprofits grow by developing effective strategies, building strong donor relationships, and creating sustainable communities that drive world-changing impact.

As the host of the *Masterpiece Women* podcast, Tina gives women leaders a platform to share their stories of redemption and transformation. Through her leadership and personal journey, she inspires individuals to rise above challenges, embrace their identity, and lead with confidence. Tina is the author of *My Freedom Climb,* a book that uses mountain climbing analogies to guide women in overcoming obstacles through faith. She is committed to seeing women and organizations thrive and achieve success.

www.tinarains.com

A Summer of Restoration

By Tina Rains

Restoration and healing come when we invite Jesus into our lives. But does that mean we no longer struggle with the enemy's schemes? No, we will continue to battle until we reach heaven.

In Ephesians 6:11, God instructs us to *Put on the full armor of God, so that you can take your stand against the devil's schemes* (NIV). By wearing God's armor, we are fully equipped to overcome whatever the enemy throws at us—whether it's doubt, confusion, or even sin.

My most challenging struggle has always been in my mind—questioning my worth, value, and ability. I know I'm not alone. I've shared my story with women worldwide and have found that this internal battle is something many of us face. The enemy often attacks our thoughts. Does that mean we aren't healed? Absolutely not. If you're feeling that God has forgotten you or hasn't restored you, I promise He is working to restore everything the enemy has stolen. One day, you'll look back and see all the ways He's been working on your behalf.

This past summer, I was feeling defeated. Life wasn't going as I had dreamed, especially professionally. After spending two years building a business I thought God had called me to, it failed. I started to doubt myself, to question my worth as a leader and businesswoman. But those lies were just distractions, ploys from the enemy trying to hold me back from the incredible plans God has for me. This summer, though, God reminded me of His goodness and faithfulness.

Jeremiah 29:11 says, *"For I know the plans I have for you," declares the Lord, "plans to prosper you and not to harm you, plans to give you hope and a future"* (NIV). Even when life feels uncertain, we can trust that God has the best plans for us.

My journey began with a trip to New Mexico, where I grew up. We were driving into Hobbs, NM, when I saw a sign that read, "Home of the Hobbs Eagles." In an instant, memories rushed back—memories of feeling worthless, abused, and shamed. I had worked through these feelings in counseling, so I found myself asking God, "Why am I crying?"

The memories of Hobbs—the place where I faced some of the darkest times in my life—started flooding back. I recalled my childhood poverty and the abuse I suffered. But I also thought about the courage I found when I stood up to my stepfather, telling him that if he ever touched me again, I would have him arrested. He took off soon after, leaving my mother heartbroken and financially destitute. At just 12 years old, I felt like I was carrying the weight of the world on my shoulders. Yet, now, as I sat in that same place, I realized my tears were tears of gratitude. Gratitude for how far I had come, for God's restoration, and for all that I had survived. Psalm 147:3 says, *He heals the brokenhearted and binds up their wounds* (NIV). That was my story, my testimony of God's healing.

That was the first time I had returned to Hobbs feeling whole. All those years ago, I had left feeling like a broken girl with little hope. Now, I felt valued, loved, and provided for. Even though I had struggled professionally and felt defeated in recent months, the undeniable truth of God's work in my life—the restoration and healing—was overwhelming. Only He could have done this. As it says in Philippians 1:6, *Being confident of this, that He who began a good work in you will carry it on to completion until the day of Christ Jesus* (NIV). God has not finished with me yet. The restoration He's brought into my life is ongoing, and I can't wait to see what He does next.

Isaiah 61:3 speaks to this: *To console those who mourn in Zion, To give them beauty for ashes, The oil of joy for mourning, The garment of praise for the spirit of heaviness* (NKJV). This verse became so real to me as I saw God's power at work in my life. The transformation He brought about is a testament to His grace and power. Even though the journey isn't over, I'm filled with awe for how far He's brought me. Every day, I see His healing and beauty in new ways.

As we drove through town, the tears kept coming and turned into sobs at one point. My husband was worried, sensing something was deeply wrong, but I couldn't stop crying. I began explaining to him that my tears weren't just about the past but were tears of gratitude for everything God had done. He had used even the pain, the poverty, and the abuse to allow me to help others more effectively. I wasn't just crying for that broken little girl anymore—I was crying because I had been healed, restored, and transformed.

God had brought me so far—from the shattered girl who left Hobbs to the woman I am today: a woman with a loving husband, a family, and the joy of traveling and experiencing new adventures. In that moment, I was reminded that my pain had become my purpose. Romans 8:28 says, *And we know that in all things God works for the good of those who love him, who have been called according to his purpose* (NIV). This verse has been true in every step of my journey. God has worked through everything—good and painful—to shape me for His glory and to bless others through my story.

That moment of reflection in New Mexico became a powerful reminder of God's healing touch. It was there, when I was 12, that I first encountered the love of Christ. After my stepfather left, a friend invited my mom to church. That night, she accepted Christ; the very next day, my brother and I did too. That was the moment everything changed for us. My mom's radical transformation marked the beginning of our family's restoration. If she hadn't surrendered to God in that moment, who knows where we would be today. But God...

As I returned to Hobbs, it wasn't just about revisiting my childhood. It was about recognizing the transformation God had done in me. Where there was once shame, I now had confidence. Where there was once resentment, there was now forgiveness. I was returning with more than just memories; I was returning with a renewed spirit and a sense of gratitude for all God had done.

And as I prepared to meet my biological father and brothers for the first time, a whirlwind of emotions swirled inside me—nervousness, excitement, and overwhelming gratitude. Just a few months earlier, I had discovered them through a DNA test. Now, here I was, about to meet them in person. It was nothing short of miraculous. For years, I had prayed for a father who would love me the way I had always wanted to be loved. Psalm 68:5 tells us, *A father to the fatherless, a defender of widows, is God in His holy dwelling* (NIV). God had been my Father all along, filling that void in my heart. But now, He was blessing me with an earthly father—a gift I had stopped praying for years ago.

In Hobbs, we met my half-brother and his wife, who welcomed us with open arms. As we shared stories from our childhoods, I couldn't help but be overwhelmed by the fact that I was standing in this place that once held so much pain—and now, it was a place of healing. I could see God's fingerprints all over my story. What was once broken, He had made whole. What was once hopeless, He had restored. And the beauty of it all? It was just the beginning of what He will continue to do in my life.

As I drove through the streets of Hobbs, I pointed out the home where I grew up and the high school I graduated from and shared recollections from those years. It was a journey down memory lane, but this time, it was different. This time, it was filled with peace and gratitude rather than pain and sorrow. Over and over, the word "restoration" echoed in my heart. The Lord had indeed restored the years that the enemy had stolen, and He had used them for His glory. The Lord's words from Joel 2:25 came alive in my heart: *"I will repay you for the years the locusts have eaten"* (NIV). What an incredible promise! God had not only repaid me, but He had done so in ways I could never have imagined. Driving around with my brother was one of those amazing ways.

As I continued to share stories with my brother, I was filled with emotions and awe at what the Lord had done in my life. It was true—every trial, every heartache, God had used for good. And now, I was here, in this place of past pain, sharing about God's goodness and His restoration of my life with my brother. The Lord had done great things—He had transformed my pain into purpose, my sorrow into joy, and my loss into restoration. And now, I was blessed to witness Him at work as I shared with my brother.

Wow! We serve an incredible God, a truly good Father. This summer continued to reveal the goodness of our Savior in ways that took my breath away. A few days after our time in Hobbs, we headed to Colorado to meet my dad. Meeting my father was an unexpected blessing and a beautiful gift from my heavenly Father just when He knew I needed it. His timing is always perfect.

My dad is a kind and generous man, quiet and reserved but with a heart full of warmth. He is an amazing patriot who served our country well. I am quite proud of him. He is an adventurer as well. I guess I know where I get it from now. We spent several days getting to know each other, and his words were like honey to my soul. He shared that after learning more about me— doing research and even listening to my podcast—he felt that any father would be proud to call me his daughter. Hearing those words, words I had longed to hear my whole life, was the best gift I could have imagined.

Yet, as incredible as it was to hear those words, I realized how much more important it is to hear from my heavenly Father, *"Well done, good and faithful servant"* (NIV). Matthew 25:23 resonates deeply in my heart because it captures the ultimate affirmation I long for. I don't have to do anything to obtain His love—I already have it. I am loved without having to perform, yet I strive to please my Father because of that love.

What made this meeting with my dad even more special was the fact that I went into it without any expectations. I didn't need anything from him; I just wanted to know him. And it was wonderful. He cooked for us, took me on a scenic tour of his beautiful community, and even took me on a date. I couldn't have asked for more. The simple things he did meant so much to me, not because they were extravagant, but because they were thoughtful. Several times, he noticed things I mentioned that I liked, and he was sure to bring them with him on the next visit. He was intentional. I loved it. Even as I sit here writing this, I am blown away by the fact that he is in my life.

His thoughtfulness reminded me so much of my heavenly Father. Just as my father listened to us, God listens to our requests, desires, and petitions. Philippians 4:6 teaches us, *Do not be anxious about anything, but in every situation, by prayer and petition, with thanksgiving, present your requests to God* (NIV). Though the answers may not always come in the timing we desire, God always answers. He cares about the things we care about, and this summer, He showed me that in so many ways. There were moments of sadness as I learned my father had lived just miles away from me when I was a very young girl; at times I caught myself imagining what it would have been like to have my father during my childhood. I believe God allowed me to experience transformation and reveal Himself to me before meeting my father in New Mexico so that I wouldn't let the enemy steal my gratitude for what God had done—how He used the pain and gave me purpose. Things might have turned out very differently if I hadn't gone through that experience before meeting my father.

As I reflect on this experience, I am reminded of Psalm 37:4, which says, *Take delight in the Lord, and He will give you the desires of your heart* (NIV). God has been so faithful, and this summer was a testament to His unending care and love for me. What a loving Father we serve! I continue to build a relationship with my earthly father, and I am more hopeful and excited than ever to do the work my heavenly Father has for me.

Throughout the summer, God revealed Himself in both small and huge ways—from granting us favor with parking spaces to displaying His majestic beauty in the mountains, rivers, and breathtaking landscapes as we traveled through the U.S. and Canada to orchestrating divine connections. When we look for God and pay attention, we can see Him everywhere. This summer has been a gift, restoring my soul in ways I can't even describe. It has renewed my excitement to serve God, serve others, and build stronger relationships with my family. I am so grateful.

In these past months, I've experienced a profound shift—a divine restoration. The summer journey had not only been about reconnecting with family and friends but also about seeing God's handiwork in ways I never imagined. From my time with my brother in Hobbs to meeting my dad in Colorado, God revealed the true beauty of restoration lies not just in mending brokenness but in transforming it into something glorious.

We all have experienced pain and heartache in some form. Perhaps it's the ache of a broken relationship, the sting of rejection, or the emptiness left by dreams unfulfilled. It can be easy to let these wounds define us, reacting as if we'll never fully recover or find peace. But God promises that what the enemy meant for harm, He will turn for good. As Romans 8:28 affirms, *And we know that in all things God works for the good of those who love Him, who have been called according to His purpose* (NIV).

God has shown me, time and again, that He uses our wounds to shape us into the women He created us to be. What the enemy meant to discourage me, God used to deepen my faith, broaden my purpose, and renew my heart. When I look back at the painful moments of my life, I now see them as the very stepping stones that led me closer to the person I am today.

Throughout the summer, God didn't just restore the relationships I thought had been lost forever; He restored my understanding of who I am in Him. As I spent time with my earthly father, I realized that my deepest longing was not just for earthly affirmation but for the approval of my heavenly Father. I am His daughter, chosen and loved, and that love is what truly sustains me.

So, I encourage you today: Look for the restoration God is working in your life. It may not come in the form you expect, and it may not happen on your timeline. But know this—God is always working behind the scenes, weaving a story of redemption that only He can tell. As you embrace your journey and trust His plan, He will transform your pain into purpose, your sorrow into joy, and your brokenness into restoration.

I've witnessed this transformation in my own life, and I know He is doing the same in yours. When we surrender our hurts and struggles to God, He takes them, heals them, and uses them for His glory. Trust Him with the details of your life because He is the master storyteller, and His plans for you are far greater than you could ever imagine.

What have you experienced? How has God used it in your life? This chapter is meant to encourage you to see the beauty in the details of your own story. Be encouraged, knowing that no matter the circumstances, God's love is constant, and His restorative power is limitless. He is faithful to restore everything the enemy has stolen. Your story is still being written, and it is a beautiful one.

Keep walking in faith, keep trusting in His promises, and watch as He unfolds His plan for your life—step by step, detail by detail. You are being restored, and His glory is being revealed in and through you.

Your pain is your purpose. God is restoring what the enemy has stolen, and the very things meant for your destruction, He will use for His glory. What a gift we have in our Father—the peace, joy, and love that only come from knowing Him intimately. There is nothing better. Jesus loves you, and so do I! Be blessed!

Heather R. Cockrell

Heather R. Cockrell was born and raised in South Carolina, but Birmingham, Alabama, became home when she relocated with her job over 25 years ago. There, she met her husband of 22 years, Duane; they have been blessed with three amazing children—Alex, Danielle, and Denise.

Though Heather has been in the corporate world for over 30 years, she discovered her true calling as a women's empowerment coach through serving in numerous women's ministries and pursuing ministry leadership training at Highlands College.

Heather is a coach and mentor with a passion for enabling women to discover and embrace their true God-given identity and empowering them to step into the unique calling that God created them to fulfill for such a time as this! Through this passion, God birthed Sister to Sister, which is Heather's one-on-one coaching and women of faith networking ministry.

You can find her and Sister to Sister on social media or at sistertosister.life.

True Identity, True Healing

By Heather R. Cockrell

Daughter. Employee. Wife. Mother. Adulterer. These labels defined my identity for the first four decades of my life.

I hadn't planned to be unfaithful to my husband. Who does? I had big hopes and dreams for our future together. I was a successful career woman with three healthy, amazing children and a successful, talented husband. He was the best person I knew—intelligent and funny. Stable and steady. I knew he'd be a good husband and father; being with him felt like being home. I adored him. We owned a beautiful home in a nice neighborhood—from the outside, we seemingly had it all together. Seven years into our marriage, it all came crashing down. How had I gotten to that point? To the end of potentially losing everything I had built—my marriage, my kids, and my home?

When I look back on the breakdown in my marriage, I recognize that it started even before we got married—in our dating years. They say opposites attract, and that was certainly the case for us. I'm spontaneous, have very little brain-mouth filter, and love jumping in and taking risks. He's logical, analytical, and definitely risk-averse.

He wasn't all that affectionate or communicative, and I was the exact opposite. I always verbalized everything I felt and thought about him, but he didn't do the same. This translated into me thinking that I loved him more than he loved me from the very beginning. And I knew I was a lot. "Extra," you might say. I knew he was a better person than me. He was more grounded. And while I had a trail of mistakes in adulthood, he seemed to have very few. I knew I didn't deserve him. I could live with being the one that loved him more. I really could. I was lucky to have him.

We had been dating for almost two years when I found out I was pregnant. I was 30 and was devastated at this turn of events. Most of my friends had been married for years and had already started their families. That was never my goal. I was focused on my career. A husband and a family were never high on my priority list. I was fine continuing to date and maybe moving in together at some point, but I didn't have plans beyond that. How could I have let this happen? I mean, seriously, who gets pregnant at THIRTY unintentionally??

I didn't know what to do, and I was panicking. In his true logical, analytical nature, he suggested we take two weeks apart to individually process the situation and figure out what we wanted to do.

After two weeks, we got back together, and I blurted out, "I want this baby—let's move in together."

He calmly said, "I want this baby—let's get married."

I loved him and was carrying his child—marrying him wasn't a hard sell. And so when I was five months pregnant with our son, we said, "I do."

I had never been so happy. I enjoyed so much of what was happening. Most of my pregnancy was good; we were creating a home together, decorating the nursery, and having baby showers thrown for us. This was my parent's first grandchild; they were ecstatic about becoming grandparents despite us being a bit out of order by getting pregnant before marriage.

Still, a nagging question surfaced from time to time in the back of my mind: *Had he really wanted to marry me, or was he just being honorable?* But I was happy, so I pushed it aside and moved on.

We adored our little boy. A few years later, we were ready to expand our family. We bought a bigger house, and I got pregnant again, but I had a miscarriage and lost our baby. About a year after we recovered from that loss, we started trying again and soon found out we were having twins!

While that was exactly what we wanted, we had no idea what was in store. Having three children under the age of five and no family close by to help was rough. Taking care of twins was really demanding. We barely remember their first year because we were so sleep-deprived. I was physically and mentally exhausted all the time from trying to take care of the kids and the house and working full time. And with three kids in daycare, we were financially strapped. I had nothing left at the end of the day and resisted any of my husband's attempts at intimacy—I just wanted to sleep. He resented me for leaving him at a physical deficit, and I resented him for resenting me because my best wasn't good enough!

Couldn't he see all that I was juggling? Couldn't he see all that I was accomplishing? Why was nothing I did good enough for him? I received no recognition for my efforts and no compliments on my outfits or career advancement. I needed to hear words that affirmed I was a good wife, a successful career woman, smart, capable, and desirable to my husband. I wanted to know that he DID want to be married to me and not someone else and be reassured I was all he ever wanted and needed in a wife. But those words never came. And I felt more and more unloved and unappreciated.

In my heart and mind, I answered that nagging question that had come up from time to time: *Did he marry me just because I was pregnant?* I was sure the answer was Yes.

Day after day and week after week, the resentment grew between us. I couldn't say anything without him getting defensive, and I'm sure he felt the same way. I felt alone and unloved. So, when someone else started paying attention to me—noticing all the effort I was making and complimenting me instead of taking me for granted—I fell into a sinful situation.

If I thought I was hiding the affair, I was wrong. I'm not sure I even attempted to cover my tracks all that much. I've often wondered if I wanted my husband to catch me so our marriage could be done and over with. I hated what I was doing, but my need to be loved, treasured, and appreciated had consumed me.

My husband found some emails, and his suspicions were confirmed. I was having an affair. But not just an affair with a random person that he didn't know. No, I was having an affair with my best friend's husband—someone we spent a lot of time with, went out to dinner with, invited to our home, and whose home we had visited together.

The day my husband found out began better than most. I had taken the day off from work and was heading to meet my mom and a friend who were in town visiting when my phone dinged with a text message from my husband. He said he knew about the affair. And that he had told my best friend. I started to shake. I thought I was going to throw up. What had I done? And what was I going to do?

I texted my mom to tell her I couldn't meet her, and I drove back home. I have no recollection of that drive. I think I was in shock.

I sat on the porch for hours, staring into space and trying to process the situation and figure out what to do. How would I pick up my kids from daycare and act like everything was normal? How would I cook dinner and bathe the kids with my husband standing right there? What was he going to say? Would he tell me to leave? Would he pack up the kids and leave me? I just wanted to get in my car and drive away. Far, far away from the damage and destruction I had caused.

By the grace of God, my husband didn't make me leave, and he didn't leave me. He didn't take my babies from me. We somehow made it through those first days and weeks. I answered his questions about how it all happened and what had happened, and I asked him to forgive me, and miraculously, he did. It was a major wake-up call for us both. We realized we each played a part in how we had gotten there. Thankfully, we both wanted to try and save our marriage and family. We had a lot of work to do but no idea where to start.

We tried counseling, but that didn't stick. We went to church a few times, but we had no real path forward to heal fully. We were trying, and we were grateful to still be together. We had good and bad days, successful vacations, and good times with the kids, but the root of the issues remained. The resentment was still there. And we did not invite God to be part of our healing.

The turning point for me came when I was riding in the car with my daddy. Due to his declining health, we had moved him close to us, and I was taking him to a doctor's appointment. He knew I was unhappy—it wasn't like I tried to hide it. I complained quite often to my family about it. But my daddy, in particular, had a front-row seat to my damaged marriage.

On the way home from the doctor's visit, my daddy asked if he could give me some marriage advice. Um, marriage advice was not something I necessarily wanted from my dad, nor did I think he was all that qualified to give it, quite honestly. He was born during the Depression, tough as nails, and thought women had their place in society (which was more on the barefoot and pregnant side than the corporate working woman side)—and he was pretty vocal about his opinions. Figuring I was going to hear his advice anyway, I reluctantly agreed to listen.

He told me he knew my husband didn't do or say everything I wanted him to but reminded me that he was a good man and a good father. He called attention to the fact that my husband provided well for our family, wasn't out drinking and coming home late, and loved and cared for me and our children. My dad suggested that I focus on the good things my husband WAS doing and not what he WASN'T doing. He also suggested that I focus on doing more for my husband rather than focusing on what he was or wasn't doing for me.

While I wanted to full-on eye roll my daddy because what I heard was that I was selfish and our marital problems were ALL my fault, the seeds that he planted that day began to take root. My husband *was* a good man, and he did all those things that my daddy said he did. Literally everyone I knew liked him. Did I see him for who he was, or was something skewed within me? I didn't switch gears overnight, but I started focusing more on the positive things my husband was doing and expressing gratitude for them. I also began doing little things for my husband to make his life easier and happier.

Slowly, over time, my perspective began to change. My heart began to soften, and I started falling in love again. My husband saw the change and started responding to it. We knew it was going to take a lot of work. We also understood that to heal and save our marriage fully, we had to move God from being an outlier in our lives—the One we prayed to before meals or said a quick prayer to at night—and instead invite Him to reside at the very center of our lives and our kids' lives.

> This is what the Lord says... "You will seek me and find me when you seek me with all your heart" (Jeremiah 29:10, 13 NIV).

With that intent, we began searching for a church home, which was not an easy task as my husband and I both had a lot of church hurt from our childhoods and were very skeptical about getting involved in a church again. But on one of those Sunday mornings when we were trying out a new church, I was sitting in the back row up in the rafters when I had a full-on Holy Spirit encounter.

You see, even though my marriage was starting to heal, and I had confessed my sin and had been forgiven by my heavenly Father, my husband, and (if you can believe it) my best friend, I was still carrying the weight of guilt and shame. Early on, after my husband and my friend found out about the affair, as I drove to work or took the kids to school, I was literally shocked

Restoration: God Brings Beauty from Ashes

that there wasn't a flashing neon billboard proclaiming "Heather is an adulterer!" around every corner. It was never far from my thoughts. I carried it around like a big scarlet letter "A" on my chest. I walked in such shame ALL the time. I carried it around on my shoulders, and it was a very heavy burden, let me tell you. I walked through the days with my head down, trying to hide and hoping no one noticed the sin that seemed to cover me like a shroud everywhere I went. I just knew everyone could see it on me.

As I sat in the back of that church that Sunday morning, the Holy Spirit revealed He wanted a relationship with me. I don't remember what the message was about or even who gave it, but I do remember the speaker saying, "Are you feeling burdened? Are you tired of carrying the weight of sin all by yourself? You don't have to. You weren't meant to." As I listened, chains broke off me. I had been so very weary and burdened, but I felt the weight of my sin fall off in an instant. The pastor reminded me that my Lord and Savior had died to separate me from my sin and make me pure. My true healing began in that moment. I started to hear my heavenly Father's voice tell me who I was instead of the voice of the enemy placing labels on me.

Trust in the Lord with all of your heart and lean not on your own understanding; in all your ways submit to Him, and He will make your paths straight (Proverbs 3:5-6 NIV).

I began to realize that I had been putting a responsibility on my husband that he wasn't equipped or even created to provide. I had been looking to him for confirmation of who I am and what I'm worth. I now know that confirmation comes ONLY from my heavenly Father. *He* says who I am— not my sin, not my shame, and not my husband.

That realization altered the course of my life, my marriage, and my family. Not only did I fall in love with my husband again, I grew to love him more than I did when I married him. We've now been married 22 years. On our 20th wedding anniversary, in the presence of God, friends, and family, and with our three beautiful children standing beside us, we renewed our wedding vows on a beach in Aruba, where we went on our honeymoon.

Our marriage isn't perfect. We are still working on it and us, but we know it will continue to get better and better because we are now centered on godly principles. I pray every day to be the wife and mother He has called me to be. Not only did He save my marriage and my family, but He has redeemed my sin for His glory; now, I am using those hard lessons I learned to help other women walk in their true identity in Christ.

I never knew this kind of peace and joy was even possible, and I'm so incredibly thankful for it each and every day. My Father has forgiven me; His Son has redeemed me and delivered me from a life of guilt, stress, and shame; and He has turned my feelings of being unseen, unloved, and unappreciated into a life of love, peace, joy, contentment, and fulfillment. God has shown me that having an identity in Him changes everything—not only how we see ourselves but also how we walk through life and serve Him in every season. The labels the world puts on us do not define us. The labels we put on ourselves do not define us. I no longer live under the erroneous labels I carried for 40 years. I now walk in the TRUE identity that my Father has given me.

Who does He say that I am?

I am His daughter. I am a mother. I am a leader. I am a servant. I am a coach. I am a warrior. I am a shepherdess. I am a gardener for His kingdom.

Will you allow Him to define you, too?

"Blessed is she who has believed that the Lord would fulfill his promises to her!" (Luke 1:45 NIV).

Marriage Restoration *Is* Possible

By Kimberly Anne Kahn

> *And the two shall become one flesh'; so then they are no longer two, but one flesh* (Mark 10:8 NKJV).

God created marriage to be sacred, precious, and pure. In marriage, two separate identities become one as a permanent covenant relationship is established. However, many couples experience hardships during marriage that leave them wondering if restoration is possible. By inviting God into our brokenness, we can harness transformational faith to fill us with hope, inspiration, and wisdom as we witness God's healing power at work.

My husband and I got married in April. In all his goodness, my husband wanted me to have my dream wedding. We found the perfect venue, set on several acres of land with a beautiful white barn surrounded by lakes on both sides and even a few cows. I knew when we walked into the barn and saw crystal chandeliers hanging from the ceiling that this was the place. It was stunning! Our wedding was truly a dream! Our honeymoon was the best seven days we ever spent together.

To my surprise, things quickly changed after we returned from our honeymoon. We began to argue over the littlest things that we usually could have shrugged off. The transition of moving in together, readjusting the house to fit his belongings, and trying to introduce his two cats to my three was overwhelming. So it was understandable that we'd have some tensions as we united into one home. However, the arguing didn't end; it became

Restoration: God Brings Beauty from Ashes

worse. The fighting became hurtful as we pointed fingers at one another. Lies crept in, and trust began to fade. Our marriage was being destroyed by triggers from the wounds we had from childhood. The more we fought, the further we moved God from the center of our marriage. It became so bad that after five weeks of marriage, my husband left, saying he wanted a divorce.

Alone in my empty home, I sat and cried. I prayed for God to give me direction, and something within me told me that God wasn't done with our marriage. The Lord said, "Don't give up." I believed the Lord spoke to my husband's heart, giving him comfort, love, and hope not to give up either.

I reached out to my husband, asking for forgiveness for contributing to the fighting, and he, too, asked for forgiveness. In that moment, we both experienced the profound power of forgiveness. Forgiving one another allowed God to begin working in us to heal our hearts from our past, allowing us to move forward and rebuild our relationship.

Over time, the Lord has softened our hearts through intensive marriage counseling. He's restoring the broken pieces of the past and making us whole in Christ as we continue to put Him in the center of ourselves and the relationship. We are embracing the healing journey as Christ navigates. The Bible says,

For nothing will be impossible with God *(Luke 1:37 ESV).*

God desires to heal every broken marriage, and He will if both partners willingly yield to and humble themselves before Him and each other.

Most importantly, God wants you to come to Him with a willing heart and do as He instructs. If you are seeking restoration in your marriage, you must first seek God with your whole heart and obediently follow His path as He holds you close and guides you. Trust His timing and His direction.

If you're facing struggles in your relationship, remember these key principles:

- Seek God first and keep Him at the center of your relationship. God is our life source in every situation we come against.

  But seek first his kingdom and his righteousness, and all these things will be given to you as well (Matthew 6:33 NIV).

- Pray for your spouse daily, no matter the current circumstance.

  I urge, then...that petitions, prayers, intercession and thanksgiving be made for all people...that we may live peaceful and quiet lives in all godliness and holiness (1 Timothy 2:1-2 NIV).

- Practice forgiveness, remembering that both you and your spouse are God's masterpieces who deserve respect and love.

  Bearing with each other and forgiving one another if any of you has a complaint against another, even as Christ forgave you, so you must also do (Colossians 3:13 NKJV)

  Let love be without hypocrisy. Abhor what is evil. Cling to what is good (Romans 12:9 NKJV).

- Surround yourself with godly counsel.

  The way of a fool is right in his own eyes, But he who heeds counsel is wise (Proverbs 12:15 NKJV).

God loves marriage. He desires and is able to redeem and restore marriages as we submit to and honor Him and each other. Trust in His timing. Believe He is working for you. And allow His love to restore your marriage.

. . . .

Jennifer L. Cooper

Jennifer Cooper is a mother of two: a grown daughter and a teenage son. She loves her home to be filled with laughter from them and their friends. They keep her active, as they regularly work out together and navigate life's daily challenges. Together, they also "share" a dog and a cat.

Jennifer enjoys trying new things and looks forward to exploring new foods, experiences, and traveling. Recently, she discovered she loves paddleboarding and is returning to school to earn her master's degree. She regularly worships and serves in her neighborhood church, believing every day presents an opportunity to serve, love, and laugh with others.

When she's not working as an art director in marketing, doing schoolwork, or exercising, Jennifer is committed to getting 7 to 9 hours of sleep each night without interruptions from needing to use the bathroom or sweating before sunrise.

Becoming a Woman of God

By Jennifer L. Cooper

There are many things I want to know when I die. The questions that most often swirl around my head center on one word: "Why?" I'm fascinated by God's ways, such as Him putting people in our path for a certain season or a reason that wasn't evident at the time, so I'm sure I'll ask Him how many times I crossed someone's path before our lives actually intersected. And I will have lighter questions like, "Where and how did I lose that earring? How many times was it in plain view? Did I walk past it without seeing it?"

Now faith is confidence in what we hope for and assurance about what we do not see (Hebrews 11:1 NIV).

I don't know about you, but by nature, I have very limited vision. I can barely see the tree right in front of me, let alone the forest. But I've learned we each have a choice: we can choose to walk in faith, putting our trust in God to lead the way, or we can walk by sight—making decisions based on logical reasoning, validated feelings, and what we think we are seeing. God is not kidding when He declares, *"For my thoughts are not your thoughts, neither are your ways my ways"* (Isaiah 55:8-9 NIV).

From middle school until well after college graduation, my dad was the meat market manager at the largest grocery retailer in our small town, which is also where I held my first job. Once, my dad shared with me that one of the vendors told him, "If you're not careful, your daughter will become a woman of the world." In my own naiveté, I mistakenly took this as a compliment. I visualized a woman who traveled the world, accomplished great things, and knew what she wanted. It took me another decade to discern what a "woman of the world" really meant and that I'd like to learn more about being a "woman of God."

> We also glory in our sufferings, because we know that suffering produces perseverance; perseverance, character; and character, hope (Romans 5:3-5 NIV).

> To appoint unto them that mourn in Zion, to give unto them beauty for ashes, the oil of joy for mourning, the garment of praise for the spirit of heaviness; that they might be called trees of righteousness, the planting of the Lord, that he might be glorified (Isaiah 61:3 KJV).

Beauty for ashes. The first time I heard this scripture, the words seemed to leap off the page. Over twenty years ago, on Tuesday nights, 10-15 ladies, mostly young moms, would gather in a cozy family room. I was probably one of the "older" moms, and I was still new to walking in faith instead of walking by sight.

Every week, different women would bring desserts to the Beth Moore video Bible study at my friend's home. Beth Moore's humor and Texas accent made it easy for me to stay engaged. She had a way of bringing God's Word to life for me that nobody had ever done before. She applied God's Word and His principles to her everyday walk and talk. Often, it felt like we were transported to other lands. Beth would say, "Now, over here..." and point to scripture. Or "And over there..." pointing out more scripture and historical context, making it easy to apply the text to everyday life.

After the video, we'd review our homework assignment from the prior week. The Bible study was about more than gaining knowledge. The multiple pages of thought-provoking questions challenged us to grow in our faith as we learned to relate God's Word to our everyday lives. Our discussions illuminated opportunities to use God's teachings in our current walk and our walks yet to come, instilling a sense of hope and optimism for our personal growth.

I will forever be grateful for those Bible studies in my sweet friend's home. She had three young children, but she sacrificed one night a week for us when she could have chosen to do so many other things—such as nothing at all—a true luxury in any mom's life, especially one with several children.

I didn't fully understand that these weekly meetings were healing me from past hurts, preparing me for future struggles, and growing me as a woman of God. But God knew. The ladies in the group became an integral part of my life—helping, encouraging, supporting, and pointing me in the right direction when crises inevitably arose.

Just as the mountains surround Jerusalem, so the Lord's wraparound presence surrounds his people, protecting them now and forever (Psalm 125:2 TPT).

When I was two, my mom and my biological dad separated. They were officially divorced by the time I was four, and my mom and I moved from New Jersey to my mom's hometown in Florida. I was an only child and a latchkey kid. We didn't have much of a routine, and we moved a lot. There were no pep talks to prepare me for a new place or school. Instead, my mom would pick me up from whatever friend or family member I was visiting, and we'd go to a new place where I'd find my belongings. The following day, she'd drive me to my new school, dropping me off at the front door and leaving me to find my way. There weren't any school tours, orientations, or teacher meet-and-greets.

Mom remarried when I was almost nine. That was when my Aunt Linda, my new stepdad's sister, and her family came into my life. Aunt Linda had two children—one was the same age as me, and the other was younger. Aunt Linda and her children prayed together before meals and at bedtime, which was all new to me.

Shortly after Mom remarried, we settled down, and life seemed more stable. I excelled academically and graduated from high school with many of the same kids I had gone to 5th grade with. However, life at home was filled with strains that can accompany a step-parent family dynamic.

Growing up, our family had an *Upper Room* or *Our Daily Bread* devotional to peruse. Ironically, my mom and aunt kept these monthly publications on a table beside the toilet. I guess they both figured the location would increase the possibility of them being read; after all, in there, we were a trapped audience with nowhere to go—and we didn't have cell phones.

But the fruit of the Spirit is love, joy, peace, forbearance, kindness, goodness, faithfulness, gentleness and self-control. Against such things there is no law (Galatians 5:22-23 NIV).

The summer before I was to start my first year away at college, a mole my mom had on the bottom of her foot since childhood started bleeding and wouldn't heal. This was in the late 80s. She rationalized it didn't heal because she often walked barefoot in our backyard. (This was well before the A, B, C, D warning signs for melanoma—Asymmetrical, Border, Color, Diameter.) None of us knew what was headed our way.

On a hot and stormy summer afternoon, my mom went to a well-known dermatologist for a biopsy. A few days after the biopsy, we learned that the simple mole she'd had since childhood was the beginning of stage-4 melanoma cancer.

> *If I go up to the heavens, you are there; if I make my bed in the depths,*
> *you are there. If I rise on the wings of the dawn, if I settle on the far side*
> *of the sea, even there your hand will guide me, your right hand will*
> *hold me fast* (Psalm 139:8-10 NIV).

We were entering into uncertain territory. My mom was 42, I was 18. I wasn't sure how this new season would play out, and I still didn't know much about God or His Word. I certainly didn't understand the Jesus connection yet. All my years growing up, my mom would tell me how much she loved me. She would expand on the depth of her love by saying, "I love you so much, I would die for you." I probably ignored, dismissed, or rolled my eyes when she'd say this. Additionally, she'd tell me I didn't belong to her. *Excuse me?* Instead, she would say she was merely the vessel I passed through. I only knew what she meant much later in life when I had my own children.

> *"Before I formed you in the womb, I knew you, before you were born, I*
> *set you apart"* (Jeremiah 1:5 NIV).

For the next seven years, we tried to live life as normally as possible. For the first four years, I was often away at college. After graduating, I returned home for a year, moved out for a year, and then was married soon after. All this time, my mom endured treatments, surgeries, and experimental therapies, all with many resulting side effects, including her hair falling out. I accompanied her to several specialist appointments and a weekly support group. Members of the group would not return, and we would later learn that they had passed. I always felt like the "big bad wolf" was lurking behind the door, just waiting for my mom.

There was a lot of holding my breath and walking on eggshells until my mom passed away. She died about two months after my first wedding anniversary—a month after my 25th birthday. My birthday was the last time she went out of the house for fun.

In her final two weeks, my mom was admitted to a hospital in a nearby city. I stayed by her side night and day. When her doctor left the room after a visit, I followed behind and stopped him in the corridor. "How much time are we looking at?"

Without skipping a beat, looking straight into my eyes, he said, "Two weeks would be asking a lot."

I had never known what "having your heart ripped out" meant until that moment. Exactly two weeks later, my mom, the ever-constant, loving force of my life, was gone forever.

To say I had "anger" or "absolute rage" toward God doesn't adequately describe how I felt. He had ripped my mom from me. She was my everything, my source of comfort and unconditional love, someone I spoke to at least four to five times a day.

I turned away from God, but honestly, how is it possible to turn away from someone I was never facing in the first place? *Did this happen because I never truly sought God but instead looked within to the throne of my own heart?* For the next 60 or maybe 90 days, I felt like I was free-falling, sliding ever faster down a greasy slope to the bottom. I began to understand how people can migrate to excessive drinking or drug use, acts of infidelity, eating disorders, or other addictions to numb or distract from the pain. I wanted the pain to stop. Somehow, by the grace of God, I didn't succumb to any of those behaviors, but I could sense the pulling. Everything was difficult. It was like God was saying, "Okay, you want to do this by yourself?" and further motioning to me to "go right ahead."

The simplest of tasks became nearly impossible. I'll spare you the many paragraphs it would take to share all the ways it became difficult; suffice it to say that every step and breath was heavy. Maybe you've experienced this yourself.

Knowing God as I do now, and being a parent myself, I know He wasn't far from me, but it sure felt that way.

"My grace is sufficient for you" (2 Corinthians 12:9 NIV).

Then, one day, I came home to an empty house after a very long, miserable day at work. I dropped to my knees and looked up.

"I give up. I can't do this by myself. I don't know how this works, but I can't do this by myself anymore."

From that afternoon, one step at a time, life started changing. I went back to school, and God put people on my path to walk with me through my pain. My husband and I moved from my hometown to another city. Ironically, we moved into a neighborhood just a few houses down from where my mom spent time with her high school friends. There, we soon found a church, a home, and a community, and I started growing in my walk with the Lord as I learned the power of forgiveness and that God's grace is greater than all our sins. The ladies from my friend's Beth Moore Bible study helped me.

You will again have compassion on us; you will tread our sins underfoot and hurl all our iniquities into the depths of the sea (Micah 7:19 NIV).

At one point, God brought me to a devotional from 2020, a digital version of Our Daily Bread, the very same publication my aunt and mom would leave for us in the bathroom. In it was written, "Holocaust survivor Corrie ten Boom knew the importance of forgiveness. In her book *Tramp for the Lord,* she says her favorite mental picture was of forgiven sins thrown into the sea. 'When we confess our sins, God casts them into the deepest ocean, gone forever...I believe God then places a sign out there that says No Fishing Allowed.'" [1]

It's been said God is the great "Way Maker." He is in the habit of "making a way" where it looks like there isn't one. His answers often don't look like anything a resourceful girl like me could come up with. As someone who has been led and ruled by my own validated feelings and logical reasoning, I sensed He was saying, "You can handle this on your own, or you can do this My way and have a very different result. It's your choice."

My mom being diagnosed with cancer when I was 18 and dying when I was 25 was as tragic as all the grownups around me were saying at the time. However, I know without a doubt that had it not been for my mom dying, I would have never sought out the Lord. Before that, I didn't need Him. Or so I thought. I had my mom for comfort and guidance and my own grit and determination to depend on. Until I didn't. When my mom said she would die for me, she kind of did. It took the pain of losing her for me to finally be knocked to my knees and look up and look outside my own resources.

"Be still and know I am God" (Psalm 46:10 NIV).

Now, I look at my twenty-five-year-old daughter, knowing how crucial the ages of 18 to 25 can be. The trajectory of my own life could have been very different—for bad or for good. For a long time, I was a "woman of the world"—the very label the vendor at that grocery store warned my dad about so many years ago.

Becoming a "woman of God" doesn't mean our validated feelings and logical reasoning don't have their place in our lives—it simply means that we correctly prioritize those things below God. Your vice may be your success, your kids' accomplishments, or your reputation. Whatever it is that threatens to pull you from God, please be aware of the danger of putting

Restoration: God Brings Beauty from Ashes

your faith in anything but God. When we put anything ahead of God, and those things are taken away or threatened—which will inevitably happen—we can lose our hope because we placed our hope in the wrong things all along.

I can't say that I understand God completely, nor would I be able to debate you on all the theologies. But I do know and love God. And I know He knows and loves me. And somewhere, somehow, by His grace alone, I was able to receive Him and His plan for me. And that's really all that matters.

I don't have to know all the answers.

You don't have to know all the answers.

We only need to be willing to surrender to Him, His will, and His ways. Trust Him. He is willing and able to exchange all the ashes this world has to offer for a beauty that He will reveal when we walk in faith and not by sight as a woman of God.

---

[1] Pye, Amy Boucher. "No Fishing Allowed." Posted August 23, 2020." Our Daily Bread. https://www.odbm.org/devotionals/devotional-category/no-fishing-allowed

Karla Avielle

Karla Avielle is an actress, teacher, and filmmaker living in Spokane, Washington.

Karla studied acting at The American Academy of Dramatic Arts in Los Angeles, California, and has an Elementary Education Degree with an endorsement in Reading.

Karla is a professional actor with numerous credits in film, television, and theater. In 2022, Karla won the award for "Best Actress" at the Great Lakes Christian Film Festival for her starring role as Angela Carmichael in the feature film *The Text*.

In 2019, she and her team produced *Why She Smiles*, a moving documentary about a faith-filled young woman with a rare, terminal disease. The film won numerous awards and was picked up for distribution by Bridgestone Multimedia Group. Karla is a born storyteller.

Karla has three grown children whom she absolutely adores. She is teaching once again and is currently working on her memoir. Karla is thrilled to share part of her story in *Restoration: God Brings Beauty from Ashes*.

The Naming of Karla Jean

By Karla Avielle

"In every story, in every life, there are moments of death that take away our name, and rename us strangers, orphans, or widows. At the moment of being unnamed, we are thrown into our story." [1]

If you look at the back of a tapestry, you will see a mess of colors and threads intersecting with no apparent rhyme or reason. But upon turning the tapestry over, a splendid, cohesive piece of artwork is revealed, and it is clear that every thread was meticulously placed to create the beautifully finished tapestry.

One of my mother's favorite stories was that of a young woman who visited a weaver's school and saw students making beautiful patterns. The young woman asked, "When you make a mistake, must you cut it out and start from the beginning?"

A student answered, "No. Our teacher is such a great artist that when we make a mistake, he uses it to improve the beauty of the pattern."

As she told the story, my mother would explain, "That is what God does with our mistakes and sorrow. He can use them to make the pattern of our lives more beautiful." That went along with one of her favorite metaphors: "My life is a tapestry. The colorful and sometimes dark threads are woven from the people and experiences that have made me who I am."

I learned to fear my father at an early age. I have one memory of being left alone with him when I was about six years old. Mom prepared me for her absence by gushing, "It will be so much fun! You'll go out to ice cream and to the park! It will be just the two of you!"

My little-girl heart got so excited imagining all the fun we'd have. We would hold hands as we walked through the park, eating our ice cream. He would push me on the swings! Maybe he would even call me his little Pixie Princess!! I allowed my heart to hope.

My mother left the next day, and I waited expectantly for my dad to announce our fun plans. I don't remember what I did that set him off. Whatever it was enraged him. In an instant, he transformed into a huffing, puffing, red-faced monster. He grabbed me, put me over his knee, and began spanking me, striking my bottom with his open hand repeatedly. I screamed and cried, which only enraged him more. When I fell silent, he finally stopped. He barked at me, "Go stand with your nose in the corner!"

I stood there, nose pressed into the corner, heartbroken and terrorized and sobbing uncontrollably. He bellowed, "Stop that crying, or I'll give you something more to cry about!!"

My shoulders shook as I stood there devastated. Somehow, I had ruined everything. I was a bad girl. I vowed that I would never do anything to make him angry again. I would do whatever it took to make him love me so he wouldn't want to hurt me. I forced the terror deep inside and built a wall around it so it wouldn't escape and overwhelm me.

The next day, my father knelt in front of me and said, "I'm sorry I lost my temper with you yesterday. I didn't mean it."

I wanted his love so much that even this tiny crumb of guilt-induced tenderness caused my heart to melt.

He continued, "I bought you something! He held out his gift. It was a yellow-haired rag doll wearing a beautiful dress and a little yellow hat. I gasped with delight and reached for her, but he held her back, "Don't tell your mom that I got so angry with you, ok? It will be our little secret."

I took the yellow-haired bribe and ran to my room thinking, *Maybe he does love me!*

As mom was getting me ready for a bath, she noticed the bruises and welts all over my back and bottom and gasped, "What happened?!"

I didn't answer. I couldn't tell the secret, or Daddy would take my doll away. Even worse, he might get angry and hit me again!

"Karla, did your dad do this?"

I didn't say it out loud, but my tears told the secret. She knew. And she never left me alone with him again.

All my life I have ached with longing for the love of my father. My relationship with my dad was mainly spent trying to elicit any love or affection from him—the lack of which became the deepest wound that subconsciously propelled every choice I made in life.

My mother tried to compensate for my dad, lavishing love and encouragement on me. She often told me the story of my miraculous birth.

"Once upon a time, there was a mommy and a daddy who wanted to have a baby more than anything. But their dream of having a child wasn't coming true. The momma knew that with God, all things are possible. So, one Sunday she went to church and had the pastor pray that she would have a baby. 'You will have a baby in June!' the pastor said. And YOU were born on June 5th! You were our miracle baby! Always remember that you are special, Karla. God has a beautiful plan for your life!"

I am wanted; I am special; I am loved. That was what I told myself each time my father's rejection caused my heart to break. That was my identity. Until it wasn't.

Here is how I discovered the true story of me.

A year after my mother passed away from cancer, my childhood neighbor and friend came to town, and we agreed to meet for dinner. Brent offered his condolences on the death of my mom. "I'm so sorry about your mom, Karla. I know how close you two were. My dad died of cancer four years ago."

I replied, "Mom was my best friend. She was the one person on this earth who knew me completely and still loved me. We told each other everything. I miss her every day."

Then Brent said something that changed my past and my future simultaneously. "You know, my older brothers were pretty convinced that your mom and my dad had a thing going on."

Although this news completely blindsided me, it was suddenly as if a movie played in slow motion before my eyes. Memories, pieces of conversations between my mom and me, my sisters teasing me about the "milkman bringing me," and my mother's confession about having an affair all seemed to merge into a bizarre Lifetime movie. And somehow, I just knew. I put my head in my hands, took a deep breath, and said, "Brent, I think you're my brother."

Weeks later, when the DNA test confirmed that my dad was not my biological father and Brent's dad was my true father, I was devastated.

My relationship with my mom had been built on trust, openness, love, and admiration. She was my safe place, my refuge. And now, the most sacred relationship, the one I had defined myself by, was a lie. I had learned to put a protective wall around my heart with my dad, but I loved and trusted my mother so completely that there was not an inch of a protective wall between my heart and hers. And for an unwalled heart, betrayal is excruciatingly painful.

A panic-inducing guilt engulfed me as I thought that maybe keeping the secret of "me" all those years was what caused the intestinal cancer that took my mom's life. *Did the secret of "me" kill my own mother?*

I became unnamed in an instant. I lost my identity. My view of myself changed. I was not the gift from God. I was not special. My miracle baby birth story was just a lie to cover up my mother's affair. I not only lost my name but had now renamed myself my mother's killer. The waves of panic continued as I now realized that the heartbreak I had endured all those years as I tried to make my father love me was for nothing. HE WAS NOT EVEN MY FATHER.

All the while, my real father had lived just eight houses down the street. But now, he was dead. And with his death, any chance of a loving embrace, any chance of looking into his eyes and seeing myself there, and any chance of being wrapped in a warm and loving embrace by my father were all stripped away. My mother's secret-keeping took two priceless gifts from me—the gift of father and a truthful identity. My mother had kept from me what I needed to know more than anything else: Who I am, where I came from, and how I am just...like...him—the father I never knew.

I was angry at my mother, but I was furious with God. *Why God? WHY was it so important that I find out the truth?* Over time, I understood. God knew that knowing the truth about my earthly father's identity would send me on a journey of healing with my heavenly Father. It was the most important journey I would ever take.

According to The Fatherless Daughter Project[2], you can become a fatherless daughter through the physical death of your father, your parent's divorce, abandonment, addiction, verbal or physical abuse, or through the emotional unavailability of a father who lives with you but is not concerned or invested in you. At age 59, I discovered I was a "fatherless daughter." I began to understand that my lack of boundaries, emotional numbing, relationship troubles, and the constant battle with feeling unworthy of love are all common struggles for fatherless daughters.

I didn't know how to receive love from God—I could read about it, talk about it, and even preach about it, but I could never fully accept it. I had no background knowledge from my relationship with my dad to draw from. My picture of Father God was intertwined with my view of my earthly father. I had projected the character flaws of my dad onto God. How could I love or receive love from a God I perceived to be like the angry, unavailable, and abusive father I had grown up seeing?

The first step in my healing journey was to go to counseling to learn how to allow myself to fully grieve the loss of a tender word or touch from my father. I deeply mourned the fact that my dad never picked me up to hug me, reached for my hand as we walked, looked at me with adoration, wiped away a tear, or comforted my hurting heart. As I allowed myself to name my wounds and lay them in the lap of my Abba—my Daddy, Poppa, my all-loving Father God—I was able to picture my Father God weeping with me.

I spent time each morning writing in my journal and pouring my heart out to God, allowing Him to tear down the walls that kept me from genuinely loving and seeing Him for who He is. I clung to Isaiah 49:16, *See, I have engraved you on the palms of my hands; your walls are ever before me* (NIV).

As I spent time with God, imploring Him to teach me about Himself as my loving Father, the picture I had in my mind of what the love of a father looks like changed. And as I drew near to my Abba, the walls that surrounded my heart fell away. I also recognized and forgave myself for trying to find love in the arms and beds of men offering me the "false father." I discovered I had been looking for the love of my Abba. I relaxed in His love as He drew me to Himself with loving kindness.

> The Lord appeared to us in the past. He said, "I have loved you with a love that lasts forever. I have kept on loving you with a kindness that never fails" (Jeremiah 31:3 NIRV).

Restoration: God Brings Beauty from Ashes

Knowing the truth allowed me to see my dad in a different light. Every time he looked at me, instead of seeing his "Pixie Princess," he must have seen a painful "Pixie Reminder" of my mother's betrayal. In his later years, he gave me a rare glimpse of his childhood. "My mom believed children should be seen and not heard," he said. "There were no hugs, no being told, 'I love you.' It got a bit lonely."

In that moment, I pictured my dad as a little boy longing for love and affection. It did not excuse his behavior, but it did allow compassion to fill my heart.

I forgave my mother as well. She, too, was a fatherless daughter. She was the child of an alcoholic father who had suddenly died when she was 10 years old. I realized that my mother had given me the gift of identity—the gift of Father—when she taught me about Jesus. She knew that my Abba's love would never leave me. She had full confidence that the Master Weaver would make something beautiful of my life.

My Abba journey has shown me my Father's heart. He is the Father who will never leave me or forsake me (Deuteronomy 31:6-8), the Abba who longs to quiet me with his love and rejoice over me with singing (Zephaniah 3:17), and the Father who is close to the brokenhearted and saves the crushed in spirit (Psalm 34:18) In a way, we are all fatherless daughters—searching to fill a void that only He can fill. But the truth is none of us are Fatherless daughters—we are all treasured daughters of the one, true Father who will go to any length to FIND us, LOVE us, and bring us HOME.

Our stories are never just for ourselves. My story is for ALL who feel they are a fatherless daughter. All who ache with longing hearts for the love their earthly father was never able to give. It is for the abandoned, the abused, the ashamed, and the invisible daughter. It is for the women seeking love in all the wrong places, arms, and faces as they experience the creeping numbness that protects them from the pain of a shattered heart. My story is for the daughter who is simply longing to be truly seen, loved, and accepted just as she is. Abba has an invitation for each of us: *"Come to me, all who are tired and are carrying heavy loads. I will give you rest"* (Matthew 11:28 NIRV).

Amid my Abba journey, my second marriage, so full of passion and promise, burned to the ground, leaving me mourning with a pile of gray soot with which to paint my face. The death of a marriage is nothing less than heart-wrenching, disorienting, doubt-producing torture. But because of my journey with God, by the time my husband served me with divorce papers, God had mercifully allowed me to fully see and understand what I had been searching for all along.

I had been looking for my love story in the faces of men all my life. I learned that my love story was not to be found in the face of an earthly father, lover, husband, brother, or friend.

I finally understand deep in my soul. I am the daughter of my Abba, The Beloved. Together, we are the love story. My greatest shattering—that of being unnamed, became my greatest source of healing.

From the ashes of my torched name, Abba brought beauty and restoration.

First Samuel 7:12 tells of Samuel setting up an Ebenezer Stone, a stone of remembrance, to commemorate God's help in the Israelites' victory over the Philistines. Like Samuel, I wanted to commemorate my journey from recognizing that I am not a fatherless daughter but Abba's Child. I decided my Ebenezer Stone would be a new last name with deep significance. I chose the last name Avielle, which in Hebrew means God is my Father.

I am not defined by the ever-changing seasons around me, nor should I be guided only by the voices from within. Rather, my identity must continue to be found in the love of my Creator Himself. I am loved. Deeply loved. And when I let that love define who I am, I am suddenly free to be myself.

My name is Karla Jean Avielle, and I am my Father's Daughter.

---

[1] Dan Allender, To Be Told, (Waterbrook, 2005), 43
[2] Deanna Babul and Karin Smithson, *The Fatherless Daughter Project: Understanding Our Losses and Reclaiming Our Lives*, (Avery Publishing Group, 2016).

Restoring a Friendship

By Kimberly Ann Hobbs

Surviving a broken friendship can be brutal, but there is hope and guidance about how to restore a godly friendship; it begins by being obedient to God and His Word. If we desire true restoration in our broken friendship with someone, God will step in to help and guide us when we turn to Him. God does not want us to have bad feelings and hatred for any human being, let alone a friend. We can look to the scriptures about how to restore a friendship biblically.

One of the first ways God instructs us to repair damage in a relationship is through forgiveness. If we have a brother or a sister that we feel has issues with us or us with them, we need to go to that person in love. Pray to God over your friend and, as the Holy Spirit empowers you, let go of the hurt and allow the Holy Spirit to speak into your wound with His mercy. Ask Him to lead you back to the person you have an issue with for a restoration in friendship. Give your hurting heart to God, then go as He directs you.

> *"No matter how many times in one day your brother sins against you and says, 'I'm sorry, I am changing; forgive me,' you need to forgive him each and every time"* (Luke 17:4 TPT).

Even if your friend doesn't say they are sorry to you, the Bible instructs us to cover them in love. We are to forgive others, just as God forgave us with tremendous love while we were still in sin, even dying on the cross for us. We can rise above any situation as God has called us to by demonstrating true love—the same love Jesus showed us when we were undeserving.

Restoration: God Brings Beauty from Ashes

Go to Jesus and release your wound and your pain to Him.

Now, this is the goal: To live in harmony with one another and demonstrate affectionate love, sympathy, and kindness toward other believers. Let humility describe who you are as you dearly love one another. Never retaliate when someone treats you wrongly, nor insult those who insult you, but instead, respond by speaking a blessing over them—because a blessing is what God promised to give you. For the scriptures tell us: Whoever wants to embrace true life and find beauty in each day must stop speaking evil, hurtful words and never deceive in what they say. Always turn from what is wrong and cultivate what is good; eagerly pursue peace in every relationship, making it your prize. For the eyes of the Lord Yahweh rest upon the godly, and his heart responds to their prayers. But he turns his back on those who practice evil (1 Peter 3:8-12 TPT).

Remembering that not one of us is perfect can help us display love towards our friends. And love, as 1 Peter 4:8 teaches, *covers over a multitude of sins* (NIV).

> And do not grieve the Holy Spirit of God, with whom you were sealed for the day of redemption. Get rid of all bitterness, rage and anger, brawling and slander, along with every form of malice. Be kind and compassionate to one another, forgiving each other, just as Christ God forgave you (Ephesians 4:30-32 NIV).

I'm not saying that doing all this to restore a broken friendship is easy. On the contrary, it requires obedience, strength, and courage! You must be honest and willing to forgive and be forgiven. Even if it feels a bit awkward, try to reach out regularly and work on what brought you and your friend together to begin with. Put extra effort into your friendship and show them love and, if necessary, forgiveness, as God instructs us in His Word.

As you go through this process, remember to pray with an open spirit.

Reflect on "the good" from your friendship, sincerely apologize when necessary, give space if needed, and always remember that your actions speak louder than your words. As you graciously work toward restoration, stand strong against the temptation to get frustrated if they don't respond to you on your timeline. Trust God's timing and what His Word and voice instruct you to do, and then respond with your heart. Continue to pray— pray again and again and again, expressing your gratitude to God for placing your friend in your life. Know that God is with you and is moving in response to your obedient heart. Be vulnerable and trust that He will cover your earnest desire to reconcile with your friend if it is in His will.

Finally, if the friend does not choose reconciliation with you after all your attempts to honor God's Word towards her, trust that God may be removing that person from your life for a reason. God's ways are higher than our ways. He sees what we don't. Trust His process of restoration, knowing He is in control and His plan is always perfect.

. . . .

Gierda Senat

Gierda Senat is God-fearing and has the spirit of trust, grace, and gratitude. As a devoted mother, loving wife, and doting grandmother, Gierda's family is at the heart of her inspiration, fueling her creativity and nurturing her compassionate spirit.

Gierda's educational journey after high school began with a Unit Secretary Certification in 1991. She further honed her skills at Johnson & Wales University, earning an Associate's Degree in Hotel Management in 1998 and later expanded her expertise with a focus on Medical Billing and Coding from Everest Institute in 2009.

Gierda's professional experience includes six years in the hotel industry, dedicating over a decade to serving the Miami-Dade County community from 2000 to 2013.

Gierda is a genuine people person, always connecting with those around her. Her caring nature and belief in the power of community shine through in her life and work. Gierda encourages readers to trust in their own journeys, reminding them that questioning the why of life's challenges is unnecessary when you can choose to be thankful for the lessons learned along the way.

Gierda invites you to trust in God and the purpose and direction He has planned for your life!

From Rags to Riches

By Gierda Senat

BELIEVING...

This is the story of believing that all things are possible with almighty God at the forefront of your life. It's a journey of understanding that storms are temporary and God places us where we need to be for a reason. Never doubt the power of believing in God and in yourself.

> Jesus looked at them and said, "With man this is impossible, but not with God; all things are possible with God" (Mark 10:27 NIV).

I was born in Nassau, Bahamas, to a mother of Haitian descent who migrated to the Bahamas in search of a better life. Growing up, she worked hard selling candies, chips, and sodas in the 1970s. My parents saw an opportunity for a brighter future and sent me to the United States at the tender age of nine to live with my aunt, hoping to provide me with better educational prospects. Upon my arrival, my aunt already had six children, which made me the seventh. She supported our large household as a seamstress, while my father occasionally sent money to cover my expenses.

As I grew older, I felt a longing for a better life. At just 16, I decided it was time to carve my own path. I can remember the exact day I left my aunt's house. Standing in front of the door, I declared, "As of today, I'm an adult, and I will conduct myself as such." This moment marked a significant turning point in my life as I entered my independence and embarked on the responsibility that came with it.

Through every challenge and every triumph, I can honestly say that I held onto my faith. I never let go, even in the rough storms that life can sometimes bring!

> And we know that in all things God works for the good of those who love him, who have been called according to his purpose (Romans 8:28 NIV).

This truth has been my anchor, been with me through the storms, and led me to a life filled with so much hope and possibility. Believing in God and myself has opened doors I never imagined, and I committed to continue to live with bold faith at the forefront.

I WILL KEEP BELIEVING...

When I left home, I had no idea where I would live or what my future would hold. However, I quickly realized that God always places a shining light in our paths. For me, that light was Mr. Brown (now deceased), who found me a place to stay and picked me up every day for school and work.

I faced a lot of hard things, and I faced them head-on, but I was determined to pursue my education. I was told I would not graduate from high school, let alone attend college. Yet, I refused to let those words define me. I chased that dream even harder!!

During high school, I became pregnant at the age of eighteen with my first child. I attended school throughout my pregnancy, never missing a day.

The struggles were great, but my resolve was greater. At nineteen, while five months pregnant with my second child, I walked across the stage to receive my high school diploma. This achievement was a testament to what I always believed—that I could do all things through Christ who strengthens me (Philippians 4:13). It was a powerful reminder fueling my perseverance and faith to overcome even the most challenging obstacles.

In 1998, I graduated from Johnson and Wales University with an associate's degree in Hotel and Restaurant Management and a certificate in Unit Secretary. My education journey didn't stop there. I continued to pursue my dreams by enrolling at Everest Institute to study Billing and Coding. Every single step I took fueled my desire to change my life for the better, relying on Christ's strength to lead me through every storm.

I learned early on that perseverance is key. KEEP GOING!! Each setback became a setup for a comeback, and I embraced the notion that nothing is impossible with God. Jeremiah 29:11 reassured me along the way, *"For I know the plans I have for you," declares the Lord, "plans to prosper you and not to harm you, plans to give you hope and a future"* (NIV). This verse became my anchor, constantly reminding me that God has a purpose for my life, even when everything feels uncertain. I am grateful for every opportunity and every storm, as they have shaped me into the person I am today. I know it's due to my bold faith and determination that I continue to chase my dreams and trust all that God has for me.

After a very challenging ten-year marriage ended in failure, I welcomed my third child into the world, still holding on to the hope that I could make a meaningful difference in my life and the lives of others. I was determined to work on myself, my career, and my relationship with Christ. I knew God had a plan for me, even despite the trials I faced. I learned that trusting God and the process and remaining faithful during the storms is most important.

At that point in my life, God led me to Primerica, a financial firm dedicated to changing lives by providing financial education and opportunities.

In 2008, a friend introduced me to her coach, who presented a business opportunity that piqued my interest.

Although I didn't have the initial investment fee, I felt compelled to act. I made the difficult decision to sacrifice a bill to cover the cost of a background check, sensing in my spirit that my breakthrough was finally on the horizon. Something was about to shift! That took a lot of believing and faith.

That weekend, I attended the class as instructed, and there I met my knight in shining armor. Little did I know that this encounter would lead to a beautiful marriage that has now lasted for 15 years. This experience reaffirmed for me that everything happens for a reason; we must not interrupt God's plan for our lives—His intentions are always good.

In the years that followed, I devoted myself to personal growth and nurturing my family. I discovered that by putting God first and trusting His timing, I can transform my life. Each hard, long step I take brings me closer to the person I am meant to be.

Today, I stand firm in my faith and continue to pursue opportunities that align with my purpose, knowing and *believing* that with God, all things are possible.

My husband, Teshler Senat, and I tied the knot in August 2009, bringing together our two families. His daughters—Ruth and Cindy, and my three children—Shawn, Jeffrey, and Richelle, formed a blended family right from the start. As a bonus parent, I took on an active role in raising our children, and over the past six years, our family has continued to grow.

My husband made me a heartfelt promise, saying, "Baby, if you stand by me and keep our family united, I will ensure you're taken care of for the rest of your life." He has truly kept that promise, making it his mission to treat me like a queen every single day.

Together, we started our Primerica journey, helping other families plan their financial futures while working on our own! We went on to achieve the rank of Regional Vice President. However, our path was not without its challenges.

There's a popular saying that a breakdown often comes before a breakthrough. As we worked to build our financial powerhouse, we encountered our share of challenges, much like many entrepreneurs do, but we remained resilient throughout all of it!

In late 2013, I faced one of the saddest days of my life when my mother passed away. The grief was overwhelming; to add to the sorrow, my husband's sister also passed away that same year. We were heartbroken, but I held on to my faith even tighter, trusting that God had a greater plan for this, too. In the midst of this turmoil, I made the decision to move to Orlando to continue building our business.

We never gave up; because of this perseverance, God transformed our trials into triumphs. We were promoted to Senior Vice President, one of the most prestigious positions within Primerica. We have received several accolades since then, including becoming members of the company's esteemed "Wall of Fame."

> *And we know that in all things God works for the good of those who love him, who have been called according to his purpose* (Romans 8:28 NIV).

This beautiful scripture has been a guiding light in our life together, reaffirming that every setback can lead to a greater purpose. Our story stands as a testament to the power of faith and perseverance and that trusting and *believing* in God and following His path allows us to grow and reap the benefits of our obedience.

Today, we enjoy a wonderful lifestyle, experiencing the finest flavors from around the world, traveling extensively, and gaining knowledge in various fields, all while staying deeply connected to our families and communities. This reflects our faith in God, His plan for our lives, the amount of growth we've undertaken, the seeds we've planted before reaping the rewards, and our commitment to lift and support those in need.

It doesn't mean things are always easy, but it does mean that God will be right there with us. We are living proof that with God at the center of our lives, we can overcome anything and achieve remarkable things.

YOU CAN DO ANYTHING...

Having the right mindset and a strong work ethic is instrumental in achieving anything meaningful in life. However, it's also crucial to have a clear vision of your goals and to seek mentorship to help you reach those goals. The difference between knowing what to do and actually succeeding is having the courage to take action every day. Having God with us has provided guidance and strength, which has been essential to fulfilling our purpose. We also sought advice from those who have succeeded before us. As history shows, if we want to be successful, we should learn from those who have already achieved it. One saying that has guided us is by Jim Rohn, who said, "Discipline is the bridge between goals and accomplishment."

Throughout our journey, we've learned the importance of being consistent in our daily actions and sharing those skills with others. Zig Ziglar once said, "You can have everything you want in life if you help enough people get what they want." We live by that principle.

We've come to understand that "success is not a straight path, but a series of good habits practiced over time," as one of our business partners has observed from the beginning of our careers. We overcame challenges simply by consistently doing the right things, which set us apart from others. Our coaches, Charlemont & Marlene, have played a huge role in our success, and we are forever grateful for their support.

The world will try to place labels of disgrace or limitation on you, but it is ultimately up to you to believe otherwise. You can do anything you put your mind to! Just because you encounter trials and challenges does not mean that God's plan for your life isn't perfect. I grew up in a world where I was expected to be a statistic, but by trusting in God, *believing* God, and following His path for me, I have achieved incredible things alongside my husband.

Today, my husband and I are blessed to coach a large and diverse team, empowering our associates to reach new heights while helping our clients attain financial independence. This has taught me that the secret to success lies in doing your part, remaining steadfast, and pushing through the hard things, no matter how difficult or daunting they may seem.

You, too, can achieve your goals and dreams if you are willing to believe in yourself and in the plan God has for your life.

As Hebrews 13:16 reminds us, *Do not neglect to do good and to share what you have, for such sacrifices are pleasing to God* (RSV). This verse is a call to action, encouraging us to extend kindness and generosity to others. By uplifting those around us and sharing our resources, we not only honor God, but we also create a ripple effect of positivity in our communities. God has called you to be His light on this earth to others!

> *You are the light of the world. A city set on a hill cannot be hidden. Nor do men light a lamp and put it under a basket, but on a stand, and it gives light to all in the house. Let your light shine before men, so that they may see your good works and give glory to your Father who is in heaven* (Matthew 5:14-16 RSV).

We are called to be light and hope and inspiration, setting the path for others through our actions and words.

In a world filled with darkness, let your light shine so bright. Believe in the purpose God has for you and share that light with others. When you do, you will not only transform your own life, but you also will contribute to a brighter, more hopeful future for those around you.

God will be right there with you. No matter what. With faith, perseverance, and a commitment to doing good, you can overcome any label society may place on you and fulfill the incredible destiny God has designed for your life.

BELIEVE IN YOURSELF...

I am truly thrilled to share my story with women all over the world. To the beautiful woman reading this, I want to remind you never to stop believing. Believe in yourself, believe in a loving and beautiful God, and trust that He empowers you to achieve the impossible. Life may present you with challenges and storms, but I assure you, you will make it to the other side where victory awaits you.

When you face doubt, whether from others or from within, let it ignite a fire in you to pursue your dreams even more fiercely. If someone tells you that you can't accomplish something, use that as motivation to push harder, not to prove them wrong but to build a stronger sense of self and faith.

Hold tight to the truth of God's Word, which assures us that we can do far more than we can think or imagine through His power (Ephesians 3:20). Remember, our God is a God who never gives up on us, and He equips us to overcome any obstacle.

As you go through the storms in your life, hold tight to the belief that your struggles are not in vain. In moments of doubt, remind yourself of the promises in Scripture and believe you are capable of achieving your dreams.

So, dear friend, keep going, and never, ever give up. Your purpose is unique, and your story matters. Thank you for allowing me to share my journey with you, and I hope that one day, I will have the privilege of reading yours.

Together, let us uplift and encourage one another, celebrating the victories and embracing the challenges, knowing that we are never alone in this journey. Trust in God and trust in yourself, for the best is yet to come. Your story is still being written—for such a time as this!

You've got this!

> For if you remain silent at this time, relief and deliverance for the Jews will arise from another place, but you and your father's family will perish. And who knows but that you have come to your royal position for such a time as this? (Esther 4:14 NIV).

Carol Ann Whipkey

Carol Ann Whipkey is a best-selling published author. She is a Christ follower, and much of her retired time is devoted to serving in the Women World Leaders ministry as a writer and encourager through her uplifting, joyful spirit, guidance, and love for writing.

Carol has enjoyed her career as a beauty consultant and worked in an accounting position at UPS until retirement.

She is an artist trained by the world-renowned wood carver Joe Leanord, whose work is in the New York Museum of Art and Disney in Paris and the USA. As a hobby, Carol spends much of her time carving horses, birds, and other commissioned work that comes her way.

Carol lives in her own park-like setting on 52 acres in Thompson, Ohio, with her husband, Mel. She is the mother of four, which includes her first-born child Kimberly Hobbs of Women World Leaders, and is the grandmother of seven and great-grandmother of eight.

Lessons from the Ashes

By Carol Ann Whipkey

I thank God for the wonderful opportunity He provided to be part of this book. As I prayed and accepted the honor, I thought about the story I might share. Of course, my restoration story of the moment Christ came into my life was first to mind, but it didn't seem to be the one God was laying on my heart. My faith in Jesus Christ as my Savior IS my ultimate restoration story; I must say that before continuing.

Thinking of a topic, I dove into the archives of my journals from years and years of notes. I reflected on the many lessons I've learned from studying the Bible and how I've grown in my relationship with God. The restoration from fear, chaos, and calamities in my life has been a process of overcoming and eradicating that has taken many lessons. I'm about to share one of those lessons.

But where was the journal and story I wanted to share? I couldn't find it, so I prayed and went to bed. When I woke up, God had something completely different on my mind. He moved me to write about something opposite of what I looked for. I had never journaled this story because of how frightened it made me. In fact, I had tried to forget it. But the impulse from God was so strong that I began to write it out immediately.

A few years after I came to know Jesus as my Savior, I was still teetering on giving up things that pleased me in this world. I was a free-spirited woman, doing whatever I wanted to do whenever I wanted to do it, without many barriers.

One day, a sweet friend called and asked me to bring my Ouija board to her home. I didn't think twice about it because I didn't understand the depths of what I was playing with. Thinking this would be the perfect opportunity to try this thing out and have some fun, I acted impulsively. I had no idea there was a spiritual existence around me, nor did I understand the devil's antics threatening to destroy my newfound faith. He was prowling around my life, seeking to take me away from Christ.

I had purchased the Ouija board a while back and put it away. I always wanted to see if it really worked; this was my opportunity! My friend, Mary Alice (Mac for short), had a husband named Jim. Jim had a friend who had disappeared "out of the blue" without any answers years before. He was still considered a "missing person" by authorities because he had never been seen again, nor was his body ever found. Mac and I felt this would be the perfect opportunity to test the board and see if it could really tell us something about where Jim's friend was. Excited, I gathered up my board and left for Mac's house.

Mac and Jim lived in a two-story duplex home. Jim, Mac, and the children lived in the bottom part, while Mac's mom and dad lived upstairs in the top half. As I walked inside the house, Ouija board in hand, Mac told me her husband had to go to work as he was on the afternoon shift. Unfortunately, he couldn't join us. But he gave Mac some details about his friend so we could find out his whereabouts.

We sat down to play and began by asking some fun questions we knew the answers to. Wow, it worked great! Everything it spelled out was accurate answers and 100% truthful. Next, we began asking questions we didn't know answers to. That primed us to feed the board details. When we felt confident with what we saw, we got to the big question we'd ask, "Where is Jim's missing friend?" We did it!

The board began to answer. It told us that he had drowned in Canada.

"Yeah, right!" we said.

We sat there thinking a bit deeper and kept going. We started getting very eerie feelings around us. Our hairs were rising, goosebumps erupted, and fear crept up on our bodies. We decided to stop and only do "fun stuff," but the feeling of being "freaked out" was not dissipating. I was the one who was directing this thing by placing my hands lightly on the pointer. The movement took me to letters or numbers that spelled information. We were hooked, yet scared. We really wanted to know if Ouija was telling us the truth about Jim's friend, so we decided to ask it a very personal question.

We asked a question about Mac's elderly dad, which only his mom and dad knew the answer to. We asked, "Ouija, what was Mac's father's nickname when he was a little boy?"

The board began to move, pointing and spelling out the name "Cookie."

We thought it was an odd name, so Mac immediately ran upstairs to ask her mom for the nickname that was never discussed, knowing her mom was the only other person alive who knew that information.

Mac came running back down the stairs, screaming, "Yes! It's right, it's right!"

This thing now had our full attention! We continued asking all sorts of questions. We continued for hours, trying to cover up being truly frightened with bursts of laughter and jokes. We became sucked into this game because of its accuracy and power.

"Do not turn to mediums or necromancers; do not seek them out, and so make yourself unclean by them. I am the Lord your God" (Leviticus 19:31 ESV).

Deeply enthralled with Ouija, we had no thought as to what was happening in our midst when suddenly, the phone on the kitchen wall rang loudly, startling us!

Mac got up and answered the phone. The person on the other end asked, "Is there someone there who is playing with a Ouija board?" Mac motioned me toward the phone (this was long before cell phones were a thing).

Immediately, we both thought this might have been someone playing a joke on us. But the only people who knew what we were doing were Mac's parents and Jim. Her parents were not the type of people who joked. They were elderly people who minded their business. And Jim was at work, so we knew it wasn't him. Before we could answer anything, the caller spoke further. He stated he got the phone number from his Ouija board, which he had just been playing with. We remained silent. He proceeded to tell us that the vibes he got were so strong he had to call the number to find out who we were and why we were playing.

My girlfriend Mac was as petrified as I was; she immediately handed me the phone. Talk about shivering chills; they penetrated my entire body. The man said some things about the Ouija board. I spoke up multiple times, asking, "Who is this? Tell us again how you got this number!" He just kept talking, as if he didn't even hear us, telling us there are two types of Ouija boards—white and black. He said we had a black one. He was right!

At that point, all I wanted to do was hang up, go home, and get to my safe place. We were scared beyond words. I can't explain how petrified I was. I felt responsible for being the one who brought this thing into their home!

I was so afraid to even get into my car by myself, so Jim, who had returned from work, offered to drive me home. But I needed my car the next day, so I asked him if he would trail behind me to make sure no one was following me. I prayed all the way home. As I pulled into the driveway, I waved at Jim and darted inside the house, leaving Ouija board in the car!

I looked out the window as Jim left our driveway. In my house, my husband was sound asleep, and all the kids were in bed. I didn't want to wake anybody up, but I had the most unsettling feeling I have ever had in my life. I didn't want to be alone. I felt like someone was lingering around me, watching me, lurking, and hovering over my body. I felt sensations I'd never felt before. Even as a little child, but now a full-grown adult, I had never been that scared. Home was the place where I would run whenever I felt this way. My home was a safe place, always, but this scenario wasn't the case. After hours of trembling and fear, I finally fell asleep. Even as I continue to write this, knowing Jesus is with me, I have shivers remembering the horror of how I felt.

The next day, I woke up, and everything was normal. When my husband got up, I told him what had happened with the board. He seemed not to be as weirded out as I was, so we brushed it off, laughed a little, and then put it to rest. He went to work. As I got the kids off to school, I started my day.

Then the house phone rang. I answered it. There was a person on the other end who said, "Don't hang up." I can't remember all he said, but I do remember him saying, "You have a black Ouija board you opened. Get rid of it. NOW! Black ones are extremely dangerous!"

Oh, dear Lord, I gasped. *How did this person get my number? Who is this person? What does it mean that I have a black Ouija board? How does he even know who I am, where I live, or my phone number? How does he know I have this thing?*

Many thoughts raced through my head in that moment. The sporadic calls from random people really got me scared. I can't remember exactly what I said to that caller, but it was something like, "I believe in Jesus, and don't ever call me again!"

At the moment, I could not understand why this was happening to me. *Is it to see if I really believe in God? Am I willing to compromise my Christianity by playing with evil spirits?* Thoughts were racing. *Is there validity in what the board was telling me or what the phone calls meant?*

All I wanted to do was just get rid of the board. PERIOD!

I went outside and tried throwing it in the rubbish can. I later decided to get it out, thinking someone else might get it and try to use it. I just wanted it destroyed. I didn't know how I'd do it, so in my desperation, I went and hid it in an untouched place in the garage, figuring I'd have my husband dispose of it properly.

Time passed. To be honest, it must have sat out there for some time as my husband was so busy, and I eventually forgot about it. That is, until the day my son Michael brought it back into the house.

When I saw it in his possession, I panicked! I screamed at him, startling him as much as it had startled me to see it tucked under his arm. He was headed out to play with it when I yelled, "Get rid of that thing now. Get it out of this house!" He was shocked to see me panicked. I told him to go outside and bury it because it was evil. Quickly, I told him what had happened to his Aunt Mac and me when we played with it and why we needed it out of our house!

My son was shaken; he immediately went outside, taking the board with him. What I didn't know was that when he had found it, he had gathered his friends to play with it, and intense, scary things had happened to them, too. Afraid, Michael took it to the back of our yard with his friends. They decided to burn it to get rid of it; all the kids stood around and witnessed what happened next.

What started as a tiny little one-flame fire in the backyard of our house raged up in a flash the moment Ouija was set on top of the little flame. The fire exploded with magnitude. In an instant, the flames came jumping out with fierce anger, every kid being targeted. Michael described it, saying the flames were like bony fingers on a witch's hands trying to lash them. While the human-like horror images leaped out of the fire, cries and terrible screams came from within. The kids were all so scared they didn't know what to do except back up; as soon as they did that, with a flash, the fire instantly went out. It was completely gone! It went from a raging fire with piercing sounds to a heap of ashes before their eyes. Neighborhood mothers saw the intensity and height of the flames and came barreling outside to see what happened. As everyone approached the area, all that remained was a heap of ashes. The Ouija board had completely vanished.

God was there all the time. He never left the children. My son testifies to this day how God intervened and protected them from both the board and the fierceness of the explosion of the fire. God eradicated that board to ashes within seconds.

As I was writing this, I called my son and asked him to re-explain the story as he recalled. He assured me everything I have written here is exactly how it happened. He will never forget the fear and the intensity of playing with that board. He said it was evil stuff, and crazy things happened while he and his friends were playing with it. They would never forget it and still recall "the time when...." I never realized that something like this could be so real. Evil exists.

My takeaway is this: the devil tries to lure us towards himself in many ways. I was just playing a game with a friend, having no idea what I was dabbling in. But Satan was playing right there with us. He will try to reach us however he can.

God tells us not to mess with things that can distract us, hurt us, or even kill us. There is a spirit world, and the enemy of our soul will try to stir demonic activity that can easily detour us. I opened the door to something I thought was fun and harmless. I learned such a lesson through it that, even today, I thank God for protecting my children and me. God brought restoration through it. I thank Him for forgiving and protecting me in my ignorance. God restored my walk with Him, using my terrifying lesson to bring me closer to Himself. I found a place of peace I never wanted to leave. Now, I focus only on His Word. All the truth I will ever need to know is found inside the Bible. I learned to stay far away from any evil, even if it "promises" knowledge.

> He has preserved our lives and kept our feet from slipping
> (Psalm 66:9 NIV).

God protects and covers us with His own blood, which He shed for all of us. Beauty comes from ashes when God is involved! He wants us to run to Him when we are afraid. God continuously teaches us through every situation, no matter where we are or what we do.

Be on guard. The spirit world is real.

> Stay alert! Watch out for your great enemy, the devil. He prowls around like a roaring lion, looking for someone to devour. Stand firm against him and be strong in your faith (1 Peter 5:8-9 NLT).

God protects His own. The phone call warned us, but the accuracy of the board game had lured us in. As a young Christian, I didn't think there could be any harm in playing a game. I wasn't aware the evil one was trying to get me or my children, but God was in the midst, watching. He opened my eyes to see. He gave me the Holy Spirit, who put the fear of God inside of me.

> Through our faith, the mighty power of God constantly guards us until our full salvation is ready to be revealed in the last time
> (1 Peter 1:5 TPT).

God restored my soul. He will hear any of us at any point when we are afraid. Call on Him. If you mess up, confess to Him. Call out His name, and He will rescue you and restore you. Restoration with God will help you steer clear of evil. When you ask to be forgiven, He forgives, and you'll not need to fear again. With me, when fear set in, I was doing something wrong. I needed God to rescue me and my family, so I called out to Him for that.

God took care of me. He protected my son as well as our friends and allowed all of us to learn a lesson from the evil that was surrounding us. When the fire happened, the ashes came, and thank God for them. Beauty did come from the ashes that day! The board was gone, and a lesson was learned! God devoured the enemy in that flame, and it was gone! God brought peace in its place.

God can restore anything we do and bring beauty from ashes. He can restore us to a closer walk with Him. My story shows that evil will be burned to ashes, but the beauty is what I learned: God is and will always be triumphant. The evil one has no place in our life! We must tell the devil, "Don't mess with me! I'm God's chosen."

> *And I will cut off sorceries from your hand, and you will have no more tellers of fortunes* (Micah 5:12 ESV).

God is the God of restoration. He brings beauty from ashes. And I am grateful I can learn from the ashes.

Afterword

In these stories and teachings, you've seen that experiencing God's restoration involves asking Him for forgiveness and healing and then opening your heart to His power and mercy.

> Let my passion for life be restored, tasting joy in every breakthrough you bring to me (Psalm 51:12 TPT).

God restores people from pain through His love, grace, and the power of the Holy Spirit. Our prayer as a team of writers is that, as you have read *Restoration,* you have found comfort in God's presence and begun your own healing through a deepened relationship with Him. The message in the stories and teachings the Holy Spirit empowered us to share is clear: God always offers spiritual growth and a renewed sense of hope, even amidst our suffering. He alone provides a path to beauty so we can leave the ashes of trauma behind.

As we close, we ask that you be fully aware of the process God has offered you. Your next step is to bring all your struggles and hurts to Him in prayer, acknowledging your vulnerability and HIS ability to heal. Yes, God can restore whatever you've lost when you invite Jesus to come into your life. Trust Him as He gathers up the pieces of charred ash and allows them to disappear into His perfect peace, offering you the most beautiful picture of who He is.

God wants to bring us each healing and restoration, but we must remember we also have a part to play in the process. You cannot hold on to your "ashes" and still receive God's beauty. You must move forward and leave all the bitterness, self-pity, unforgiveness, and anything else that stands between you and your Savior behind. Release it into God's hands through prayer and petition with thanksgiving. Immerse yourself in scripture, prayer, and the guidance of the Holy Spirit. Know that as you pray about your circumstance, memorize scripture, and speak out loud to the Lord, He will hear you.

> *Don't worry about anything; instead, pray about everything.*
> *Tell God what you need and thank him for all he has done*
> (Philippians 4:6 NLT).

If you tend to focus on everything that has gone wrong, PLEASE STOP. Change your attitude and mindset. Choose joy and maintain a positive, grateful outlook. Choose to mentally set your mind on all the powerful things God has done in your life as you, with faith, trust in everything He will do as you move forward from here with Him.

> *Stop imitating the ideals and opinions of the culture around you,*
> *but be inwardly transformed by the Holy Spirit* (Romans 12:2 TPT).

The stories we've presented are meant to inspire you to see God's redemptive work in your own life. God's love and grace provide everything you need to heal you from your past with a renewed heart and perspective. May you deepen your faith and rely more fully on God as your source of comfort, guidance, and strength through challenging times. Please allow God to navigate your pain and help you find healing, just as you have seen Him restore the individuals in these stories. He will demonstrate His power and faithfulness when you fully surrender to His will for your life.

We can trust God's promises because He is faithful and true to His Word. And He will never change.

God brings beauty from ashes for all His children. That means He will bring you complete restoration through His authoritative power.

> *He will give a crown of beauty for ashes, a joyous blessing instead of mourning, festive praise instead of despair* (Isaiah 61:3 NLT).

May God bless you!

More WPP Anthologies!

Men, families, communities, and countries must be on guard as courageous and battle-ready warriors. Men of God are each commissioned to be vigilant conquerors, prepared to lead the fight to overcome evil. The valiant authors in *Fit 2 Fight* share how they have overcome using the weapons that ensure victory no matter what we face.

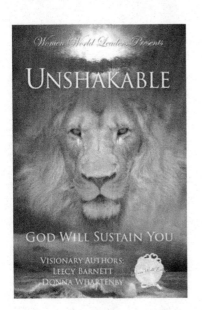

God longs for you to have ferocious faith grounded in His unwavering love. Get ready to be encouraged as you open the pages of *Unshakable: God Will Sustain You*. Through true stories written by faithful and resilient women, you will witness God's sustaining power available to those who rely on Him.

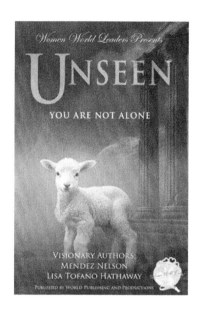

The authors of *Unseen: You Are Not Alone* share their struggles of feeling isolated and unnoticed and detail how our awesome God helped them overcome every obstacle to find what truly matters: Him. These stories and devotional teachings shed light on the truth of your significance and value. You are never alone!

Despite all the adversities we face throughout our lives, God is the source of our hope. As you read the pages of this book, you will see firsthand how God brings *Hope Alive* to every person who is yearning for a reason to go on. Like a broken tree in a dark place is primed for new growth, God can use the rich soil of your dark place to prepare a new life to sprout in you.

The authors of *Miracle Mindset: Finding Hope in the Chaos*, have experienced the wonders of God's provision, protection, and guidance. These stories and teachings will ignite a spark within you, propelling you to encounter the marvel of God's miracles, even in the chaos.

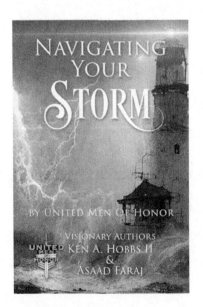

Life is full of storms and rough waters. The stories in *Navigating Your Storm: By United Men of Honor* will give you the ability to see the light of God and navigate your storm victoriously.

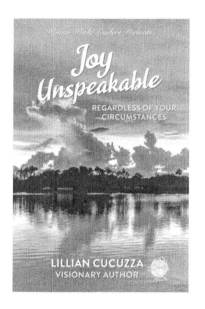

With *Joy Unspeakable: Regardless of Your Circumstances,* you will learn how joy and sorrow can dance together during adversity. The words in this book will encourage, inspire, motivate, and give you hope, joy, and peace.

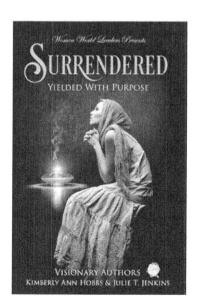

Surrendered: Yielded With Purpose will help you recognize with awe that surrendering to God is far more effective than striving alone. When we let go of our own attempts to earn God's favor and rely on Jesus Christ, we receive a deeper intimacy with Him and a greater power to serve Him.

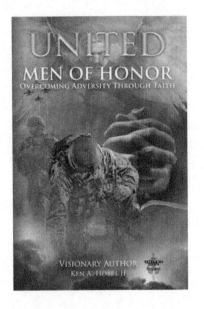

United Men of Honor: Overcoming Adversity Through Faith will help you armor up, become fit to fight, and move forward with what it takes to be an honorable leader. Over twenty authors in this book share their accounts of God's provision, care, and power as they proclaim His Word.

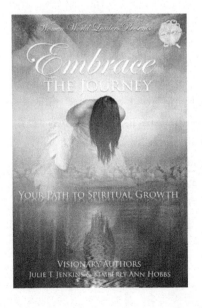

Embrace the Journey: Your Path to Spiritual Growth will strengthen and empower you to step boldly in faith. These stories, along with expertly placed expositional teachings will remind you that no matter what we encounter, we can always look to God, trusting HIS provision, strength, and direction. .

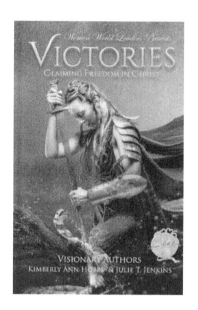

Victories: Claiming Freedom in Christ presents expository teaching coupled with individual stories that testify to battles conquered victoriously through the power of Jesus Christ. The words in this book will motivate and inspire you and give you hope as God awakens you to your victory!

WPP's Mission

World Publishing and Productions was birthed in obedience to God's call. Our mission is to empower writers to walk in their God-given purpose as they share their God story with the world. We offer one-on-one coaching and a complete publishing experience. To find out more about how we can help you become a published author or to purchase books written to share God's glory, please visit: **worldpublishingandproductions.com**

Heartbeat of a Survivor tells the story of Nita Tin, a Buddhist born and raised in an opulent lifestyle in Burma. As her country came under the control of a ruthless military dictator, Nita's whole life changed. Forced to flee her home, her soul was soon set free in a greater way than she ever dreamed possible.

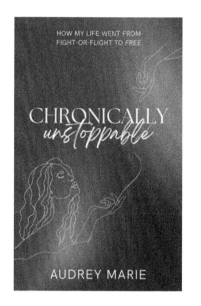

At seventeen, Audrey Marie experienced a sudden and relentless excruciating firestorm of pain. *Chronically Unstoppable* tells of her true-life journey as she faced pain, developed strength, and battled forward with hope.

The world has become a place where we don't have a millisecond to think for ourselves, often leaving us feeling lost or overwhelmed. That is why Max Gold wrote *Planestorming!*—a straightforward guide to help you evaluate and change your life for the better. It's time to get to work and make the rest of your life the BEST of your life.

Riley Rossey is not your everyday bullied student, but one who discovers how to utilize his talents to assist other shy and picked-on individuals. Journey with Riley as he meets bullying head-on and becomes a God-given blessing to so many in *The Bullied Student Who Changed All the Rules* by Robert M. Fishbein.

Made in the USA
Coppell, TX
05 July 2025

51506124R10197